Women in Business

Women in Business

Special Issue Editors

Paola Demartini
Francesca Maria Cesaroni
Paola Paoloni

MDPI • Basel • Beijing • Wuhan • Barcelona • Belgrade

MDPI

Special Issue Editors
Paola Demartini
Roma Tre University
Italy

Francesca Maria Cesaroni
University of Urbino Carlo Bo
Italy

Paola Paoloni
Sapienza University of Rome
Italy

Editorial Office
MDPI
St. Alban-Anlage 66
4052 Basel, Switzerland

This is a reprint of articles from the Special Issue published online in the open access journal *Administrative Sciences* (ISSN 2076-3387) form 2018 to 2019 (available at: https://www.mdpi.com/journal/admsci/special_issues/Women_Business)

For citation purposes, cite each article independently as indicated on the article page online and as indicated below:

LastName, A.A.; LastName, B.B.; LastName, C.C. Article Title. *Journal Name* **Year**, *Article Number*, Page Range.

ISBN 978-3-03921-638-3 (Pbk)
ISBN 978-3-03921-639-0 (PDF)

Contents

About the Special Issue Editors

Paola Demartini is Full Professor of Business Administration and Corporate Governance at Roma Tre University, Department of Business Studies. She is the Head of the Roma Tre Corporate Governance Lab. Her main research fields concern sustainability performance and accountability, gender in business studies and entrepreneurship. Author and co-author of several essays in international scientific journals, she has authored over 100 scholarly publications. She has been co-ordinator or member of research teams supported by funding agencies such as the Italian MIUR, the Finnish Tekes, the Croatian Ministry of Tourism and she is now involved in a Horizon2020 research project granted by the European Union. Since 2015, she is included in the official Register of independent Experts issued by the Italian Ministry of Education, University and Research, for the scientific evaluation of national and international research projects. She is the member of the editorial board of several scientific journals and since 2018 she is co-editor in chief of *Piccola Impresa/Small Business*, a scientific journal devoted to entrepreneurship research and Chief Editor of the Series: *Corporate Governance and Business Scenarios*, published by Roma TrEPress.

Francesca Maria Cesaroni is Full Professor of Business Administration at the University of Urbino Carlo Bo, Department of Economics, Society, Politics, Urbino (PU), Italy. She is the Director of the Bachelor Degree in Economics and Management, School of Economics, Department of Economics, Society, Politics, University of Urbino, Italy and she teaches Advanced Accounting and Entrepreneurship and small business at the School of Economics, University of Urbino. Her main research topics include SMEs, entrepreneurship, women-owned firms, family firms, succession process. She is the editor and author of several essays in international scientific journals. She is the member of the editorial board of several scientific journals and since 2018 she is the co-editor in chief of the journal *Piccola Impresa/Small Business*. Since 2016 she is the Scientific responsible of UniurbLab, the Contamination lab of the University of Urbino, http://contaminationlab.uniurb.it, a teaching program aimed at promoting student entrepreneurship. She is the Director of the Research Centre on Entrepreneurship and Small-Medium-sized firms, University of Urbino, Italy. Since 2017, she is the Italian vice-president for ECSB-European Council of Small Business.

Paola Paoloni, is Full Professor at The Sapienza University Faculty of Economy, in Rome. She teaches Business Administration and Strategic decisions. Her research interest includes general management, financial reporting, female entrepreneurship and intellectual-based management. She is the head of "Ipazia" Scientific Observatory of gender studies. She is author and co-author of several articles and books on above mentioned research areas and she attended as a speaker at many international conferences. She is member of: SIDREA (Societa Italiana di Ragioneria e di Economia Aziendale); NCP new club Paris –task force women; AIDEA (Accademia Italiana di Economia Aziendale). She is a member of the Editorial Board of some academic journals like: *Open innovation: Technology, Market, and Complexity; China-USA Business Review* journal. She is Vice-President of the Society of Open Innovation Technology. She is scientific director of the Observatory on Gender.

administrative
sciences

MDPI

Editorial

Why and How Women in Business Can Make Innovations in Light of the Sustainable Development Goals

Paola Demartini

Department of Business Study, Roma Tre University, 00154 Roma RM, Italy; paola.demartini@uniroma3.it

Received: 20 August 2019; Accepted: 21 August 2019; Published: 25 August 2019

1. Introduction

In 1999, Amartya Sen wrote, " . . . women are increasingly seen, by men as well as women, as active agents of change: the dynamic promoters of social transformations that can alter the lives of both women and men". Moreover, he points out that an increase in women's participation does not only generate results for women in general—a reward on its own merit—but it also provides social benefits as women are a major influence on social change, innovation and the development process (pp. 201–2).

Innovation, indeed, is a matter of change in the life of individuals, organisations and institutions driven not only by scientific and technological advances but also by societal expectations, values and demands (Phills et al. 2008; Cajaiba-Santana 2014; van der Have and Rubalcaba 2016). However, innovation has had a critical and sometimes controversial impact on our society (Godin 2015). What makes the difference is its finalisation and the socio-economic and environmental impact that it produces on the fabric of our society and the physical environment in which we live (Edler and Fagerberg 2017). Innovation as an end and not a means should promote a change that reduces inequalities and promotes well-being as stated in the Sustainable Development Goals (SDGs), which are "a universal call to action to end poverty, protect the planet and ensure that all people enjoy peace and prosperity" (United Nations 2015).

In detail, according to SDG 5: *Achieve gender equality and empower all women and girls*, women are both the target that policymakers and institutions should pay attention to, through innovative reforms and policies aimed at reducing the inequalities that exist at all levels (see Table 1), and also the means by which to foster innovation and the development of our society (UN Women 2017).

Table 1. Goal 5: Achieve gender equality and empower all women and girls.

5.a Undertake reforms to give women equal rights to economic resources, as well as access to ownership and control over land and other forms of property, financial services, inheritance and natural resources, in accordance with national laws.
5.b Enhance the use of enabling technology, in particular information and communications technology, to promote the empowerment of women.
5.c Adopt and strengthen sound policies and enforceable legislation for the promotion of gender equality and the empowerment of all women and girls at all levels.

In light of these propositions, this editorial develops in two directions.

The first introduces the reader to the more general theme of the relationships between gender conditions and economic development and argues that gender inequality leads to a net loss, both economically and in terms of quality of life (Klasen and Lamanna 2009; Duflo 2012). Not only does gender inequality have economic and social effects on women but also the community as a whole (Klasen 2002; Kabeer and Natali 2013). Accordingly, eliminating gender inequality could lead to a radical change within the global economy, not only in terms of economic growth and GDP but also, and above all, in terms of the redistribution of wealth and increased well-being for the entire society (King and Mason 2001; Benería et al. 2015). For this reason, the gender issue has become a point on the agenda of economic policy, both globally and nationally (Cornwall and Rivas 2015).

This premise is important because it is also the underlying pillar of the flourishing of research on both gender inequalities and women in business in recent years (Henry et al. 2016; Paoloni and Demartini 2016).

The second direction introduces the reader to the individual contributions of this book, which mainly concern the most advanced categories of women in business, namely, women entrepreneurs and professionals. Hence, the specific objective is to offer insights to researchers, policymakers and all those interested in reducing gender inequalities and supporting the process of female empowerment and leadership (Cornwall and Rivas 2015).

Finally, the primary purpose of this editorial is to present a picture of both directions and summarise a macro and microeconomic perspective of why and how women in business can make innovations in light of the SDGs.

2. Gender Inequalities and Economic Development: A Macro Perspective

In a nutshell, gender inequalities, i.e., the result of social organisation and cultural tradition, take the form of fewer opportunities for women to access and use tangible and intangible resources than men, which limits women's chances of gaining more power both in production and consumption of wealth.

Gender differences are also reflected in the different spending and consumption patterns within the family, with women more strongly promoting investments in children's human capital (Roushdy 2004). The control of women regarding income and wealth is important as a tool for the well-being of children. In fact, the greater control of women concerning income increases spending on assets that also benefit the rest of the family (Schady and Rosero 2008; Rubalcava et al. 2009). For example, it is noted that the share of land owned by women is positively associated with higher spending on food among rural families; that is, if mothers have more land ownership, fewer children are severely underweight (Allendorf 2007).

Advancing gender equality is critical to all areas of a healthy society, from reducing poverty to promoting health, education, protection and the well-being of children and future generations (Abu-Ghaida and Klasen 2004).

Speaking specifically of women in business, we focus on the role that women can have, as workers or as entrepreneurs in a business. Concretely, inequalities can manifest themselves at various stages of a woman's life, especially before entering the workplace, through educational and experiential paths differentiated by gender that limit/influence the acquisition of knowledge, skills and competences by women. The effect of these inequalities translates into greater difficulty for women to establish companies in the most innovative and profitable sectors (BarNir 2012) and enter into the work world in roles with greater prospects (Beede et al. 2011). Once they enter the labour market, with equal responsibilities, women are on average less remunerated than men (Bobbitt-Zeher 2007) and have more difficulty in making a career, a phenomenon well known in the literature for which the term "glass ceiling" has been coined (Cotter et al. 2001; Broadbridge and Weyer 2007). Even for women entrepreneurs, the greater difficulty in accessing, accumulating and using human capital as well as financial resources can limit the success of the company and has fuelled the debate in the literature on "the gender underperformance hypothesis" (Fairlie and Robb 2009). However, beyond ethical reasons, there is an economic rationale for which women must be able to express their potential in the business world. Indeed, the full participation of women in labour forces would add percentage points to most national growth rates—double digits in many cases (https://www.un.org). In general, women's and girls' empowerment is essential to promote social development (United Nations 2018; Duflo 2012).

In this context, development can also be read as economic and human development. Economic development, commonly captured by per capita GDP, is included in the ISU (Human Development

Index), a synthetic measure of human development. In fact, this index measures the average results of a country in the three fundamental dimensions of human development: a long and healthy life, access to knowledge and a decent standard of living (WorldBank 2001).

In the following, we refer to two models that explain and empirically test the impact of gender conditions on economics. What differentiates these models the most is the indices used as a representation of gender conditions:

- The Gender Inequality Index (GII), created by the Human Development Relations Office of the United Nations Development Program (HDRO 2018);
- The gender discrimination index within social institutions (Social Institution and Gender Index, SIGI), created by the OECD Development Centre (2014).

Commonly, these two models lead to identical results, confirming the hypothesis that gender inequality causes damage to the community in terms of lack of development (Ferrant 2011; Ferrant and Kolev 2016).

For the model that uses GII, gender inequality refers to disparity between individuals due to gender. This multidimensional concept contains various aspects that can vary from one country to another depending on the level of development, as well as the social and cultural characteristics and, finally, the institutions. For economic reasons, gender inequality is important because it creates a distortion analogous to a distorted tax. In fact, men less gifted and skilled than women may have better access to education, political, social and economic resources, labour markets and, as a result, economic opportunities. Thus productivity, capital accumulation and technological progress are negatively affected by all the forms in which gender inequality appears (Ferrant 2011, pp. 22–25).

For the model that uses SIGI, discriminatory social institutions are implemented through formal and informal laws, attitudes and practices that limit women's and girls' access to opportunities in terms of rights, justice and empowerment. These are captured in a multifaceted approach from the SIGI variables that combine qualitative and quantitative data, taking into consideration both de jure and de facto discrimination of social institutions. The results show that gender discrimination in social institutions prevents economic development beyond its effects on gender inequality, reducing countries' income levels. This effect is stronger for low-income countries and appears to work by reducing total factor productivity and reducing the level of education and labour participation among women. Furthermore, the analyses show that the loss of income associated with current levels of discrimination could be substantial, estimated at up to $12 trillion, 16% of current global revenues (Ferrant and Kolev 2016, p. 28). At the same time, the authors estimate that a gradual dismantling of gender discrimination in social institutions could bring about significant economic benefits, leading to an annual increase in the global income growth rate from 0.03 to 0.6 per cent points by 2030 (ib: 30).

In summary, both models demonstrate that among the reasons for which local and international policies must be oriented decisively to the abatement of gender inequality, there is also the economic loss and the lack of development caused by it.

The limitations of these empirical analyses must also be remembered. Gender inequality is a social construct and society is a complex environment, in which it is difficult to circumscribe and isolate elements. So, although having an index for gender inequality is very useful and indispensable for quantitative analyses, this indicator is not entirely exhaustive in describing the phenomenon.

However, the empirical evidence that there is a positive relationship between the reduction of gender inequalities and economic development explains why the topic is on policymakers' agenda. But an agenda is not sufficient to put forward results; therefore, it must be translated into targeted and effective actions.

For this reason, in addition to macro-economic analyses, it is essential to develop research on how the women's situation evolves to offer concrete indications and tools to policymakers so that they can operate effectively in single cultural, economic, social and political contexts. Understanding "how" requires a qualitative research approach with in-depth analyses of case studies to understand such a complex phenomenon. Accordingly, the papers of this book mean to offer a contribution to the theme of women in business from a micro perspective.

3. Women in Business as Actors of Change and Innovation: A Micro Perspective

The role of women in entrepreneurship, management and corporate governance is regarded as central to the development and welfare of economies. Since the early 1980s, there has been increased interest in women managers and entrepreneurs, often from an interdisciplinary approach combining, for example, sociology, psychology, management and organisational studies and economics. Nowadays, research on women in management and organisations is continuously and rapidly evolving (Paoloni and Demartini 2016). Research on the way women face new business challenges within organisations as entrepreneurs, owners and managers, as well as workers, can contribute to understanding the new drivers affecting value creation dynamics in our knowledge-based society. Accordingly, this book tries to offer some insights on how women create, process and share knowledge in their business activity through the application and exploitation of novel creative ideas and solutions.

Specifically, contributions will focus on the following topics:

- Female entrepreneurship challenges in the innovative sectors;
- Women's participation in the ownership, management and leadership of family business;
- Women's opportunities and difficulties in professional careers;
- Ideas and thoughts for overcoming gender inequalities.

The choice of the field of study that female students and male students make is perpetuating gender segregation in labour markets, with women underrepresented in the business sector and concentrated in the areas of health, well-being, education and administration. For this reason, it is interesting to analyse the challenges that women face when they enter advanced and extremely competitive sectors.

In this book, three articles deal with female entrepreneurs in high-tech and innovative sectors.

The first article by Paola Demartini is titled: *Innovative Female-Led Startups. Do Women in Business Underperform?* The spur of innovative startups has provided an unprecedented opportunity for female entrepreneurship. However, mainstream literature on startups has elaborated a gender performance gap hypothesis. Considering the speed of technological, social and cultural changes that have taken place in this millennium, the author wonders if this gap can still be found today, with particular reference to new technology-based ventures (Berger and Kuckertz 2016). The research results reveal that as far as financial performance is concerned, innovative female-led startups do not lag behind male ones in terms of dimension, company profitability, efficiency and financial management. However, findings confirmed that female businesses raise, on average, a lower amount of financial resources in comparison to men. To fully understand the value that female entrepreneurs can create, the author deems that future research should extend the assessment of female business performance outside the mainstream field and consider indicators referring to well-being and societal impact.

Indeed, a famous professional report (Startup Genome 2018) tackled the issue in its latest survey looking at how female and male founders might differ as far as their goals are concerned. Unsurprisingly, women are more likely to be oriented toward goals with a societal impact than men. In fact, they say they want to *"change the world"* with their startups, while men seem to be more market-oriented and more likely to say their primary mission is to *"build high-quality products"* (ib: 41).

The aim of the second paper *"Female-Owned Innovative Startups in Italy: Status Quo and Implications"* by Paola Paoloni and Giuseppe Modaffari is to provide an overview of the current literature on this business phenomenon with regard to gender studies and to point out what has happened in the Italian context. The absence of complex organisational structures in female startups is demonstrated by the results found in the literature which deals with the different problems encountered by the entrepreneur in doing business (Neill et al. 2015). By comparing the results that emerged in Paoloni-Demartini's study (2016) on female entrepreneurship, the authors have found the same difficulties common to the entrepreneur in starting their business. These concern, above all, the difficulty in facing the startup phase, the undercapitalisation of the company and the difficulties in accessing credit, the latter also confirmed by the empirical research carried out within the Italian economic context.

Therefore, from both papers, the suggestion to policymakers to support women entrepreneurs' access to credit emerges. This theme is relevant for all startups, but it is even more important for high-tech companies and particularly so for women who often suffer from the prejudice of not being in charge of business enterprises with performances similar to those of men.

The third paper by Katherina Kuschel, *"Women Founders in the Technology Industry: The Startup Relatedness of the Decision to Become a Mother"*, explores the decision to become a mother among women in the technology industry, particularly if there is an "optimal context" regarding startup development. Findings suggest two sources of "mumpreneurs" in technology ventures: (1) women who created a startup while young and childless, postponing maternity until the business was "stable" and (2) mothers who created a technology venture as a strategy to gain higher levels of flexibility and autonomy than they experienced in the corporate world. The results of this work contribute to theory development by revealing the "startup-relatedness" of family decisions by women founders in the technology industry.

Hence, this research shows that competencies and skills that allow women to become successful entrepreneurs in the technologically advanced sectors do not guarantee equality. In fact, if childcare costs remain high, it will not be economically viable for women to work full time. Furthermore, as long as culture penalises women, who decide or are socially bound to take a break to have a child or assist elderly relatives, and as long as women continue to bear the brunt of unpaid domestic work, it will be difficult for them to realise their full potential in the labour market and in business.

This specific topic is addressed in the paper titled *"It's Always a Women's Problem! Micro-Entrepreneurs, Work–Family Balance and Economic Crisis"* by Francesca Maria Cesaroni, Maria Gabriella Pediconi and Annalisa Sentuti. Gender inequality in the division of family work is vastly corroborated and work–family balance is an important topic in the female entrepreneurship field of research. Even if work–family balance should be a necessity indiscriminately perceived by all women and men who have a paid job, it is a particularly pertinent issue for women, called to find an equilibrium between work and family. This study analyses the situation of men and women entrepreneurs in the Italian context in order to investigate how the economic crisis has affected the work–family balance. Findings show that the work–family balance of women entrepreneurs does not seem to have been particularly affected by the crisis. Difficulties in managing relations between firm and family are more structural, that is, mostly related to the person's family condition and the disparity of roles between men and women in the family context, than conjunctural. This result seems to suggest, mainly to policymakers who deal with gender equality and supporting policies of work–family balance, the opportunity to manage the question considering two aspects: gender culture and services to be offered to support the family.

Hence, the provision of services is a necessary but perhaps insufficient condition to support women entrepreneurs and female workers. A cultural change, which modifies the common way of thinking about the division of roles between men and women within the family, is also necessary.

The difficulties women face in career advancement is the topic addressed by three contributions. The issue of women's participation in top management and boardroom positions has received increasing attention in the academic literature and the press but, the pace of advancement for women managers and directors continues to be slow and uneven.

In the paper *"Women Career Paths in Accounting Organisations: Big4 Scenario"*, Adriana Tiron-Tudor and Widad Atena Faragalla analyse the gender issues present in the accounting profession, and more precisely, on the career paths one could follow in the accounting profession. Findings reveal that the most disputed career path in the literature is working in a large auditing firm. In this context, gender discrimination is very much present through glass ceiling phenomena, double standard, motherhood and the aftermath that comes with it. Indeed, the findings show that motherhood is an important reason why women do not advance to partners as easily or as fast as men. The overall findings revealed that breaking through the ceiling and overcoming all the obstacles to reaching the top level, for women, is still difficult.

Strictly related to the latter issue is the paper *"Women's Role in the Accounting Profession: A Comparative Study between Italy and Romania"* by Mara Del Baldo, Adriana Tiron-Tudor and Widad Atena Faragalla. Historically, in most countries, the accounting profession has always been male-dominated. Liberal professions such as lawyers, engineers, architects and doctors share the common trait of conservatism. The accounting profession, which is also a liberal profession, is no exception. Starting from this premise, this work aims to provide, using a historical and institutional perspective, a picture of the past and current "journey" in the accountancy profession of women chartered accountants and auditors in Italy and Romania. Drawing from the theoretical framework of gendered construction of the accounting profession, the paper points out issues affecting the presence and degree of representativeness and the role of women within the National Chartered Association and their continued under-representation in Italy and Romania.

In this stream of research, Katherina Kuschel and Erica Salvaj present, in their paper titled *"Opening the "Black Box". Factors Affecting Women's Journey to Top Management Positions: A Framework Applied to Chile"*, a framework of the factors that, at the individual, organisational and public policy level, affect both career persistence and the advancement of women in top management positions. In Chile, only 32 per cent of women "persist", or have a career without interruptions, mainly due to issues with work–family integration. Women who "advanced" in their professional careers represent 30 per cent of high management positions in the public sector and 18 per cent in the private sector. Only 3 per cent of general managers in Chile are women. Hence the authors draw business leaders' and public policymakers' attention to designing organisations that retain and promote talented women in top positions.

Two articles that offer insights for further developments and research studies bring this book to an end.

The first article, titled *"Adoption of Gender-Responsive Budgeting (GRB) by an Italian Municipality"* by Giovanna Galizzi, Gaia Viviana Bassani and Cristiana Cattaneo, offers insight to public officers on how an instrument can be a real help to overcome gender inequalities. Over the past few decades, many governments throughout the world have promoted gender-responsive budgeting (GRB). With its focus on equality, accountability, transparency and participation in the policy-making process, GRB shares some relevant principles with public governance principles. In detail, the case study shows that, when GRB is fully developed, the stakeholders involved are both internal and external, and these multiple actors, in pursuing gender equality, cooperate to achieve a shared, public aim. In this way, GRB gives effectiveness to the public decision-making process, contributing to greater incisiveness in the local government's management and creation of a gender-sensitive governance process.

Finally, the paper *"Female Entrepreneurship in Perspective: A Methodological Issue"* by Paola Paoloni and Gabriele Serafini proposes some questions for scholars. A methodological approach to the concept of female entrepreneurship has not yet been studied: Is female entrepreneurship an individual or collective concept? Is it considered a social or natural variable? The authors try to clear up these alternatives, which are preliminary questions for future research on female entrepreneurship. The term female relates to gender issues and collective characteristics but only when placed next to the term *entrepreneurship*, which is usually intended as an individual variable (Parker 2018, p. 300). However, the authors state that research on female entrepreneurship has not yet investigated whether it is an individual or collective variable and whether it has a social or natural derivation. Furthermore, inquiry on female entrepreneurship can be intended as a gender-based field of research, or research on the standardised qualities and functions of standardised human beings, rather than research on a particular function that characterises individuals. Hence, the originality of this research consists in its fourfold classification of the concept of female entrepreneurship, intended as a preparatory step to the analysis of its characteristics and measures.

Funding: This research received no external funding.

Conflicts of Interest: The author declares no conflict of interest.

References

Abu-Ghaida, Dina, and Stephan Klasen. 2004. The costs of missing the Millennium Development Goal on gender equity. *World Development* 32: 1075–107. [CrossRef]

Allendorf, Keera. 2007. Do Women's Land Rights Promote Empowerment and Child Health in Nepal? *World Development* 35: 1975–88. [CrossRef] [PubMed]

BarNir, Anat. 2012. Starting technologically innovative ventures: Reasons, human capital, and gender. *Management Decision* 50: 399–419. [CrossRef]

Beede, David N., Tiffany A. Julian, David Langdon, George McKittrick, Beethika Khan, and Mark E. Doms. 2011. Women in STEM: A gender gap to innovation. *Economics and Statistics Administration Issue Brief.*. [CrossRef]

Benería, Lourdes, Günseli Berik, and Maria Floro. 2015. *Gender, Development and Globalization: Economics as If All People Mattered.* Abingdon-on-Thames: Routledge.

Berger, Elisabeth S. C., and Andreas Kuckertz. 2016. Female entrepreneurship in startup ecosystems worldwide. *Journal of Business Research* 69: 5163–68. [CrossRef]

Bobbitt-Zeher, Donna. 2007. The gender income gap and the role of education. *Sociology of Education* 80: 1–22. [CrossRef]

Broadbridge, Adelina, and Birgit Weyer. 2007. Twenty years later: Explaining the persistence of the glass ceiling for women leaders. *Women in Management Review* 22: 482–96.

Cajaiba-Santana, Giovany. 2014. Social innovation: Moving the field forward. A conceptual framework. *Technological Forecasting and Social Change* 82: 42–51. [CrossRef]

Cornwall, Andrea, and Althea-Maria Rivas. 2015. From 'gender equality and 'women's empowerment'to global justice: Reclaiming a transformative agenda for gender and development. *Third World Quarterly* 36: 396–415. [CrossRef]

Cotter, David A., Joan M. Hermsen, Seth Ovadia, and Reeve Vanneman. 2001. The glass ceiling effect. *Social Forces* 80: 655–81. [CrossRef]

Duflo, Esther. 2012. Women empowerment and economic development. *Journal of Economic Literature* 50: 1051–79. [CrossRef]

Edler, Jakob, and Jan Fagerberg. 2017. Innovation policy: What, why, and how. *Oxford Review of Economic Policy* 33: 2–23. [CrossRef]

Fairlie, Robert W., and Alicia M. Robb. 2009. Gender differences in business performance: Evidence from the Characteristics of Business Owners survey. *Small Business Economics* 33: 375. [CrossRef]

Ferrant, Gaëlle. 2011. How Gender Inequalities Hinder Development: Cross-Country Evidence. HAL Id: halshs-00609828. Available online: https://halshs.archives-ouvertes.fr/halshs-00609828 (accessed on 23 July 2019).

Ferrant, Gaëlle, and Alexandre Kolev. 2016. *Does Gender Discrimination in Social Institutions Matter for Long-Term Growth? Cross-Country Evidence.* Working Paper No. 330. Paris: OECD Publishing, Available online: https://doi.org/10.1787/5jm2hz8dgls6-en (accessed on 23 July 2019).

Godin, Benoît. 2015. *Innovation Contested: The Idea of Innovation over the Centuries.* Abingdon-on-Thames: Routledge.

HDRO. 2018. Technical Notes. UN Development Programm. Available online: http://hdr.undp.org/sites/default/files/hdr2018_technical_notes.pdf (accessed on 23 July 2019).

Henry, Colette, Lene Foss, and Helene Ahl. 2016. Gender and entrepreneurship research: A review of methodological approaches. *International Small Business Journal* 34: 217–41. [CrossRef]

Kabeer, Naila, and Luisa Natali. 2013. Gender Equality and Economic Growth: Is there a Win-Win? *IDS Working Papers* 2013: 1–58. [CrossRef]

King, Elizabeth, and Andrew Mason. 2001. *Engendering Development: Through Gender Equality in Rights, Resources, and Voice.* Washington, DC: The World Bank.

Klasen, Stephan. 2002. Low schooling for girls, slower growth for all? Cross-country evidence on the effect of gender inequality in education on economic development. *The World Bank Economic Review* 16: 345–73. [CrossRef]

Klasen, Stephan, and Francesca Lamanna. 2009. The impact of gender inequality in education and employment on economic growth: New evidence for a panel of countries. *Feminist Economics* 15: 91–132. [CrossRef]

Neill, Stern, Lynn Metcalf, and Jonathan L. York. 2015. Seeing what others miss: A study of women entrepreneurs in high-growth startups. *Entrepreneurship Research Journal* 5: 293–322. [CrossRef]

OECD Development Centre. 2014. SIGI Methodological Background Paper. Available online: https://www.oecd.org/dev/development-gender/Backgroundpaper_cover.pdf (accessed on 23 July 2019).

Paoloni, Paola, and Paola Demartini. 2016. Women in management: Perspectives on a decade of research (2005–2015). *Palgrave Communications* 2: 16094. [CrossRef]

Parker, Simon C. 2018. *The Economics of Entrepreneurship*. Cambridge: Cambridge University Press.

Phills, James A., Kriss Deiglmeier, and Dale T. Miller. 2008. Rediscovering social innovation. *Stanford Social Innovation Review* 6: 34–43.

Roushdy, Rania. 2004. Intrahousehold Resource Allocation in Egypt: Does Women's Empowerment Lead to Greater Investments in Children? Paper presented at Economic Research Forum. Available online: https://erf.org.eg/wp-content/uploads/2017/04/0410_final.pdf (accessed on 23 July 2019).

Rubalcava, Luis, Graciela Teruel, and Duncan Thomas. 2009. Investments, Time Preferences, and Public Transfers Paid to Women. *Economic Development and Cultural Change* 57: 507–38. [CrossRef]

Schady, Norbert, and José Rosero. 2008. Are Cash Transfers Made to Women Spent Like Other Sources of Income? *Economics Letters* 101: 246–48. [CrossRef]

Startup Genome. 2018. Global Startup Ecosystem Report 2018. Available online: https://startupgenome.com/reports/2018/GSER-2018-v1.1.pdf (accessed on 15 August 2019).

United Nations. 2015. Transforming our World: The 2030 Agenda for Sustainable Development. Available online: https://sustainabledevelopment.un.org (accessed on 23 July 2019).

United Nations. 2018. Gender Equality: Why It Matters. Available online: https://www.un.org/sustainabledevelopment/wp-content/uploads/2018/09/Goal-5.pdf (accessed on 23 July 2019).

UN Women. 2017. SDG 5: Achieve Gender Equality and Empower All Women and Girls. Available online: https://www.unwomen.org/en/news/in-focus/women-and-the-sdgs/sdg-5-gender-equality (accessed on 23 July 2019).

van der Have, Robert P., and Luis Rubalcaba. 2016. Social innovation research: An emerging area of innovation studies? *Research Policy* 45: 1923–35. [CrossRef]

WorldBank. 2001. *Engendering Development through Gender Inequality in Rights, Resources and Voice*. Washington, DC: World Bank.

administrative sciences

MDPI

Article

Innovative Female-Led Startups. Do Women in Business Underperform?

Paola Demartini

Department of Business Studies, Roma Tre University, 00154 Roma RM, Italy; paola.demartini@uniroma3.it

Received: 29 October 2018; Accepted: 15 November 2018; Published: 18 November 2018

Abstract: The spur of innovative startups has provided an unprecedented opportunity for female entrepreneurship. However, the mainstream literature on startups has elaborated a gender performance gap hypothesis. Considering the speed of technological, social, and cultural changes that have taken place in this millennium, we wonder if this gap can still be found today, with particular reference to new technology-based ventures. A financial analysis has been conducted on a sample of innovative Italian startups, and the following variables have been used to assess the company's success: (i) size, (ii) profitability, (iii) efficiency, (iv) financial structure, and (v) financial management. Our results reveal that as far as financial performance is concerned, innovative female-led startups do not lag behind male ones in terms of dimension, company profitability, efficiency, and financial management. However, findings confirmed, even for our sample, that female businesses raise, on average, a lower amount of financial resources in comparison to men.

Keywords: Innovative female startups; underperformance hypothesis; gender gap; high tech female entrepreneur

---

1. Introduction

Female businesses are one of the fastest growing entrepreneurial populations in the world, and can make significant contributions to the innovation, employment, and wealth creation of all economies around the world (Brush et al. 2009; Hughes et al. 2012; Jennings and Brush 2013; Block et al. 2017). They also offer an answer in terms of self-employment to overcome the crisis of unemployment afflicting certain economies.

However, the empowerment of women in the main entrepreneurial ecosystems (Berger and Kuckertz 2016) is still contained in both the more developed and emerging countries, never exceeding 18% of the population of startups (Startup Genome 2018). In rational terms, the fact that women do not actively participate in the economic growth of GDP is undoubtedly a loss not only of wealth, but also of competitiveness, especially in a knowledge economy in which the entrepreneurial capital is increasingly a precious resource for the development of a country (Erikson 2002; Demartini and Paoloni 2014).

Another interesting aspect, to emphasise the contribution that women can make to a knowledge economy, is that in most advanced economies (but not only), the level of female education is comparable to that of men. Moreover, it has also grown in areas of knowledge known as disciplines of science, technology, engineering, and mathematics (STEM), which is traditionally a male domain (Beede et al. 2011).

Starting from the undisputed statistical evidence of a lower quantitative presence of female business owners, we are interested in understanding the strengths and weaknesses of female entrepreneurship today. Our study specifically aims at discussing the mainstream literature that found a gender gap, known as "*the gender underperformance hypothesis*" (Du Rietz and Henrekson 2000; Gatewood et al. 2003 for a literature review). In fact, most of the previous studies have found evidence at the aggregate level that female entrepreneurs tend to underperform compared to men (Rosa et al. 1996; Fairlie and Robb 2009).

Our study focuses on measuring the success of female companies, with particular reference to new technology-based ventures (Kuschel and Lepeley 2016). The latter are worthy of special attention because they can offer new business models and management styles useful for those who (entrepreneurs, consultants, politicians, trade associations, educators) are concerned with fostering the development of female entrepreneurship.

Our research question is as follows:

- Are innovative female-led startups less successful than male ones?

In the literature, there are two diverging views.

The mainstream literature, in line with the theory of resources (Alvarez and Busenitz 2001), considers that this gap is attributable to the limited resources of female startups, mainly due to the insufficient previous professional experience of the founders (Fairlie and Robb 2009) and a greater difficulty in accessing the capital market (Gatewood et al. 2009) and social networks (Aldrich 1989; Autio et al. 1997).

Other authors justify the lower profitability of female companies in the light of a lower risk appetite of women compared to men (Harris and Jenkins 2006). Because of this different attitude, female entrepreneurs are more oriented towards making choices that are positioned on a different and lower point on the risk-return curve (He et al. 2008).

On the other hand, there is an emerging stream of research, which considers that women in business, entrepreneurs and executives, aim for different goals, compared to those of men, being more interested in achieving a work-life balance, workers' well-being, and community welfare with respect to mere corporate profit (Justo et al. 2015). For this reason, the success of women's businesses cannot be measured and evaluated with the conventional performance indicators used in previous studies.

Our research draws on this debate and analyses the financial performance of a selected sample of innovative female-led startups. Considering the merciless speed of technological, social, and cultural changes, we wonder whether the performance gap mentioned above is still true for startups born after the world's financial crisis.

We develop our analysis in the Italian context in which law 221/2012 (known as Italy's Startup Act) has been introduced with the purpose to provide a favourable environment for the establishment and growth of innovative businesses. Since the latter must be registered in a special section of the Company Register, we had the opportunity to gather information about governance and financial data from a selected universe where businesses ought to be characterised by a high innovative and technological value. In detail, most of those female entrepreneurs work in knowledge-intensive business services, such as software production, scientific research, and other professional and technical services. In the past, all these activities have been a "male domain".

Our findings show that, even in Italy, female startups account for only 12% of the whole selected population. However, looking at the aspects taken simultaneously as a proxy of success (size, profitability, operational efficiency, and financial management), our results reveal that innovative female-led startups have similar performances to those of their male counterparts.

Therefore, we deem that a benchmark population should be used to study this phenomenon more thoroughly to find out about new female governance styles. This understanding can help not only female entrepreneurs, but also policymakers, when allocating resources to encourage innovation and educators and when training entrepreneurs to enhance the competitiveness and sustainability of their new ventures.

The paper is structured as follows. In Section 2, a brief review of the relevant literature is presented. Section 3 details the methodology, and Sections 4 and 5 summarise the findings of our preliminary analysis. Finally, Section 6 provides a research agenda for more in-depth investigation in the future.

2. Literature Review

Literature regarding entrepreneurship is particularly interested in explaining the drivers of entrepreneurial success (Song et al. 2008; Ayala and Manzano 2014; Boyer and Blazy 2014), and how women and men business owners perceive success (Kirkwood 2016). When considering the gender variable, the bulk of the extant research generally assumes that female entrepreneurship is less successful than male entrepreneurship (Du Rietz and Henrekson 2000; Fairlie and Robb 2009; Klapper and Parker 2010; more recently, see Brixiová and Kangoye 2016; Shinnar et al. 2018). However emerging research is challenging the so called "female underperformance hypothesis" (Robb and Watson 2012; Zolin et al. 2013; Justo et al. 2015; Aidis and Weeks 2016; Farhat and Mijid 2016).

In the following section, two diverging streams of research on female business performances will be analysed (see Figure 1).

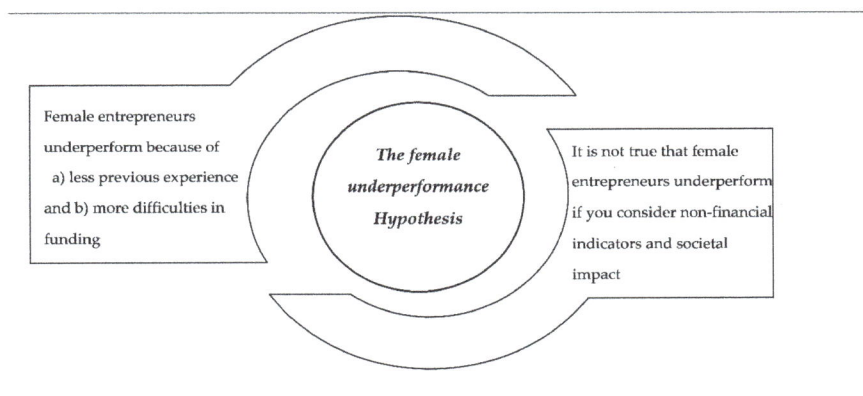

Figure 1. The academic debate on the "female underperformance hypothesis".

2.1. Research Supporting the "Female Underperformance Hypothesis"

Some studies have shown that women-owned businesses have a lower ability to achieve success and lower survival rates, sales, profits, and employees (Kalleberg and Leicht 1991; Rosa et al. 1996; Du Rietz and Henrekson 2000; Robb and Wolken 2002; Fairlie and Robb 2009).

In particular, focusing on the empirical evidence of Fairlie and Robb (2009), which is one of the most quoted, business success is evaluated by simultaneously taking into consideration three different proxy variables, which are:

- The closure rate, expressed by the exit rate of companies from the market;
- the company size, expressed in terms of sales volumes and average number of employees; and
- profitability, expressed by the company's ability to generate profits.

The analysed sample consists of companies whose performance refers to the period, 1992–1996. Information on the characteristics of business owners has been gathered by the U.S. Census Bureau. The differences between the two universes are evident:

- Female companies have lower survival rates than male companies: The average probability of closure between 1992 and 1996 is 24.4% for female-owned businesses and 21.6% for male companies;
- women-owned businesses tend to be smaller. In fact, they have sales roughly 80% lower than the average sales of male-owned firms; and
- finally, only 17.3% of female businesses have a fiscal year profit of at least US $10,000, compared to 36.4% of male companies.

From the analyses conducted by Fairlie and Robb (2009), the main factors explaining the diversity of performance between the two business universes emerge: (a) Previous work experience of the founders; (b) the level of education of the entrepreneurs; and (c) the amount of the initial capital.

Starting from the first, previous work experience of the entrepreneurs is a fundamental element, which can be associated with companies with better performances. Previous work experiences, in fact, increase human capital, in terms of skills and knowledge (Lentz and Laband 1990, Fairlie and Robb 2007), a useful tool for obtaining better business results. Concerning skills and knowledge, the issue of the level of education cannot be overlooked; the higher the level of education of the entrepreneurs, in fact, translates into better business results (Bates 1997; Åstebro and Bernhardt 2003; Headd 2003). As far as human capital is concerned, gender-based differences in newborn businesses also emerge in other studies. In fact, whereas male entrepreneurs leverage their industry and occupational background, women tend to leverage general human capital based on education and employment opportunities (BarNir 2012).

The last factor listed above, the total amount of initial capital, becomes relevant since the best performance is associated with businesses that are launched with the highest amount of startup capital (Bates 1997; Headd 2003; Coleman and Robb 2009; Robb and Coleman 2010). In their analysis, Fairlie and Robb (2009) consistently found that female entrepreneurs start their activities with less capital, in terms of both equity and loans, than men, which also explains the worst performances of female-owned businesses.

Although they are not able to verify it in their statistical analyses, the authors conclude by stating that other variables could explain the differences in gender performance. Among these are different objectives that women entrepreneurs pursue, which may have implications for business outcomes, different motivations and reasons to launch a new venture (Kourilsky and Walstad 1998; Blanchflower et al. 2001), and a different attitude towards risk (Bird and Brush 2002; Watson and Robinson 2003; Maxfield et al. 2010).

2.2. Research Challenging the "Female Underperformance Hypothesis"

In recent years, the number of scholars that challenge the "female underperformance hypothesis" has grown. Some authors, such as Robb and Watson (2012), suggested size adjusted performance measures, knowing that female-owned firms tend to be smaller than their male counterparts. Farhat and Mijid (2016) employed a matched sample approach to determine whether there is a gap in success, between male- and female-owned businesses. Based on their analysis of survival rate, profitability, growth, and financial capital injection measurement, they did not detect any gender gaps in terms of business performance.

There is also another school of thought of authors who believe that it is not true that women are less successful. Their studies are not based on statistical analysis disavowing previous results. The underpinning idea is that conventional indicators that measure the firm's success/failure (such as the rate of closure/survival) are not grasping the specificities of women's businesses. This is true for two reasons.

Some authors argue that it is necessary to introduce new, more expressive indicators of the real impact of female entrepreneurship. Following Aidis and Weeks (2016), high-impact female entrepreneurship is defined as firms headed by women that are market-expanding, export-oriented, and innovative, and whose assessment is focused on new indices, such as the Gender-Global Entrepreneurship and Development Index (GEDI 2018).

Other authors, instead, drawing on feminist theories (Ahl 2006; Ahl and Marlow 2012), suggest a new perspective to understand the statistical evidence. As an example, Justo et al. (2015) reject the female underperformance hypothesis by challenging the assumption that female-owned startups are more likely to fail. They argue that female entrepreneurs are actually more likely than male entrepreneurs to exit voluntarily for personal reasons and other professional/financial opportunities. This shows that the same indicators used in previous research can be interpreted differently, in light of the personal goals of entrepreneurs and how they perceive success. For example, Cliff (1998) shows that because women are more concerned about the quality of interpersonal relationships as a measure of business success than about quantitative indicators, they give a lower value to business growth than males.

Our empirical research develops from this debate and aims to challenge the gender underperformance hypothesis by analysing the financial performance of a sample of innovative Italian, female and male startups, thanks to the possibility of consulting an archive established by law since 2012 (known as Italy's Startup Act). Compared to previous surveys, our study contributes to previous literature by focusing on technology-based ventures.

3. Methodology

The goal of our empirical research is to evaluate the performance of a selected female and male innovative startup sample, by analysing some key indicators based on the Fairlie and Robb (2009) proxy of "business success", which allow us to confirm or refute the results of previous studies.

3.1. The Sample Selection

The sample selection is the result of the combined and simultaneous adoption of two databases: The Italian Company Register, in which there is a specific section for innovative startups, also with information related to the gender characteristics of their governance; and the AIDA database (https://aida.bvdinfo.com/), which contains financial data for a wide range of Italian limited liability companies.

As of February 2018, there were above 8,500 innovative startups registered in the special section of the Company Register. These companies must, among others, meet the following requirements:

- Have their headquarters in Italy or other EU countries, but with at least one production site branch in Italy; and
- produce, develop, and commercialise innovative goods or services of high technological value (See Appendix A for detailed characteristics).

As of 30 June 2018, the AIDA database has contained 3352 innovative startups, which were subsequently subject to filters relating the date of establishment and availability of the financial statements for at least two financial years, in order to have a sample consistent with our research purposes.

The first filter related to the date of establishment provides for the selection of all the innovative startups registered between January 2012 (the year of introduction of the Startup Act) and December 2016. From the application of this first filter, the number of startups fell to 750.

The second filter concerns the availability of financial statements. Its application was necessary since not all the companies contained in the database publish their financial reporting. Consequently, the sample number fell further to 248 innovative startups.

With the application of the third filter, the need was to have financial data available for at least two years, so that financial reporting could demonstrate a running company. From the application of this third filter, the sample was made up of 227 innovative startups (see Table 1).

Table 1. The sample selection process.

No. of Innovative Startups	Filters
8500	*Italian innovative startups included in the official Company Register* (June 2018)
3352	*1st filter*: Innovative startups included in the AIDA database
750	*2nd filter*: Period of establishment of a company (01/01/2012–31/12/2016)
248 *	*3rd filter*: Available Financial Statements
226	*4th filter*: Financial Statements available for at least two years

* Included two companies in winding-up.

After selecting 226 innovative startups, male and female businesses were identified, thanks to the gender codification of the startups' governance (see Appendix B for code details).

By applying this additional filter, three sub-samples of companies have been identified: exclusively or predominantly male or female companies and mixed companies, whose size is shown in Table 2.

Table 2. Our sample of innovative startups by gender governance.

	Female Startups	**Male Startups**	**Mixed Male/Female Startups**	**Total.**
No.	26	131	69	226
%	12%	58%	30%	100%

Fifty-eight percent of our sample consists of companies led exclusively or predominantly by men and only 12% by women. There are 30% of companies in which governance can be defined as mixed. However, the percentage of female governance companies in our sample is very close to that of the entire population of innovative Italian startups. In fact, as of February 2018, Demartini and Marchegiani (2018) found that businesses where women have an exclusive, min, or high influence on corporate governance account for 13.14% of the universe.

3.2. Data Gathering

We polarised our analyses on firms exclusively or predominantly run by men or women. Therefore, we focused on two samples made of 26 female and 131 male businesses.

To analyse the success of the innovative startups, financial ratios were obtained from the AIDA database, which contains the financial statements of the Italian startups. When looking at the two samples, we conducted a financial analysis by focusing on the income statements and balance sheets, and cash flow statements. Data refer to the financial reporting of the fiscal year of 2016 as not all companies had already filed the 2017 financial statements.

3.3. Data Analysis

We aimed not only to compare our findings with previous descriptive statistics (see Table 3), but also to express a more comprehensive assessment of the management performance. For the last reason, a complementary financial analysis is conducted on the two aggregates of companies (see Table 4). As is well known, a financial analysis is used to analyze whether an entity is profitable, stable, and solvent (Higgins 2012).

To compare our evidence with Fairlie and Robb (2009, p. 377), the following key indicators were collected as proxy variables of business success:

- *Closure rate*: Measured by the number of companies no longer operating;
- *Size:* Measured by number of employees and annual sales turnover;
- *Profitability*: measured by EBITDA/sales.

Table 3. Business outcomes.

Variables	Fairly & Robb's Measurement	Our Measurement
Closure rate	% of firms no longer operating	No. of firms no longer operating
Size	number of employees; annual sales	No. of employees; annual sales
Profitability	% of firms with positive profits; % of firms with net profit >$10,000	EBITDA/sales

As far as profitability is concerned, it should be highlighted that while Fairlie and Robb (2009) focused on net income, the main ratio we took into consideration was EBITDA/Sales. The latter indicator is more suitable to effectively express the profitability of a startup that may not yet have reached the break-even point, being still in a launch or development phase.

Generally speaking, it is very difficult for analysts valuing early-stage deals. The difficulty lies in the fact that relatively little or even no hard historical data exists with which an investor could make an informed decision about the company's future prospects. Quantitative modelling runs into serious obstacles here; past successes are not necessarily an indication of future performance. EBITDA can be used to analyze and compare profitability between companies and industries because it eliminates the effects of financing and accounting decisions. In practice, value is often expressed as a multiple of some cash flow measure, e.g., enterprise value in relation to EBITDA.

Table 4. Other variables.

Other Variables	Measurement
Operational Efficiency	Revenues per employee, value added per employee, assets turnover ratio, working capital turnover ratio
Financial structure	Total equity; total liability and equity; leverage ratio
Financial management	Interest expenses to revenues; liquidity ratio, current ratio

To complement the previous analysis, we also focused on the following aspects:

- *Operational Efficiency*: Efficiency is assessed through the turnover ratios (assets turnover and working capital turnover ratios) and the productivity indicators (revenues per employee, value added per employee);
- *Financial structure*: Assessed through measurement of total equity; total liability and equity; leverage ratio.; and
- *Financial management*: Analysed through the liquidity ratio, current ratio, and interest expenses to revenues.

Our aim is not only to verify the total amount of financial resources that the female entrepreneurs are able to collect, but also their ability both to manage it and mitigate the risks of financial embarrassment.

A list of the main financial indicators is included in Appendix C.

4. Results

In the following section, we will present our results. The analysis was carried out concerning the two sub-samples through the measurement of the average values of the key selected indicators (calculated as the sum of the values of the indicators of the individual companies divided by the number of observations).

4.1. Closure Rate

Only two companies belonging to the male universe presented a critical financial situation in the chosen period (2012–2017), liquidation, with the consequence that these were eliminated from the analysed sample.

4.2. Size

According to the average indicators shown in Table 5, it is worthwhile to notice that female companies do not present a dimensional profile significantly different from that of male companies.

Table 5. Average company size.

Variables	Female Startups	Male Startups
Employees (No)	11	9
Sales € (Thousands)	1113	1097

4.3. Profitability

Before moving on to a detailed analysis of the ratios, we begin by declaring that there are no profound differences in terms of profitability between the two samples, although female startups show slightly better results (see Table 6).

Table 6. Profitability.

Variables	Female Startups	Male Startups
EBITDA/sales	3.33%	0.68%

The average percentage values of EBITDA/sales show that female companies have greater profitability than male ones (3.33% vs. 0.68%), contrary to what was stated in the previous literature.

4.4. Operational Efficiency

Regarding company efficiency, the analysis of the indicators reported in Table 7 shows that women's businesses are even more efficient than men's.

Table 7. Operational efficiency.

Variables	Female Startups	Male Startups
Revenues per employee, € (Thousands)	265	238
Added value per employee, € (Thousands)	54	57
Total assets turnover ratio	1.20	1.11
Working capital turnover ratio	1.98	1.67

In fact, women's startups disclose, on average, higher revenues per employee (+11.1%) (but a lower added value per employee, −4.6%). Also, the turnover ratios express a greater pace of the female enterprises to renew their assets through business revenues.

4.5. Financial Structure

The first objective of our analysis was to understand whether female businesses are characterised by greater difficulty in raising capital, as suggested by the previous literature. In the analysis of the financial statements, these difficulties were revealed by lower levels of equity and total sources of funding, or by a higher cost of debt capital applied to women entrepreneurs.

To this end, the following indicators, including total equity and total liabilities and owner's equity, were taken into consideration. Findings confirmed, even for our sample, that female businesses raise, on average, a lower amount of financial resources in comparison to men (−6.9%).

To complete the picture of the companies' financial structure, the leverage ratio (calculated as the total assets divided by total equity) was equal to 22 for female startups and 10.14 for men, shows a lower capitalisation of female companies. Therefore, the female startups of our sample, despite having a smaller amount of financial resources in general, are overall more indebted and therefore make more substantial use of leverage (see Table 8).

Table 8. Financial structure.

Variables	Female Startups	Male Startups
Total equity, € (Thousands)	284	388
Liabilities and Equity, € (Thousands)	1286	1382
Leverage ratio (times)	22.00	10.14

4.6. Financial Management

The data at our disposal did not allow us to calculate the company's cost of money, but we can highlight that female businesses have a lower incidence of interest expenses on revenues (0.88% vs. 1.02%). Finally, the liquidity and current ratios were taken into consideration. Regarding these two, the two samples present a very similar ability to manage liquidity (see Table 9).

Table 9. Financial management.

Variables	Female Startups	Male Startups
Interest expense to revenue ratio (%)	0.88	1.02
Liquidity ratio (times)	1.33	1.36
Current ratio (times)	1.54	1.55

5. Discussion

Our findings reveal that as far as financial performance is concerned, innovative female-led startups do not lag behind male ones in terms of dimension, company profitability, efficiency, and financial management. Thus, the underperformance hypothesis is not confirmed. However, on average, female-led startups have less of owners' equity and funds.

In detail, our sample of innovative female-led startups does not reflect the characteristics that have emerged from previous research (Fairlie and Robb 2009), according to which female businesses are smaller than male ones, perform less on the market, and have less stable financial standings (see Figure 2).

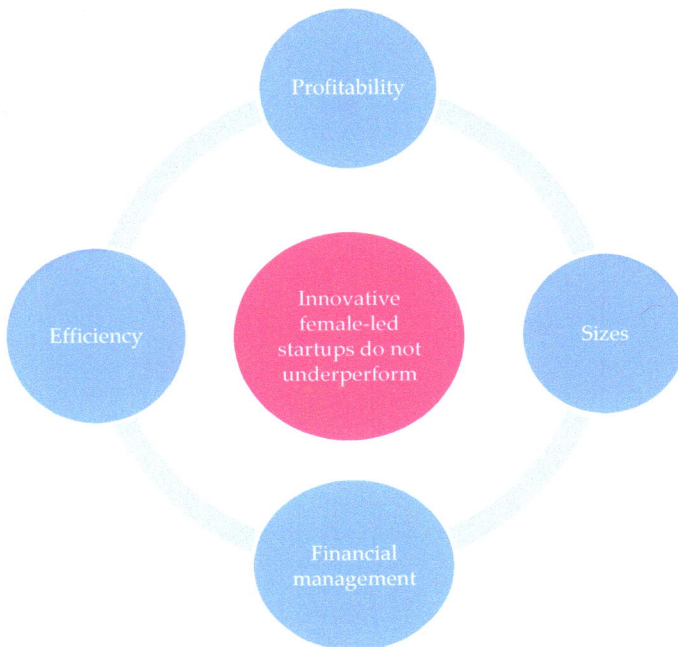

Figure 2. Testing the underperformance hypothesis. Our findings.

However, the peculiarity of our sample, which is formed by innovative new ventures, many of which operate in the knowledge-intensive business service sector, should be emphasised. It is, therefore, possible to hypothesise that the non-confirmation of the underperformance hypothesis is strongly correlated with the characteristics of the sector and the type of services offered by the companies. Indeed, we deem that where competence and knowledge are factors on which to build the company value proposition, the gender variable does not have an impact on business performance.

In the following, each variable will be discussed.

Starting with *average company size*, we have found that the dimension of women's businesses concerning sales and numbers of employees is comparable to that of men's businesses. Therefore, in our sample, the size gap, as stated in the previous literature, is not shown.

As far as corporate *profitability* is concerned, contrary to what was stated in the previous literature, female companies are not less profitable than male-owned businesses. Even in terms of *efficiency*, female companies showed even better results concerning both the revenues per employee (proxy of market effectiveness) and capital turnover (proxy of asset management efficiency).

Regarding *financial capital*, we have discovered that total equity is, on average, lower in women's businesses (confirming the analysis of Fairlie and Robb 2009). It is also true that female startups have less total liabilities and owners' capital than male startups. At the same time, it should be emphasised that female startups show, in general, efficient financial management regarding liquidity management and the incidence of interest expenses on revenues.

6. Conclusions, Implications and Future Research

Our study aimed to answer the question of whether the innovative female-led startups, founded in recent years, underperformed in comparison to the male ones. This is one of the first exploratory studies allowing us to shed light on an emerging phenomenon concerning the spur of new technology-based ventures.

Previous studies have proven women's businesses to be less successful. However, these analyses were carried out regarding data dating back to before 2000, and not to a sample of innovative companies.

With our study, we do not confirm this hypothesis, and indeed, our findings reveal a slightly better management efficiency in the female aggregate. However, it has been confirmed that, on average, female entrepreneurs raise less equity and sources of funding than men.

As far as the limits of our financial analyses are concerned, it should be noted that the conclusions reached in this research are based on the descriptive analysis of average indicators referring to fiscal year of 2016, and as fully explained in the previous paragraphs, reflect the characteristics of the selected companies. Our results, therefore, offer food for thought, but cannot be extended to the universe of innovative Italian startups, nor to other contexts.

6.1. Implications and Future Research

Traditional models are not always able to account for new phenomena. Thus, we deem that it is important for scholars to concentrate on applied research to develop new frameworks.

Regarding female entrepreneurship, we advocate that it could be important to understand the role of gender, in particular about new technology and business opportunities, especially in the knowledge intensive business service sector, ranging from artificial intelligence to big data management, and social media.

It could be worthwhile to analyse new business models and the impact of new technologies from a gender perspective both from the point of view of women as consumers, workers, and as entrepreneurs (UNCTAD 2014; Cesaroni et al. 2017).

We deem that future research should extend the assessment of female business performance outside the mainstream field of financial analysis and consider non-financial information and indicators referring to:

-     Individual and personal wellbeing; and
-     societal impact (about social performance, see Ebrahim and Rangan 2014)

Thus far, literature is more prolific on the relationships between women on boards and corporate social responsibility (Bear et al. 2010). A famous professional report (Startup Genome 2018) tackled the issue in its latest survey looking at how female and male founders might differ as far as their goals are concerned. Unsurprisingly, women are more likely to be oriented toward goals with a societal impact than men. In fact, they say they want to "*change the world*" with their startups, while men seem to be more market-oriented and more likely to say their main mission is to "*build high-quality products.*" (Startup Genome 2018, p. 41).

We are aware that a statistical analysis can be useful to describe a phenomenon, but not to answer questions regarding how women run a business. We are now considering whether we can talk about an emerging female management style based on flexibility, creativity, and resilience.

To answer that last question, a qualitative and interdisciplinary analysis is needed to study women's leadership and decision-making behaviours when running an innovative startup. In a previous exploratory survey (Demartini and Marchegiani 2018), some recurring features emerged in the management of these companies, which seem to us to be the critical success factors for their growth:

- Entrepreneurs with advanced knowledge and expertise achieved mainly in their high school educational path;
- a participatory leadership that fosters integrated thinking and participatory processes of co-creation; and
- a strong focus on personal relationships and networking as an added value of the business model.

These aspects are worthy of being highlighted and deeply investigated in future research, with special regard to successful female startups as benchmarking case studies. They could provide useful evidence for policymakers, public, private, and not for profit organisations and individuals (i.e., business angel, professionals, academics) that are interested in fostering female entrepreneurship.

Supporting female entrepreneurship is undoubtedly a useful element for sustainable growth, not only because of the economic benefit that can derive from the growth of female entrepreneurship but also because it could be a fundamental component for cultural growth, which is essential for achieving gender equality.

We envisage the following areas of improvements to support women-led innovative startups:

- Adequate funding;
- incentives to foster young women's education in disciplines of science, technology, engineering, and mathematics (STEM); and
- actions to let people know they can learn from successful models of high tech female entrepreneurs.

6.2. Funding

Venture capital and business angel financing have traditionally been advocated as important sources of financing for young innovative firms that find it difficult to access bank or debt finance. Moreover, the landscape for entrepreneurial finance has changed over the last years. Several new actors have emerged (i.e., crowdfunding, government-sponsored funds, etc.) and some of these new players value not only financial goals, but are also interested in non-financial goals (i.e., technological and community-based goals). Our research revealed that women's new businesses are even more efficient than men's and that female entrepreneurs are more likely to be oriented toward goals with a societal impact than male ones. For the above-mentioned reasons, we deem that investors should be aware of the potentiality that female led-startups own.

6.3. Young Women Education

Furthermore, we suggest that more action is needed that aims to bridge the gender gap in science, technology, engineering, and mathematics (STEM). This research could be successful to promote scientific and technical training for girls and raise the debate on new digital skills needed to create new high tech ventures.

6.4. Successful Models of High Tech Female Entrepreneurs

Finally, we deem that through inspirational keynote speakers, personal development workshops, technical classes, and networking opportunities, women in technology can connect, learn, and act on gender diversity by sharing the experiences of industry leaders and developing women's skills, both soft and technical.

Funding: This research received no external funding.

Conflicts of Interest: The author declares no conflict of interest.

Appendix A

Table A1. Italy's startup Act.

Definition and Characteristics of Innovative Italian Startups by Law 221/2012
Innovative startups are companies with shared capital (i.e., limited companies), including cooperatives, the shares or significant registered capital shares of which are not listed on a regulated market nor on a multilateral negotiation system. These companies must also meet the following requirements:

- be new or have been operational for less than 5 years;
- have their headquarters in Italy or another EU countries, but with at least one production site branch in Italy;
- have a yearly turnover lower than 5 million Euros;
- do not distribute profits;
- produce, develop and commercialise innovative goods or services of high technological value;
- are not the result of a merger, split-up or selling-off of a company or branch;
- be of innovative character, which can be identified by at least one of the following criteria:

1. at least 15% of the company's expenses can be attributed to R&D activities;
2. at least 1/3 of the total workforce are PhD students, the holders of a PhD or researchers; alternatively, 2/3 of the total workforce must hold a Master's degree;
3. the enterprise is the holder, depositary or licensee of a registered patent (industrial property) or the owner of a program for original registered computers.

Appendix B

Table A2. Italian innovative startups. Classification by gender governance.

% Owners and Directors' Gender	Governance Classification
$X = 100\%$	Exclusively Male or Female
$X > 66\% \lor X < 99\%$	Predominately Male or Female
$X > 51\% \lor X < 66\%$	Mixed Male/Female

Source: Italian Company Register.

Appendix C

List of main financial indicators

EBITDA is the acronym for Earnings before Interests, Tax, Depreciation and Amortisation.

The Total Assets Turnover Ratio is calculated as follows: net sales or revenue divided by the average total assets during the same 12 month period. It can often be used as an indicator of the efficiency with which a company is deploying its assets in generating revenue.

The working capital turnover ratio is calculated as follows: net annual sales or revenue divided by the average amount of working capital during the same 12 month period. It indicates a company's effectiveness in using its working capital.

Leverage ratio (times) compares equity to assets and is calculated as total assets divided by total equity. A high ratio indicates that the business owners may not be providing sufficient equity to fund a business.

Liquidity (quick) ratio is calculated as follows: (Cash equivalents + marketable securities + accounts receivable) divided by current liabilities.

The current ratio is calculated as follows: Current assets divided by current liabilities

Interest expense to revenue ratio = Total interest expenses divided by total revenues

References

Ahl, Helene, and Susan Marlow. 2012. Exploring the dynamics of gender, feminism and entrepreneurship: Advancing debate to escape a dead end? *Organization* 19: 543–62. [CrossRef]

Ahl, Helene. 2006. Why research on women entrepreneurs needs new directions. *Entrepreneurship Theory and Practice* 30: 595–621. [CrossRef]

Aidis, Ruta, and Julie Weeks. 2016. Mapping the gendered ecosystem: The evolution of measurement tools for comparative high-impact female entrepreneur development. *International Journal of Gender and Entrepreneurship* 8: 330–52. [CrossRef]

Aldrich, Howard. 1989. Networking among women entrepreneurs. *Women-Owned Businesses* 103: 132.

Alvarez, Sharon A., and Lowell W. Busenitz. 2001. The entrepreneurship of resource-based theory. *Journal of management* 27: 755–75. [CrossRef]

Åstebro, Thomas, and Irwin Bernhardt. 2003. Start-up financing, owner characteristics, and survival. *Journal of Economics and Business* 55: 303–19. [CrossRef]

Autio, Erkko, Robert H. Keeley, Magnus Klofsten, and Thomas Ulfstedt. 1997. Entrepreneurial intent among students: Testing an intent model in Asia, Scandinavia and USA. In *Proceedings of the Seventeenth Annual Entrepreneurship Research Conference*. Wellesley: Babson College, pp. 133–47.

Ayala, Juan-Carlos, and Guadalupe Manzano. 2014. The resilience of the entrepreneur. Influence on the success of the business. A longitudinal analysis. *Journal of Economic Psychology* 42: 126–35. [CrossRef]

BarNir, Anat. 2012. Starting technologically innovative ventures: Reasons, human capital, and gender. *Management Decision* 50: 399–419. [CrossRef]

Bates, Timothy. 1997. Financing small business creation: The case of Chinese and Korean immigrant entrepreneurs. *Journal of Business Venturing* 12: 109–24. [CrossRef]

Bear, Stephen, Noushi Rahman, and Corinne Post. 2010. The impact of board diversity and gender composition on corporate social responsibility and firm reputation. *Journal of Business Ethics* 97: 207–21. [CrossRef]

Beede, David N., Tiffany A. Julian, David Langdon, George McKittrick, Beethika Khan, and Mark E. Doms. 2011. Women in STEM: A gender gap to innovation. *SSRN Electronic Journal*. [CrossRef]

Berger, Elisabeth S. C., and Andreas Kuckertz. 2016. Female entrepreneurship in startup ecosystems worldwide. *Journal of Business Research* 69: 5163–68. [CrossRef]

Bird, Barbara, and Candida Brush. 2002. A gendered perspective on organizational creation. *Entrepreneurship Theory and Practice* 26: 41–65. [CrossRef]

Blanchflower, David G., Andrew Oswald, and Alois Stutzer. 2001. Latent entrepreneurship across nations. *European Economic Review* 45: 680–91. [CrossRef]

Block, Joern H., Christian O. Fisch, and Mirjam Van Praag. 2017. The Schumpeterian entrepreneur: A review of the empirical evidence on the antecedents, behaviour and consequences of innovative entrepreneurship. *Industry and Innovation* 24: 61–95. [CrossRef]

Boyer, Tristan, and Régis Blazy. 2014. Born to be alive? The survival of innovative and non-innovative French micro-start-ups. *Small Business Economics* 42: 669–83. [CrossRef]

Brixiová, Zuzana, and Thierry Kangoye. 2016. Gender and constraints to entrepreneurship in Africa: New evidence from Swaziland. *Journal of Business Venturing Insights* 5: 1–8. [CrossRef]

Brush, Candida G., Anne De Bruin, and Friederike Welter. 2009. A gender-aware framework for women's entrepreneurship. *International Journal of Gender and Entrepreneurship* 1: 8–24. [CrossRef]

Cesaroni, Francesca M., Paola Demartini, and Paola Paoloni. 2017. Women in business and social media: Implications for female entrepreneurship in emerging countries. *African Journal of Business Management* 11: 316–326.

Cliff, Jennifer E. 1998. Does one size fit all? Exploring the relationship between attitudes towards growth, gender, and business size. *Journal of Business Venturing* 13: 523–42. [CrossRef]

Coleman, Susan, and Alicia Robb. 2009. A comparison of new firm financing by gender: Evidence from the Kauffman Firm Survey data. *Small Business Economics* 33: 397. [CrossRef]

Demartini, Paola, and Lucia Marchegiani. 2018. Born to Be Alive? Female Entrepreneurship and Innovative Start-Ups. In *IPAZIA Workshop on Gender Issues*. Cham: Springer, pp. 219–35.

Demartini, Paola, and Paola Paoloni. 2014. Defining the entrepreneurial capital construct. *Chinese Business Review* 13: 668–80.

Du Rietz, Anita, and Magnus Henrekson. 2000. Testing the female underperformance hypothesis. *Small Business Economics* 14: 1–10. [CrossRef]

Ebrahim, Alnoor, and V. Kasturi Rangan. 2014. What impact? A framework for measuring the scale and scope of social performance. *California Management Review* 56: 118–41. [CrossRef]

Erikson, Truls. 2002. Entrepreneurial capital: The emerging venture's most important asset and competitive advantage. *Journal of Business Venturing* 17: 275–90. [CrossRef]

Fairlie, Robert W., and Alicia M. Robb. 2009. Gender differences in business performance: Evidence from the Characteristics of Business Owners survey. *Small Business Economics* 33: 375. [CrossRef]

Fairlie, Robert W., and Alicia Robb. 2007. Families, human capital, and small business: Evidence from the characteristics of business owners survey. *ILR Review* 60: 225–45. [CrossRef]

Farhat, Joseph, and Naranchimeg Mijid. 2016. Do women lag behind men? A matched-sample analysis of the dynamics of gender gaps. *Journal of Economics and Finance* 1–28. [CrossRef]

Gatewood, Elizabeth J., Candida G. Brush, Nancy M. Carter, Patricia G. Greene, and Myra M. Hart, eds. 2003. *Women Entrepreneurs, Their Ventures, and the Venture Capital Industry: An Annotated Bibliography*. Stockholm: Entrepreneurship and Small Business Research Institute (ESBRI).

Gatewood, Elizabeth J., Candida G. Brush, Nancy M. Carter, Patricia G. Greene, and Myra M. Hart. 2009. Diana: A symbol of women entrepreneurs' hunt for knowledge, money, and the rewards of entrepreneurship. *Small Business Economics* 32: 129–44. [CrossRef]

GEDI. 2018. Available online: https://thegedi.org/research/womens-entrepreneurship-index/ (accessed on 17 November 2018).

Harris, Christine R., and Michael Jenkins. 2006. Gender differences in risk assessment: Why do women take fewer risks than men? *Judgment and Decision Making* 1: 48–63.

He, Xin, J. Jeffrey Inman, and Vikas Mittal. 2008. Gender jeopardy in financial risk taking. *Journal of Marketing Research* 45: 414–24. [CrossRef]

Headd, Brian. 2003. Redefining business success: Distinguishing between closure and failure. *Small Business Economics* 21: 51–61. [CrossRef]

Higgins, Robert C. 2012. *Analysis for Financial Management*. New York: McGraw-Hill/Irwin.

Hughes, Karen D., Jennifer E. Jennings, Candida Brush, Sara Carter, and Friederike Welter. 2012. Extending women's entrepreneurship research in new directions. *Entrepreneurship Theory and Practice* 36: 429–42. [CrossRef]

Jennings, Jennifer E., and Candida G. Brush. 2013. Research on women entrepreneurs: Challenges to (and from) the broader entrepreneurship literature? *The Academy of Management Annals* 7: 663–715. [CrossRef]

Justo, Rachida, Dawn R. DeTienne, and Philipp Sieger. 2015. Failure or voluntary exit? Reassessing the female underperformance hypothesis. *Journal of Business Venturing* 30: 775–92. [CrossRef]

Kalleberg, Arne L., and Kevin T. Leicht. 1991. Gender and organizational performance: Determinants of small business survival and success. *Academy of Management Journal* 34: 136–61.

Kirkwood, Jodyanne Jane. 2016. How women and men business owners perceive success. *International Journal of Entrepreneurial Behavior & Research* 22: 594–615.

Klapper, Leora F., and Simon C. Parker. 2010. Gender and the business environment for new firm creation. *The World Bank Research Observer* 26: 237–57. [CrossRef]

Kourilsky, Marilyn L., and William B. Walstad. 1998. Entrepreneurship and female youth: Knowledge, attitudes, gender differences, and educational practices. *Journal of Business Venturing* 13: 77–88. [CrossRef]

Kuschel, Katherina, and María-Teresa Lepeley. 2016. Women start-ups in technology: Literature review and research agenda to improve participation. *International Journal of Entrepreneurship and Small Business* 27: 333–46. [CrossRef]

Lentz, Bernard F., and David N. Laband. 1990. Entrepreneurial success and occupational inheritance among proprietors. *Canadian Journal of Economics* 23: 563–79. [CrossRef]

Maxfield, Sylvia, Mary Shapiro, Vipin Gupta, and Susan Hass. 2010. Gender and risk: Women, risk taking and risk aversion. *Gender in Management: An International Journal* 25: 586–604. [CrossRef]

Robb, Alicia M., and John Watson. 2012. Gender differences in firm performance: Evidence from new ventures in the United States. *Journal of Business Venturing* 27: 544–58. [CrossRef]

Robb, Alicia M., and Susan Coleman. 2010. Financing strategies of new technology-based firms: A comparison of women-and men-owned firms. *Journal of Technology Management & Innovation* 5: 30–50.

Robb, Alicia, and John Wolken. 2002. Firm, owner, and financing characteristics: Differences between female-and male-owned small businesses. FEDS Working Paper No. 2002-18. Available online: https://ssrn.com/abstract=306800 (accessed on 17 November 2018).

Rosa, Peter, Sara Carter, and Daphne Hamilton. 1996. Gender as a determinant of small business performance: Insights from a British study. *Small Business Economics* 8: 463–78. [CrossRef]

Shinnar, Rachel S., Dan K. Hsu, Benjamin C. Powell, and Haibo Zhou. 2018. Entrepreneurial intentions and start-ups: Are women or men more likely to enact their intentions? *International Small Business Journal* 36: 60–80. [CrossRef]

Song, Michael, Ksenia Podoynitsyna, Hans Van Der Bij, and Johannes I. M. Halman. 2008. Success factors in new ventures: A meta-analysis. *Journal of Product Innovation Management* 25: 7–27. [CrossRef]

Startup Genome. 2018. Global Startup Ecosystem Report 2018. Available online: https://startupgenome.com/reports/2018/GSER-2018-v1.1.pdf (accessed on 16 November 2018).

UNCTAD (United Nations Conference on Trade and Development). 2014. *Empowering Women Entrepreneurs through Information and Communications Technologies: A Practical Guide*. UNCTAD/DTL/STICT/2013/2. New York and Geneva: United Nations publication.

Watson, John, and Sherry Robinson. 2003. Adjusting for risk in comparing the performances of male-and female-controlled SMEs. *Journal of Business Venturing* 18: 773–88. [CrossRef]

Zolin, Roxanne, Michael Stuetzer, and John Watson. 2013. Challenging the female underperformance hypothesis. *International Journal of Gender and Entrepreneurship* 5: 116–29. [CrossRef]

*administrative
sciences*

MDPI

Article

Female-Owned Innovative Startups in Italy: Status Quo and Implications

Paola Paoloni [1,*] and Giuseppe Modaffari [2]

[1] Dipartimento di Diritto ed Economia delle Attività Produttive, Università degli Studi di Roma "La Sapienza", Rome 00185, Italy
[2] Department UNISU, Niccolò Cusano University, Rome 00166, Italy; giuseppe.modaffari@unicusano.it
* Correspondence: paola.paoloni@uniroma1.it

Received: 23 August 2018; Accepted: 18 October 2018; Published: 29 October 2018

Abstract: The aim of the paper is to provide an overview of the current literature of this business phenomenon with regard to gender studies and to point out what is substantially happening and what has happened in the Italian economic context. The main research questions were RQ1: How is the phenomenon of female Startups treated from a scientific point of view? RQ2: Which is the Italian situation of this phenomenon? The methodology used is both qualitative and explorative. A bidirectional analysis has been carried out for this purpose. In order to expand the first research question (RQ1), an analysis was carried out of the articles in the EBSCO database on the topic of female startups. In order to expand the second question (RQ2), an analysis was carried out on the data concerning the phenomenon of female startups, using the register of companies held at the Chambers of Commerce which were territorially competent. Our research, carried out within the Italian economic context, demonstrates how the phenomenon of Woman Startups (WSU), even if it is widely expanding, is inherent in all the typical elements of female entrepreneurship, as reported in the literature by gender scholars. The main factors that emerge for the WSU are the small size and the undercapitalization in the startup phase. This work contributes to the expansion of studies on the topic of startups in the context of gender and can be useful to the social context, new entrepreneurs, and practitioners of the sector.

Keywords: startups; woman startups; gender analysis

1. Introduction

A startup can be defined as a particular type of innovation-focused company. In the Italian political order, a startup that has been established for no more than 60 months, has a turnover of less than 5 million Euros, has not distributed profits, and is not the result of any extraordinary operation, such as mergers or demergers, as well as having as an object social and prevalent innovative products and/or services with high technological value, is considered "innovative". This special regulatory provision arises as a way to revamp the Italian economy, following the deep economic–financial crisis of 2007. Various changes have been made since 2012 to make the startups an effective tool to revamp and improve national business performance.

In addition to these active policy measures implemented by the Italian Government, the Italian Chambers of Commerce have implemented forms of quarterly monitoring/feedback through the collection of data of the companies relating to, for example, the period of incorporation, class of share capital, legal status, etc.

With regard to this last aspect, we considered it necessary to better analyze the reality of the national territory, after a survey of the scientific literature. Our first RQ aimed to define "The situation in the literature of female startups". The starting point to answer our first question was the study conducted by Paoloni and Demartini (2016), in which, treating gender studies, they identify, schematize, and deepen the main problems that entrepreneurs have to face in carrying out their business. Our research was qualitative and started with the query, through some keywords, of the EBSCO database[1]. The cataloging of the research records according to the criteria of the Paoloni and Demartini (2016) study allowed us to understand which are the most recurring themes in international female startups and which of them academics have debated. The answer to RQ1 represents a benchmark of academic literature, for the subsequent study of data concerning the Italian economic context, namely the "Monitoring of the phenomenon in Italy", our RQ2.

In order to structure the RQ2, some official data concerning Italian startups in the second quarter of 2018 were examined and processed, which can be consulted in the special section of the register of companies held at the Italian Chambers of Commerce.

Our first contribution in the Italian economic context was one of the few pieces of evidence on the topic of "gender startups".

In order to expand on what we said, the present work is structured as follows: In the second section, the literature review will be carried out on the "gender startup"; the third section will illustrate the research methodology used to analyze the data of Italian startups, and the fourth section will show the results obtained from the analysis with regard to territorial distribution, consistency of the share capital, legal nature, and activity exercised by Italian female startups.

The present work will conclude with the contiguous observation between what the academics demonstrated and what emerged from the real data on Italian female startups, noting limitations and new and future implications of study.

2. Literature Review

For the analysis and subsequent observation of the results of the RQ1, research was conducted on the EBSCO portal; the focus of our research was "woman startups" and "female startups". In order to analyze all the contributions to the topic, our keywords were structured to include all those results that could be left out by different typing within the search engine. The question on the DB concerned the research, combined with the words "wom * star *" (for woman startups) and "female star *" (for female startups), of academic articles from 2000 to today.

The research as a whole led to 216 results on women entrepreneurship, of which only 39 dealt with the theme of woman startups (WSU).

The cataloging of the results was possible, starting from a recent study conducted by Paoloni and Demartini (2016), which represents an important benchmark on the analysis of gender studies.

The authors' work helped us to place each result on specific themes on gender studies. In the same way, in our research and analysis of the literature, we proceeded to treat the 39 results of the Woman Startups (WSU) according to the category they belong to.

A1 Corporate governance: This category includes those articles concerning the presence of women on boards of directors (Pesonen et al. 2009), board of statutory auditors or other company committees. A1 also includes research in the field of female careers (Healy et al. 2011; Tlaiss and Kauser (2011), the crystal ceiling phenomenon (Guillaume and Pochic 2009) or the phenomenon of "gender quotas".

In our search in the A1 category, we had only one result: Ebersberger and Pirhofer (2011) observed, in the startup processes of female startups, the factors of academic entrepreneurship that influence company management. The results showed how an academic approach of women in management increases value only in large startups, but produces a limited effect in small female startups.

---

[1]   Available to www.search.ebscohost.com.

A2 Female entrepreneurship: Includes all research on women's businesses, the family business, the relational capital with the activation of formal and informal relationships that a woman activates during the life cycle of her own company (Paoloni 2011), and the different problems she encounters in doing business. (Lewis and Simpson 2010; Kirkwood 2009; Hancock, 2012; Tyler and Cohen 2008)

Many articles in our research led to the A2 category. Elam and Terjesen (2010) observed the evolution of woman startups, taking into consideration macroeconomic variables, such as unemployment (unemployment), economic growth (economic growth), the health of the state (national wealth), and the degree of liberalization of economy (economic freedom). The results of the research show a distinct disadvantage and delay of woman startups in the industry sector; moreover, the disadvantage is even stronger in countries where there is a wage difference (gender wage inequality) widespread among the population, and finally, female leadership is not a symptom of success for startups.

Dechant and Lamky (2005) studied female entrepreneurship around the Gulf of Arabia (Saudi Arabia), using a sample of ten Woman Startups to observe the main obstacle factors to their business, such as capital and the finding of resources, commercial networks, and the balance between work and family (work/family balance). All this is even harder if we consider the cultural traditions of the countries of origin of the WSU, which are Islamic.

Welsh et al. (2013) studied, in the Sudanese reality, the type of support that the entrepreneurs get in relation to their personal problems, managerial skills, recourse to credit, and the level of education, the prediction of future work, and institutional support.

Barnir (2014) expanded on the effects that entrepreneurial improvisation and human capital have on common entrepreneurship. To do this, he used 3 impulse factors (impetus factors)—identified as business opportunities, mentor (guide), and the nature of work—and 4 human capital factors, namely education, employment size, managerial experience, and entrepreneurial skills.

Neill et al. (2015) dealt with women's ability to repeat business initiatives through some unknown elements that allow them to start a creative process. The authors showed how the perception of an opportunity, combined with a strong entrepreneurial mentality, increases the likelihood of creating a new initiative. Finally, Welsh et al. (2016) studied the influence on the economic development phases (SEDs) of "family support" and "personal problem" in the female startups of Canada, China, Morocco, Poland, South Korea, and Turkey. The results are useful to developing policies that promote "woman-owned business startups", understanding what barriers exist to female entrepreneurship, and what solutions to adopt at each phase (stage) for the development of the country. The themes of this latest contribution could also be merged into the A3 category, "Conflicts of interest", dealing with issues such as "family support" or "personal problem". However, due to the conclusive considerations above all on so-called "woman-owned business startups" and the relationships that the same entrepreneur is able to establish, we considered it significant to assimilate these themes to the type phenomenon of the Female Entrepreneurship treated in the A2.

A3 Conflicts of interest: Includes articles that expose and analyze the presence of conflicts between work and family, children, spouse, and how the career cycle of a woman almost always coincides with her biological cycle (Emslie and Hunt 2009; Kelan 2010; Wood and Newton 2006; McDonald et al. 2005; Ezzedeen and Ritchey 2009). It also includes inherent themes that expand on the coincidence between the age in which a company chooses its managers and their leaders and the age in which a woman generally decides to have children and is, therefore, less willing to sacrifice time to the family and more vulnerable to psychophysical fatigue. It also includes conflicts of interest between the organization of her life and that of work.

In our research, we only met one article dealing with the topic. Itani et al. (2011) offered an academic contribution by conducting a context study in Saudi Arabia where, through the analysis of female entrepreneurs present in the area, they tried to profile the local entrepreneur who encounters barriers in obtaining capital for their startup because of the gaps in the tools that should be their support, such as society and traditions, and personal and family reasons.

A4 Differences between men and women: It includes research aimed at highlighting situations of difference, for various reasons, between men and women, such as in sociopolitical contexts (Joshi et al. 2007; Swan 2010; Holvino 2010); socioeconomic (Aziz and Cunningham 2008; Van den Brink and Stobbe 2009; Van den Brink and Benschop 2012; Powell et al. 2009); geopolitical (Booysen and Nkomo 2010; Crump et al. 2007;Tienari et al. 2009; Jamali, 2009); and, finally, those differences concerning access to credit (Coleman and Robb 2009). A study of IFC & GPFI (2011)

In our research (Robinson and Finley 2007), we analyzed sex discrimination with regard to the phenomenon of entrepreneurship in rural Pennsylvania, the country with the highest number of rural residents. The authors note that women, more than men, find it difficult to find jobs in rural areas because of their need to balance work and family obligations. Muravyev et al. (2009) studied the difficulty of receiving funding for female businesses that are seen as less favored by men in providing loans. Robb and Coleman (2010) studied the financial strategy in new technology-based companies (new technology-based firms). The authors, in developing the research through the data of the Kauffman Firm Survey, found a strong financial imbalance in women's businesses more than the male ones, both in the startup phase and in the following 4 years. Women entrepreneurs employed a significant level of leverage compared to an equally significant low level of equity during the startup phase. Lee and Marvel (2014) observed the difference between male and female startups through performance measurement. The results showed that male startups have a higher capitalization and a higher level of revenues compared to female startups. Derera et al. (2014) explore the credit capital market aimed at female entrepreneurship through a context study carried out in South Africa with an interview of 50 female entrepreneurs. The results of the research revealed that women entrepreneurs experience gender discriminatory practices in requesting funds from financial institutions, thus discouraging them from venturing into nontraditional and riskier sectors. Zartaloudis (2015) analyzed gender inequality through the impact of the European Employment Strategy (EES) on Greek and Portuguese employment policies (CEP and PEP). The survey period runs from 1995 to 2009 through 44 semistructured interviews on the time available between work and family and salary differences. Kodama and Odaki (2011) observed the gender gap between men and women in starting their startup through the involvement of management courses (programs) as a value driver tool for a lasting business. The results lead us to consider that the management programs for women reduce the gender gap in the startup of a new woman startup. Brana (2013) analyzed whether microcredit can be a solution to the problem of access to credit for female entrepreneurship. The study analyzed French data referring to the period 2000–2006, with a portfolio of 3640 observations. This study showed that the male gap is found among the clienteles of MFIs.

Alina (2011) investigated, through a context study carried out on companies in Romania, whether women's businesses are more able to raise capital. The study focused on small and medium-sized startups (SMEs) and demonstrated that, in contrast to the observations of other authors, there were no significant differences between male and female startups in addressing the typical problems of the company at the beginning activities. Estrin and Mickiewicz (2011) compared the impact of institutions on female and male startups in starting a new business. The data that the authors used were from the Global Entrepreneurship Monitor survey (GEM) from 2001 to 2006 and included more than 2000 observations per year in 55 different countries. The results showed that women are more reluctant to undertake entrepreneurial activities in countries where the state sector is bigger with stronger policies.

Amatucci and Swartz (2011) studied the negotiation processes between entrepreneurs and private equity funds. The study showed how access to financial resources is one of the main topics for the growth and development of strategies for startup companies. The results showed that female startups receive a very small portion of the total investments of the EPs. Studies show that gender discrimination exists in the bargaining phases with the PE Fund even before finance is provided to the company. Armstrong (2011) studied the different approach that women and men have in the development of a new venture planning process. While men tend to have an approach linked to the effectiveness of the plan, women aim at a proprietary (owned) approach. The former is based on rational behavior of the individual, while the latter tends to have an irrational behavior linked to sensations. Coleman and Robb (2009) consider women's businesses to be of vital importance to the US economic environment, and through data provided by the Kuffman Firm Survey, they compared credit access data for this category of companies. Through the multivariate analysis of the data, they showed that startups start their undercapitalized business and only a small percentage of female businesses use external equity resources.

A5 Discrimination: It is a relevant category that emphasizes situations of discrimination in the workplace—political, economic, and social (e.g., Czarniawska et al. (2013); Dick and Hyde (2006); Baines (2010); Davey (2008); Eriksson-Zetterquist and Styhre (2008); Bird (2011).

With regard to the research on gender startups, Sequeira et al. (2016) analyzed the change of new companies in the context of Japanese and Chinese female entrepreneurship. This study focused on the concept of female entrepreneurship and their behavior in two cultures with traditional expectations on the role of gender. Berger and Kuckertz (2016) showed the positive impact that startups have in the ecosystem of new business creation. They also showed the existence of significant differences with regard to the emergence of new businesses by men or women. The latter fail to fully express their potential within the startups' ecosystem. The results of the article focused on a lack of attention at the metropolitan and national level of all those issues that act as a barrier to the birth of new entrepreneurs. Robb (2002) analyzed the survival of women's and men's businesses in the startup phase of their business. The analysis extended to the comparison of women and men, both by race and by provenance, and in all cases results showed the need to activate policy-makers for help and efficiency for a successful female entrepreneurship program.

Khan (2017) performed an overview of 80 female startups in Saudi Arabia. The report focused on the effects of motherhood and the challenges encountered in the entrepreneurial ecosystem, and also identified the role of the so-called "push or pull factors" for female startups.

A6 Other: As a residual category, it assembles all those articles that have not been included in the other previous categories.

In the residual category, we found only one record for our research. Moswete and Lacey (2015) dealt with local tourism in Botswana and looked at the phenomenon of female startups as a means of achieving the purpose of revamping the Botsawana safari.

Once the discussion of each category was concluded, the following table, which we have elaborated on, provides a quick illustration of how the individual results were allocated by category (Table 1):

Table 1. Summary of Literature.

Category	Description	Nr. Results	Nr. WSU's Results
A1	Includes those articles concerning the presence of women on boards of directors, board of statutory auditors or other company committees. A1 also includes research in the field of female careers, the crystal ceiling phenomenon or the phenomenon of "gender quotas";	8	1
A2	Includes all the researches on women's businesses, the family business, the relational capital with the activation of formal and informal relationships that a woman activates during the life cycle of her own company and the different problems she encounters in doing business	50	16
A3	Includes articles that expose and analyze the presence of conflicts between work and family, children, husband and how the career cycle of a woman almost always coincides with her biological cycle	25	1
A4	Includes those researches aimed at highlighting situations of difference, for various reasons, between men and women, such as in socio-political contexts; socio-economic; geopolitical; and finally those differences concerning access to credit	56	15
A5	It is a relevant category that emphasizes situations of discrimination in the workplace, political, economic and social	22	4
A6	As a residual category it assembles all those articles that have not been included in the other previous categories	55	2
Total		**216**	**39**

3. Research Methodology

The research started with the analysis of the DB, made available, upon request, from the Register of Companies held at the Chambers of Commerce of Italy.

The research is based on data for the second quarter of 2018, where in Italy there were 9021 startups. The cartel consists of a summary sheet and an analytical sheet.

In the summary sheet, you can see the regional geographical distribution of startups on a national basis (Table A1).

From a first observation of the Italian startup data, it is possible to notice that only 5 out of 20 regions host a number of companies that exceed 6% of the national total. In ascending order, it is possible to identify them as follow:

- Campania, with 661 startups, represents 7.33%;
- Veneto, with 832 startups, represents 9.22%;
- Emilia Romagna, with 889 startups, represents 9.85%;
- Lazio, with 921 startups, represents 10.21%;
- Lombardia, with 2.168 startups, represents 24.03%.

The data just reported will be significant in the rest of the work, when we compare the national data of startups with those exclusively reserved for female startups (woman startups—WSU).

The analytical sheet, on the other hand, proceeds to classify the companies according to the different criteria identified in the columns of the sheet. Its horizontal construction shows for each enterprise:

- Denomination: Under which the full names of each company are indicated;
- Legal Status: Under which the legal form chosen for the establishment of the startup is reported;
- Fiscal Code: Where the number of legal personality attributed to each company is reported;
- Province: Where is the abbreviation (acronym) of the province to which the startup belongs is reported;
- Municipality: Where the name of the municipality to which the startup belongs is given in full;
- Registration date in the startup section and the registration in the Business Register: As noted, the first can be prior, contextual, or after the second; additionally, the registration in the special section is maintained only for the period granted to startups (maximum one five-year period-time requirement), as well as the maintenance of the requisites required by law (residence, nondistribution of any profits, annual production value, R&D Expenses, etc.—substantial requirement);
- Starting date of the effective exercise of the activity;
- Ateco Code 2007: Identifies the business sector macroclass of each startup;
- Sector: Although in a hasty manner, reducing the options to the categories: "Services", "industry/crafts", "trade", "tourism", and, from the second quarter of 2018 onwards, also "agriculture/fisheries";
- Activities: Provides alphanumeric abbreviation with more detailed information on the macroclass to which Ateco 2007 code belongs;
- Class of production last year: Parameters identified by capital letters from A to H with values from 0 to 50,000,000 euros (Table A2);
- Class of employees last year: Parameters identified by capital letters from A to F, with values at 0 over 250 (Table A3)
- Company with a social vocation: Expresses the membership of a single startup in the sectors referred to in Article 2, paragraph 1 of Legislative Decree no. 155/2006, that is, operating in the sectors of social assistance, health care, social and health assistance, education, education and training, environmental and ecosystem protection, enhancement of cultural heritage, social tourism, university and postgraduate education, research and provision of cultural services, extrascholastic training aimed at preventing school dropout or educational and training success, and instrumental services to social enterprises. For this special type of startup, further benefits are envisaged with respect to those not belonging to the same category;
- Enterprise with a high technological value in the energy sector: Expresses its belonging to the category of a single startup that has a high technological value in the energy field, or develops and markets exclusively innovative products or services with high technological value in the energy field. Those classified with the Ateco code "72.1—experimental research and development in the field of natural sciences and engineering" that do not operate in the energy field are excluded;
- Class of capital: This important classification allows to identify the consistency of the subscribed capital for each startup. The values are expressed in Arabic numbers from 1 to 11 with values from 1 euro to over 5,000,000 euros (Table A4);
- Website: Gives evidence of each company website;
- requirements n. 1–2–3: For this important information, specific columns are dedicated within sheet 3, where the possession of the membership requirement is indicated or not within each single cell. The requirements in question refer to three of the substantive requirements summarized in the opening of the paragraph, in particular:

- requirement n. 1: Expresses the achievement of the 15% threshold of the greatest gap between costs and total value of production concerning R&D activity;
- requirement n. 2: Expresses the composition of the team, formed by 2/3 staff with a Master's degree; or from 1/3 from PhD students, PhDs, or graduates, but with at least 3 years of experience in certified research activities;
- requirement n. 3: Expresses whether the company is a depository or licensee of industrial property, or owner of registered software.

- Declaration date: This field expresses the date on which the startup has completed the information obligations scheduled every six months;
- Female prevalence-or Youth-or Foreign: Each of the three selection fields is dedicated a specific column in the spreadsheet. The values expressed are "NO", "Majority", "Strong", and "Exclusive" and are a function of the arithmetic average of the sum of the percentages of composition of the share capital and of the composition of the Board of Director (or sole Director) of the startup (Table A5).

In order to proceed with a more detailed analysis of the data, we implemented the spreadsheet by reclassifying the startups by geographical area according to their province of origin. The criteria for subdividing the national territory on a provincial basis are the same as the ones used by the National Institute of Statistics (ISTAT) to provide periodic regional performance data of startup companies, that is, considering the North, the Center, and the South as the three main Italian geographical areas. The North includes the regions of the Northwest (Liguria, Lombardy, Piedmont, Valle d'Aosta) and those of the Northeast (Emilia-Romagna, Friuli-Venezia Giulia, Trentino-Alto Adige, Veneto). The Center includes the regions of Lazio, Marche, Tuscany, and Umbria. The South includes the regions of Southern Italy or South of Italy (Abruzzo, Basilicata, Calabria, Campania, Molise, Puglia) and those of insular Italy (Sardinia, Sicily).

Abruzzo is classified as Southern Italy for historical reasons, as it was part of the Kingdom of the Two Sicilies before the unification of Italy in 1861 (Figure 1):

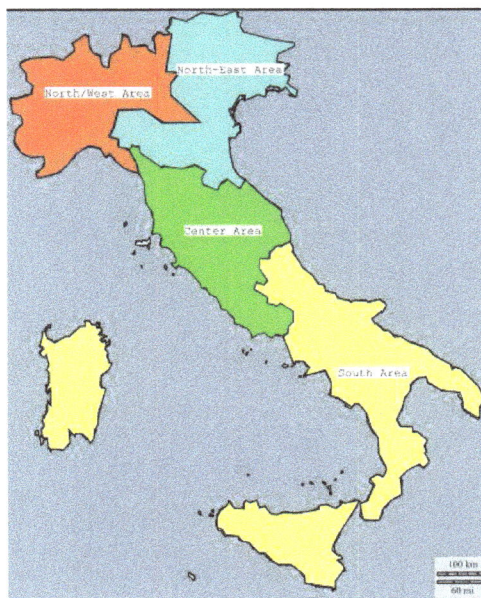

Figure 1. Geographical Macroarea.

4. Discussion

In this section, we will illustrate the data concerning the phenomenon of female startups in Italy. First of all, the WSU present in the Italian territory will be identified (Section 1) and then analyzed for each type of composition of the social structure that qualifies them as "feminine", the consistency of the social capital (Section 2), the legal status (Section 3) and, finally, the type of activity exercised (Section 4).

4.1. Italian Woman Startups and Territorial Distribution

The Table 2 below geographically shows the number of startups present in the national territory and highlights how many of these are "pink".

Table 2. Composition for geographical macroarea of women startups (WSU) and their type of relevance.

Geographical Macro-Area	Number of Italian Startup	Number of "Pink" Startups in Italy	*Relevance Exclusive*	*Relevance Strong*	*Relevance Mayority*
N/W	2834	324	86	159	79
N/E	2163	258	97	110	51
C	1977	286	103	124	59
S	2047	323	112	161	50
Total	9021	1191	398	554	239

The data show that from 9021 Italian startups, only 1191 belong to the female sex, that is, only 13.20% of the total. The data are subsequently decomposed and observed according to the percentage of share capital and chair possessed in the Board of Director by women. Therefore, it can be noted that:

- The WSU where pink representation is EXCLUSIVE (% of the share capital and % of Board of Director—or sole director—totalitarian) are 398 (33.42% of 1191);
- The WSU where pink representation is STRONG (arithmetic mean among % of the social capital and % of belonging Board of Director—or sole director—to women in the company is superior to 66%) are 554 (46.51% of 1191);
- The WSU where pink representation is MAJORITY (arithmetic mean among % of the social capital and % of belonging Board of Director—or sole director—to women in the company is superior to 50%) are 239 (20.07% of 1191).

Further data that emerge and deserve to be analyzed are the geographical distribution of female startups compared to the totality of Italian startups.

In fact, unlike that of the considered startups overall, the geographical distribution of those female startups is nearly homogeneous in the whole national territory. In the Northwest of Italy there are 324 units, followed by the area of Southern Italy with 323 units (only one less than the largest area), in reversal of the emerging data for startups overall; then, there is the area of Central Italy with 286 units, and finally the Northeast of Italy with 258 units.

The graph below clearly shows the distribution: (Figure 2)

What that makes us think is that women have a fairer distribution throughout the country, in addition to the fact that the WSU do not follow the same general distribution of startups. In fact, while the distribution of Italian startups noted the maximum record in the N/W with 2834 units and the lowest record in C with 1977, creating a differential of 857 units (9.50% of the total), the presence of female startups goes from the maximum record in the N/W with 324 units to the lowest one in the N/E with 258 units, creating a spread of only 66 units (5.54% of the total), which represents a differential of almost 4 percentage points with the evidence on Italian startups overall.

Italian's Startups: A Geographical Gender Analysis

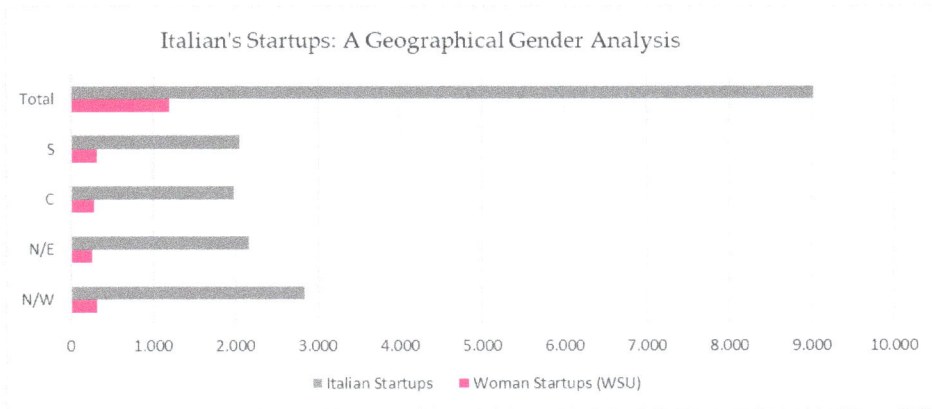

Figure 2. Distribution and the geographical location of Italian woman startups (WSU) in the s.q. 2018.

Highlighting the number of Italian female startups and analyzing the composition and distribution, the graph that follows provides a useful combined evidence of the aspects just treated: (Figure 3).

The Geographical Composition and Type of Prelevance of Woman Starups in Italy.
Second quarter of 2018

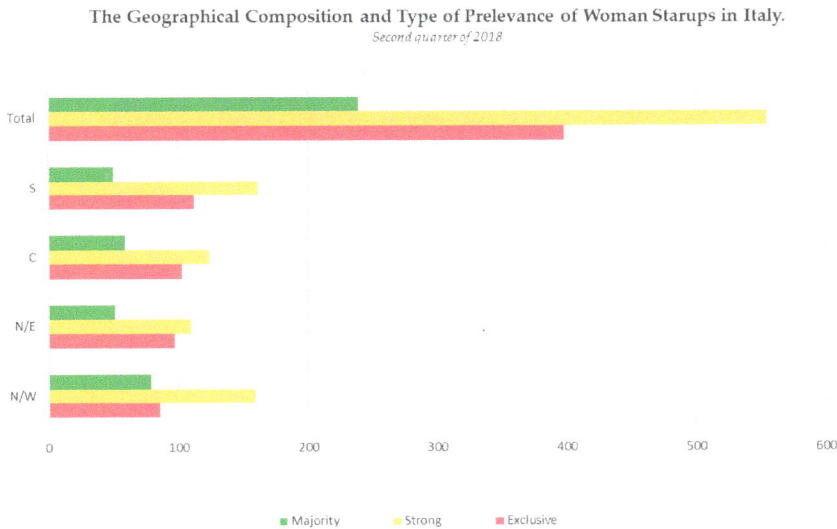

Figure 3. Composition, distribution, and type of relevance of woman startups in Italy.

From reading the graph, it is possible to understand how the WSU with exclusive, strong, and majority membership are present throughout the Italian national territory. In the following sections, we will analyze the WSU according to the class of social capital, juridical nature, and sector of activity of belonging.

4.2. The Consistency of the Italian Woman Startups Share Capital

The consistency of the share capital is one of the most delicate aspects related to the type of company being researched. The spreadsheet extracted from the register of companies, as already explained in the section dedicated to the research methodology, identifies the capital ranges and classifies them with Arabic numbers ranging from 1 to 11, in addition to a class dedicated to all those companies that have not declared the value (for a more schematic reading, see Table A4).

The national data for the second quarter of 2018 show that (Table 3):

Table 3. Class of Italian startups and the Italian woman startups' share capital.

Class of Share Capital	Italy			
	Italian Startups		Woman Italian Startups	
	unit	%	unit	%
1	106	1.18%	10	0.84%
2	1859	20.61%	321	26.95%
3	3829	42.45%	544	45.68
4	2015	22.34%	204	17.13%
5	512	5.68%	47	3.95%
6	282	3.13%	14	1.18%
7	125	1.39%	7	0.59%
8	83	0.92%	7	0.59%
9	55	0.61%	3	0.25%
10	11	0.12%	0	0.00%
11	7	0.08%	0	0.00%
Undeclared	137	1.52%	34	2.85%
Total	9021	100%	1191	100%

In Italy, there are startups for each class of capital. However, the same statement does not apply to women who stop at Class 9, with only 3 startups with a share capital ranging from €1,000,000.01 to €2.5 million.

It is also noteworthy that female startups have a higher percentage of information deficiency. In fact, out of 1191 WSU, 34 have not declared the value of the share capital, which represents, in percentage terms, 2.85% of the total; against 137 out of 9021 startups overall, equivalent to 1.52% of the total.

With reference to mode, the most common social capital class for both startups overall and for women is Class 3, with a share capital of €5000.01 to €10,000. Observing the percentage data, Class 3 represents, for Italian startups overall, 42.65% of the total, while for the female ones, 45.68% of the total.

The same similarity between WSU and startups overall is not found with reference to the less recurring capital class. For Italian startups overall, the least common class is Class 11, which hosts only seven companies with a registered capital of more than 5,000,000 (0.08% of the total), while for female startups, considering that Class 10 and 11 do not include any company, the least recurring class is Class 9, which only houses three companies with a share capital from €1,000,000.01 to €2,500,000 (0.25% of the total).

With regard to the frequency of the share capital class of the Italian WSU, there is a similarity among Italian startups overall for this aspect, too.

The trend of the share capital classes, both for women and for Italian startups overall, is a "bell curve": It gradually increases until reaching its peak in Class 3, and then slowly decreases until the minimum is reached, in Class 9 for women and in Class 11 for startups overall.

Below, we will see how Italian female startups, compared to Italian startups overall, are geographically localized in the Italian territory according to the share capital class criterion (Table 4):

Table 4. Class of Italian startups and Italian woman startups' share capital for geographical macroarea.

Class of Share Capital	N/W Area				N/E Area				C Area				S Area			
	Italian Startups		Woman Italian Startups		Italian Startups		Woman Italian Startups		Italian Startups		Woman Italian Startups		Italian Startups		Woman Italian Startups	
	unit	%	unit	%	unit	%	unit	%	unit	%	unit	%	unit	%	unit	%
1	40	1.14%	3	0.93%	24	1.11%	3	1.16%	27	1.37%	1	0.35%	15	0.73%	3	0.93%
2	457	16.13%	68	20.99%	420	19.42%	65	25.19%	423	21.40%	88	30.77%	559	27.31%	100	30.96%
3	1171	41.32%	146	45.06%	878	40.59%	124	48.06%	854	43.20%	124	43.36%	926	45.24%	150	46.44%
4	755	26.64%	78	24.07%	501	23.16%	39	15.12%	438	22.15%	50	17.48%	321	15.68%	37	11.46%
5	180	6.35%	17	5.25%	145	6.70%	11	4.26%	96	4.86%	10	3.50%	91	4.45%	9	2.79%
6	107	3.78%	5	1.54%	85	3.93%	4	1.55%	49	2.48%	0	0.00%	41	2.00%	5	1.55%
7	47	1.66%	3	0.93%	31	1.43%	2	0.78%	27	1.37%	2	0.70%	20	0.98%	0	0.00%
8	36	1.27%	2	0.62%	27	1.25%	2	0.78%	16	0.81%	1	0.35%	4	0.20%	2	0.62%
9	18	0.64%	0	0.00%	23	1.06%	3	1.16%	5	0.25%	0	0.00%	9	0.44%	0	0.00%
10	4	0.14%	0	0.00%	3	0.14%	0	0.00%	3	0.15%	0	0.00%	1	0.05%	0	0.00%
11	4	0.14%	0	0.00%	1	0.05%	0	0.00%	1	0.05%	0	0.00%	1	0.05%	0	0.00%
Undeclared	15	0.53%	2	0.62%	25	1.16%	5	1.94%	38	1.92%	10	3.50%	59	2.88%	17	5.26%
Total	2834	100.00%	324	100.00%	2163	100.00%	258	100.00%	1977	100.00%	286	100.00%	2047	100.00%	323	100.00%

In the N/W area, the highest capital class reached by the WSU is Class 8, which includes two companies with a share capital from €500,000.01 to €1,000,000

On the basis of the companies accepted, the classes of the N/W area in descending order are: Class 3 with 146 WSU; Class 4 with 78 WSU; Class 2 with 68 WSU; Class 5 with 17 WSU; Class 6 with 5 WSU; Classes 1 and 7 with 3 WSU each; and Class 8 with 2 WSU. Finally, only two WSU have not transmitted data to the register of companies relating to the size of their share capital.

In the N/E area, the highest capital class reached by the WSU is Class 9, which includes three companies with a share capital from €1,000,000.01 to €2.5 million.

On the basis of the companies accepted, the classes of the N/E area in descending order are: Class 3 with 124 WSU; Class 2 with 65 WSU; Class 4 with 39 WSU; Class 5 with 11 WSU; Class 6 with 4 WSU; Classes 1 and 9 with 3 WSU each; and Classes 7 and 8 with 2 WSU each. Finally, only five WSU have not transmitted the data to the register of companies relating to the size of their share capital.

In the C area, the highest capital class reached by the WSU is Class 8, which only includes one company with a share capital of €500,000.01 to €1,000,000.

On the basis of the companies accepted, the classes of the C area in descending order are: Class 3 with 124 WSU; Class 2 with 88 WSU; Class 4 with 50 WSU; Class 5 with 10 WSU; Class 7 with 2 WSU; and Classes 1 and 8 with 1 WSU each.

In the C area, there is a discontinuity in the classes; in fact, from Class 5, which includes ten companies, we immediately pass to Class 7, which includes 2 WSU. Class 6 is therefore vacant. Finally, only 10 WSU have not transmitted data to the register of companies relating to the size of their share capital.

In the S area, the highest capital class reached by the WSU is Class 8, which includes two companies with a share capital from €500,000.01 to €1,000,000.

On the basis of the companies accepted, the classes of the S area in descending order are: Class 3 with 150 WSU; Class 2 with 100 WSU; Class 4 with 37 WSU; Class 5 with 9 WSU; Class 6 with 5 WSU; Class 1 with 3 WSU; and Class 8 with 2 WSU.

In the Southern Italy area, there is a discontinuity in the classes; in fact, from Class 6, which includes 5 WSU, we immediately pass to Class 8, which includes 2 WSU. Capital class 7 is therefore vacant.

Finally, 17 WSU have not transmitted the data to the register of companies relating to the size of their share capital.

Some comparative considerations can be developed with regard to the four territorial areas analyzed:

-   The most "crowded" class among the four areas is Class 3, that is, the one that welcomes companies with a share capital from €5000.01 to €10,000;
-   The lowest level of information is reached by WSU in Southern Italy, reaching the peak of 17 WSU out of 323. The figure of the "nonreporting" represents 5.26% of the total number of WSU in Southern Italy;
-   The highest level of information is reached by WSU in N/W Italy, with only 2 WSU out of 324. The "nonreporting" figure represents 0.62% of the total number of WSU in N/W Italy.

The data obtained about the composition of the share capital classes of the startups mainly concern their territorial composition. To this, the analysis of the type of WSU that composes each class is added.

In the following tables, an observation was made that takes into account the type of WSU and its location in the Italian territory (Table 5):

Table 5. Type of Italian woman startups (WSU) to geographical macroarea and to class of share capital.

Class of Share Capital	Prelevance Exclusive				Prelevance Strong				Prelevance Mayority			
	N/W	N/E	C	S	N/W	N/E	C	S	N/W	N/E	C	S
1	2	3	1	2	1	0	0	1	0	0	0	0
2	27	32	35	46	28	26	39	47	13	7	14	7
3	46	42	47	45	65	52	53	82	35	30	24	23
4	7	7	10	6	51	20	25	15	20	12	15	16
5	3	5	3	1	10	6	3	7	4	0	4	1
6	0	2	0	1	2	1	0	2	3	1	0	2
7	0	0	0	0	1	2	1	0	2	0	1	0
8	0	0	0	0	0	1	0	1	2	1	1	1
9	0	2	0	0	0	1	0	0	0	0	0	0
10	0	0	0	0	0	0	0	0	0	0	0	0
11	0	0	0	0	0	0	0	0	0	0	0	0
Undeclared	1	4	7	11	1	1	3	6	0	0	0	0
Total	86	97	103	112	159	110	124	161	79	51	59	50

The significant datum that emerges from the aforementioned tables is the fact that the WSU of the "Exclusive" type, that is, those companies in which the totality of the share capital and the chairs in administration belong to women, reach Class 9 (maximum class of social capital achieved by Italian WSU), with 2 WSU in N/E Italy. In addition, the continuity of female companies with an "Exclusive" type of composition is up to Class 5, which hosts companies for each of the four territorial areas.

For the "Strong" WSU, the highest class reached is Class 9, with 1 WSU in the N/E, while for the "Majority" type, the highest class achieved is Class 8, with the coexistence of WSU in all territorial areas. With regard to this last aspect, it should be noted that for the "Strong" type, the continuity of the class occurs in Class 5, since the subsequent vacancies are in at least one of the territorial areas. For the "Majority" type, on the other hand, the continuity of the share capital is reached in Class 8. However, it is strange that the class interval between Classes 8 and 4 has at least one vacancy in at least one of the territorial areas, as well as that after Class 8, where continuity is reached, no "Majority" female startups are found.

4.3. Legal Status of Italian Female

The analysis just conducted on the social capital classes of the individual WSU by geographic area is useful for the subsequent issue that we will analyze: The legal nature adopted by the company.

The spreadsheet that contains the information in the special section of the business register provides nine legal types of business[2].

The following table shows for every company legal form, how many startups and how many WSU are present in the Italian economic context (Table 6).

The data highlight the presence of companies for each type of legal nature, albeit at least minimal, as in the case of the European Group of Economic Interest (EEIG) and European Company (EC), where there is only one startup. As far as the object of our research is concerned, there is less diversification of a business legal nature: In Italy there are no WSU with a legal status of EEIG, WSU constituted on the basis of laws of another stratum, and WSU with a juridical nature of European Companies.

The majority of Italian women's startups are set up as limited liability companies (with 941 units out of 1191, representing 79.01% of the total), followed by simplified limited liability companies (with 205 units out of 1191, representing 17.21% of the total), cooperative companies (with 36 units out of 1191, representing 3.02% of the total), single-member limited liability companies (with 4 units

---

2   The legal status concerns: European Group of Economic Interest (EEIG); Limited Liability Company; Limited Liability Company with Sole Shareholder; Simplified Limited Liability Company; Limited Liability Consortium Company; Cooperative Company; Company Formed under the laws of another State; European company; Joint Stock Company.

out of 1191, representing 0, 34% of the total), limited liability consortium companies (with 3 units out of 1191, representing 0.25% of the total), and, finally, joint-stock companies (with 2 units out of 1191, representing 0.17% of total).

Table 6. Legal form of Italian startups and Italian woman startups.

Startups (Company) Legal Form	Italy			
	Italian Startups		Woman Italian Startups	
	unit	%	unit	%
European Group of Economic Interest (EEIG)	1	0.01%	0	0.00%
Limited Liability Company (LLC)	7702	85.38%	941	79.01%
Limited Liability Company with Sole Shareholder (LLC-SS)	49	0.54%	4	0.34%
Simplified Limited Liability Company (SLLC and in Italy S.r.l.s)	1037	11.50%	205	17.21%
Limited Liability Consortium Company (LLCC)	11	0.12%	3	0.25%
Cooperative Company (CC)	144	1.60%	36	3.02%
Company Formed under the laws of another State (CFLAS)	6	0.07%	0	0.00%
European company (EC)	1	0.01%	0	0.00%
Joint Stock Company (JSC)	70	0.78%	2	0.17%
Total	9021	100.00%	1191	100.00%

The following table shows the territorial distribution of the WSU according to the legal status (Table 7).

On closer inspection:

- 941 LLC: 279 are in the N/W area, 214 are in the N/E area, 219 are in the C area, and 229 are in the S area. This type of legal status represents the most relevant for the national territory, constituting, on a local territorial base: 86.11% of the female enterprises in the N/W area; 82.95% of female businesses in the N/E area; 76.57% of female businesses in the C area; and 70.90% of female businesses in the S area;

- 205 SLLC: 40 are in the N/W area, 37 are in the N/E area, 53 are in the C area, and 75 are in the S area. This type of legal nature constitutes, for the national territory, on a local territorial basis: 12.35% of the female enterprises present in the N/W area; 14.34% of female businesses in the N/E area; 18.53% of female businesses in the C area; and 23.22% of female businesses in the S area;

- 36 CC: 2 are in the N/W area, 5 are in the N/E area, 12 are in the C area, and 17 are in the S area. This type of legal status constitutes, for the national territory, on a local territorial basis: 0.62% of the female enterprises present in the N/W area; 1.94% of female businesses in the N/E area; 4.20% of female businesses in the C area; and 5.26% of female businesses in the S area;

- 4 LLC-SS: In each of the four territorial areas there is 1 WSU. This type of juridical nature, although only present with one unit in each territorial area, has a different weight on the composition of the local economy or represents: 0.31% of the female enterprises present in the N/W and S areas; 0.39% of female businesses in the N/E area; and 0.35% of female businesses in the C area;

- 3 LLCC: One unit per territorial area is found everywhere except in the C area, where there is no WSU of this nature. Even this typology, although present in equal measure in three territorial areas, has a different weight on the composition of the local economy or represents: 0.31% of the female enterprises present in the N/W and S areas; and 0.39% of female businesses in the N/E area.

- 2 JSC: Only one unit is present in the N/W area and in the C area. This typology represents, on a local territorial base: 0.31% of the female enterprises present in the N/W area; and 0.35% of the female enterprises present in the C area.

Table 7. Legal form of Italian startups and Italian woman startups for geographical macroarea.

Startups (Company) Legal Form	N/W Area				N/E Area				C Area				S Area			
	Italian Startups		Woman Italian Startups		Italian Startups		Woman Italian Startups		Italian Startups		Woman Italian Startups		Italian Startups		Woman Italian Startups	
	unit	%	unit	%	unit	%	unit	%	unit	%	unit	%	unit	%	unit	%
EEIG	0	0.00%	0	0.00%	0	0.00%	0	0.00%	0	0.00%	0	0.00%	1	0.05%	0	0.00%
LLC	2542	89.70%	279	86.11%	1908	88.21%	214	82.95%	1660	83.97%	219	76.57%	1592	77.77%	229	70.90%
LLC-SS	14	0.49%	1	0.31%	15	0.69%	1	0.39%	7	0.35%	1	0.35%	13	0.64%	1	0.31%
SLLC and in Italy S.r.l.s	218	7.69%	40	12.35%	199	9.20%	37	14.34%	250	12.65%	53	18.53%	370	18.08%	75	23.22%
LLCC	4	0.14%	1	0.31%	3	0.14%	1	0.39%	0	0.00%	0	0.00%	4	0.20%	1	0.31%
CC	12	0.42%	2	0.62%	26	1.20%	5	1.94%	46	2.33%	12	4.20%	60	2.93%	17	5.26%
CFLAS	3	0.11%	0	0.00%	2	0.09%	0	0.00%	0	0.00%	0	0.00%	1	0.05%	0	0.00%
EC	0	0.00%	0	0.00%	0	0.00%	0	0.00%	1	0.05%	0	0.00%	0	0.00%	0	0.00%
JSC	41	1.45%	1	0.31%	10	0.46%	0	0.00%	13	0.66%	1	0.35%	6	0.29%	0	0.00%
Total	2834	100%	324	100%	2163	100%	258	100%	1977	100%	286	100%	2047	100%	323	100%

Keeping the analysis, the following tables show the sort of juridical nature chosen by each single type of WSU, that is, "Exclusive"–"Strong" or "Majority" type (Table 8):

Table 8. Type of Italian woman startups (WSU) to geographical macroarea and to type of legal form.

Startups (Company) Legal Form	Prelevance Exclusive				Prelevance Strong				Prelevance Mayority			
	N/W	N/E	C	S	N/W	N/E	C	S	N/W	N/E	C	S
EEIG	0	0	0	0	0	0	0	0	0	0	0	0
LLC	65	72	68	70	140	95	101	116	74	47	50	43
LLC-SS	1	1	1	1	0	0	0	0	0	0	0	0
SLLC and in Italy S.r.l.s	18	19	25	30	17	14	20	38	5	4	8	7
LLCC	1	1	0	0	0	0	0	1	0	0	0	0
CC	1	4	9	11	1	1	3	6	0	0	0	0
CFLAS	0	0	0	0	0	0	0	0	0	0	0	0
EC	0	0	0	0	0	0	0	0	0	0	0	0
JSC	0	0	0	0	1	0	0	0	0	0	1	0
Total	86	97	103	112	159	110	124	161	79	51	59	50

With regard to the "Exclusive" category, which is more representative for our research, the most recurring legal nature is that of a limited liability company with 275 units (sum per line). Then follow the legal nature of a simplified limited liability company with 92 units, that of a cooperative with 25 units, that of a limited liability company with sole shareholder with 4 units, and, finally, that of a limited liability consortium company with only 2 units.

Before going on to review the treatment of the "Strong" and "Majority" typologies of WSU, it should be noted that these also follow the same orientation as the "Exclusive" type, preferring the legal status of a company with limited responsibility, except in particular cases that we will soon deal with.

For the "Strong" category, as mentioned above, the most recurring legal nature is that of a limited liability company with 452 units (sum per line). Then follow the legal nature of a simplified limited liability company with 89 units, that of a cooperative company with 11 units, and, finally, that of a limited liability consortium company and that of a joint-stock company with only 1 unit each.

Concluding on the legal nature of the startups, the "Majority" category also prefers the nature of a limited liability company, reaching 214 units. There is also the nature of a simplified limited liability company with 24 units and, finally, the nature of joint stock company with only 1 unit.

4.4. Business Activities Carried Out by Italian Female Startups

In this section, we will discuss female startups from the point of view of the activity carried out. We will first illustrate to which of the macrosectors of activity the single startups belong, by ATECO code, and then we will deal in particular with those with high technological value in the energetic scope and, finally, the new phenomenon of so-called social enterprises.

With reference to the business sector, the Italian Chambers of Commerce classify startups in five macro sectors[3] and, in addition, a residual one that welcomes companies, for which it was not possible to trace that belonging.

---

[3] The Sectors are: AGRICULTURE/FISHING: It includes all the startups belonging to the primary sector operating in agriculture or in the industry; TRADE: Welcomes all those startups that, through process innovation, manage to improve the demand and supply of companies belonging to the secondary sector, acting as inter mediation between the subjects; INDUSTRY/CRAFTSMANSHIP: It welcomes all those startups that, through product and process innovation, operate in the secondary sector. All those companies that operate economic activity aimed at transforming the input into final output belong to this category. For example, we find companies that manufacture new products in the field of construction, computers and electronic equipment, means of transport, or even in the field of interior design. SERVICES: It welcomes all those startups that, through product and process innovation, operate in the tertiary sector. This category includes all those companies that offer IT services, intellectual activities, business consultancy, or specialized research and development activities; TOURISM: It welcomes all those startups that, through their activity, provide innovative services within this

The data for the second quarter of 2018 show us that (Table 9):

Table 9. Business sector of Italian startups and Italian woman startups.

Startups (Company) Business Sector	Italy			
	Italian Startups		Woman Italian Startups	
	unit	%	unit	%
AGRICULTURE/FISHING	59	0.65%	11	0.92%
TRADE	397	4.40%	68	5.71%
INDUSTRY/CRAFTSMANSHIP	1669	18.50%	197	16.54%
SERVICES	6772	75.07%	894	75.06%
TOURISM	92	1.02%	20	1.68%
Undeclared	32	0.35%	1	0.08%
Total	9021	100.00%	1191	100.00%

Observing the data, it is possible to notice that Italian startups overall operate mainly in the services sector (75.07%), and so do Italian WSU (75.06%), while the sectors in which female startups, in percentage terms on the total, are prevalent compared to startups overall are:

- The agriculture sector, where they represent 0.92% of the total against 0.65% of the generic startup observation;
- The commerce sector, where they represent 5.71% of the total against 4.40% of the generic startup observation;
- The tourism sector, where they represent 1.68% of the total against 1.02% of the generic startup observation.

The sector where the percentages of composition on the total see female startups in the minority compared to startups overall is the Industry and Crafts Industry. Female startups in this sector represent 16.54%, while an observation in the absence of gender difference tells us that this sector represents 18.50% of the total of Italian startups.

It is also useful to note that the degree of lack of information on the sector of activity of the WSU is very low: Of the 1191 female startups, only one has not declared its sector of activity.

As for the distribution in the Italian national territory of the startups operating in the various sectors, the following table provides clear evidence of the territorial location area (Table 10).

From the data provided, it can be observed that:

In the N/W Area, in order of frequency, we find:

- 254 WSU in the sector of services, representing 78.40% of the WSU allocated in the local area;
- 44 WSU in the sector of industry and craftsmanship, representing 13.58% of the WSU allocated in the local area;
- 19 WSU in the commerce sector, representing 5.86% of the WSU allocated in the local territory;
- 5 WSU in the tourism sector, representing 1.54% of the WSU allocated in the local area;
- 2 WSU in the agriculture/fishing sector, representing 0.62% of the WSU allocated in the local territory.

particular branch of the tertiary sector. Companies included in this category provide accommodation services and those typical of travel agencies and tour operator.

Table 10. Business sector of Italian startups and Italian woman startups for geographical macroarea.

Startups (Company) Business Sector	N/W Area Italian Startups		Woman Italian Startups		N/E Area Italian Startups		Woman Italian Startups		C Area Italian Startups		Woman Italian Startups		S Area Italian Startups		Woman Italian Startups	
	unit	%	unit	%	unit	%	unit	%	unit	%	unit	%	unit	%	unit	%
AGRICULTURE/FISHING	17	0.60%	2	0.62%	12	0.55%	1	0.39%	8	0.40%	2	0.70%	22	1.07%	6	1.86%
TRADE	146	5.15%	19	5.86%	72	3.33%	10	3.88%	74	3.74%	16	5.59%	105	5.13%	23	7.12%
INDUSTRY/CRAFTSMANSHIP	429	15.14%	44	13.58%	613	28.34%	61	23.64%	329	16.64%	50	17.48%	298	14.56%	42	13.00%
SERVICES	2209	77.95%	254	78.40%	1442	66.67%	182	70.54%	1541	77.95%	215	75.17%	1580	77.19%	243	75.23%
TOURISM	25	0.88%	5	1.54%	18	0.83%	4	1.55%	20	1.01%	2	0.70%	29	1.42%	9	2.79%
Undeclared	8	0.28%	0	0.00%	6	0.28%	0	0.00%	5	0.25%	1	0.35%	13	0.64%	0	0.00%
Total	2834	100%	324	100%	2163	100%	258	100%	1977	100%	286	100%	2047	100%	323	100%

None of the 324 WSU allocated in the N/W area failed to declare their sector to which they belong. In the N/E Area, in order of frequency, we find:

- 182 WSU in the sector of services, representing 70.54% of the WSU allocated in the local area;
- 61 WSU in the sector of industry and handicraft, representing 23.64% of the WSU allocated in the local area;
- 10 WSU in the commerce sector, representing 3.88% of the WSU allocated in the local territory;
- 4 WSU in the tourism sector, representing 1.55% of the WSU allocated in the local area;
- 1 WSU in the agriculture/fisheries sector, representing 0.39% of the WSU allocated in the local territory.

None of the 258 WSU allocated in the N/E failed to declare their sector to which they belong. In the C Area, in order of frequency, we find:

- 215 WSU in the sector of services, representing 75.17% of the WSU allocated in the local territory;
- 50 WSU in the sector of industry and handicraft, representing 17,48% of the WSU allocated in the local area;
- 16 WSU in the trade sector, representing 5.59% of the WSU allocated in the local territory;
- 2 WSU each in the tourism sector and in the agricultural/fishing sector, representing, for each sector, 0.70% of the WSU allocated in the local area.

The only WSU that has failed to communicate its sector of membership was in the C area, thus representing 0.35% of the 286 woman startups present in the area in question.

In the S Area, in order of frequency, we find:

- 243 WSU in the sector of services, representing 75.23% of the WSU allocated in the local territory;
- 42 WSU in the sector of industry and craftsmanship, representing 13.00% of the WSU allocated in the local area;
- 23 WSU in the trade sector, representing 7.12% of the WSU allocated in the local area;
- 9 WSU in the tourism sector, representing 2.79% of the WSU allocated in the local area;
- 6 WSU in the agriculture/fishing sector, representing 1.86% of the WSU allocated in the local territory

None of the 323 woman startups allocated in the N/E area failed to declare their sector to which they belong.

The analysis of the data obtained leads us to state that regardless of where the WSU is located, in each of the four territorial areas in Italy there are more WSU frequencies of services, followed by those of industry and crafts, then trade, and tourism, and, lastly, that operate in agriculture and fishing.

After the observation of the geographical location of the individual WSU, a further aspect that, with regard to the type of activity, must be dealt with is what kind of WSU ("Exclusive", "Strong", and "Majority") operates in each business sector.

The following table provides a first numerical evidence of the phenomenon (Table 11):

Table 11. Type of Italian woman startups (WSU) to geographical macroarea and to type of business sector.

Startups (Company) Business Sector	Prelevance Exclusive				Prelevance Strong				Prelevance Mayority			
	N/W	N/E	C	S	N/W	N/E	C	S	N/W	N/E	C	S
AGRICULTURE/FISHING	2	0	0	1	0	0	1	5	0	1	1	0
TRADE	6	5	8	7	11	3	6	14	2	2	2	2
INDUSTRY/CRAFTSMANSHIP	10	23	16	10	21	25	25	26	13	13	9	6
SERVICES	67	68	78	91	124	80	90	112	63	34	47	40
TOURISM	1	1	0	3	3	2	2	4	1	1	0	2
Undeclared	0	0	1	0	0	0	0	0	0	0	0	0
Total	86	97	103	112	159	110	124	161	79	51	59	50

The classification of the type of WSU by sector of activity represents a predominance of the "Strong" type.

For each sector it emerges that:

1.   1In AGRICULTURE/FISHING, there are 6 WSU of the "Strong" type, 3 of the "Exclusive" type, and 2 of the "Majority" type;
2.   In TRADE, there are 34 WSU of the "Strong" type, 26 of the "Exclusive" type, and 8 of the "Majority" type;
3.   In INDUSTRY/CRAFTSMANSHIP, there are 97 WSU of the "Strong" type, 59 of the "Exclusive" type, and 41 of the "Majority" type;
4.   In SERVICES, there are 406 WSU of the "Strong" type, 304 of the "Exclusive" type, and 184 of the "Majority" type;
5.   In TOURISM, there are 11 WSU of the "Strong" type, 5 of the "Exclusive" type, and 4 of the "Majority" type; the only WSU that has failed to declare in the sector it belongs to, finally, belongs to the "Exclusive" type.

Once the general discussion on the sector of activity of the WSU is concluded, the analysis of the two particular phenomena concerning the startups' activity can now be considered: High-tech companies in the energy sector and social enterprises.

Startups with a high technological value in the energy field are all those companies that increase, in the national context, the value of the so-called "Green Economy". With the following data, we will analyze, according to gender studies, where these companies are located and what kind of female composition they have.

Generally speaking, it is possible to observe how many of the startups with a high technological value in the energy sector in Italy are owned and managed by women.

The data for the second quarter of 2018 show that (Table 12):

Table 12. Italian startups and Italian woman startups operating in the high technology energy sector.

High Technology-Based Startups in the Energy Sector	Italy			
	Italian Startups		Woman Italian Startups	
	unit	%	unit	%
YES	1262	13.99%	185	15.53%
NO	7759	86.01%	1006	84.47%
Total	9021	100%	1191	100%

Only 1262 of the 9021 (13.99%) startups on the national territory are characterized by a high technological value in the energy field. With regard to gender studies, of the 1262 startups with a high technological value in the energy field, only 185 are female. The latter represent 15.53% of the 1191 WSU allocated in Italy.

Given the minimum percentage of presence in Italy, we can now move on to observe the location of this particular type of business (Table 13):

Table 13. Italian startups and Italian woman startups operating in the high technology energy sector for geographical macroarea.

High Technology-Based Startups in the Energy Sector	N/W Area				N/E Area				C Area				S Area			
	Italian Startups		Woman Italian Startups		Italian Startups		Woman Italian Startups		Italian Startups		Woman Italian Startups		Italian Startups		Woman Italian Startups	
	unit	%	unit	%	unit	%	unit	%	unit	%	unit	%	unit	%	unit	%
YES	348	12.28%	42	12.96%	345	15.95%	38	14.73%	284	14.37%	47	16.43%	285	13.92%	58	17.96%
NO	2486	87.72%	282	87.04%	1818	84.05%	220	85.27%	1693	85.63%	239	83.57%	1762	86.08%	265	82.04%
Total	2834	100%	324	100%	2163	100%	258	100%	1977	100%	286	100%	2047	100%	323	100%

With regard to the territorial area where the companies are located, it can therefore be noted that with respect to the total of WSU present in the area, those of "high technological value in the energetic field" are:

- In the N/W area: 42 WSU, or 12.96% of the total;
- In the N/E area: 38 WSU, or 14.73% of the total;
- In the C area: 47 WSU, or 16.43% of the total;
- In the S area: 58 WSU, or 17.96% of the total.

Regardless of the lack of national presence of companies with characteristics that today should be much more developed, what arouses curiosity is the fact that companies that have a high technological content in the energy field are located more in South and Central Italy than in the northern areas, which have always been considered more developed.

As for the type of the 185 WSU belonging to the sector of high technological content in the energy field, it is possible to observe that (Table 14):

Table 14. Type of Italian woman startups (WSU) to geographical macroarea and Italian companies that operate, or not, in the high technology energy sector.

High Technology-Based Startups in the Energy Sector	Prelevance Exclusive				Prelevance Strong				Prelevance Mayority			
	N/W	N/E	C	S	N/W	N/E	C	S	N/W	N/E	C	S
YES	7	12	12	20	24	16	25	23	11	10	10	15
NO	79	85	91	92	135	94	99	138	68	41	49	35
Total	86	97	103	112	159	110	124	161	79	51	59	50

- Out of the 42 WSU allocated in the N/W area, 7 are of the "Exclusive" type, 24 are of the "Forte" type, and 11 are of the "Majority" type;
- Out of the 38 WSU allocated in the N/E area, 12 are of the "Exclusive" type, 16 are of the "Forte" type, and 10 are of the "Majority" type;
- Out of the 47 WSU allocated in the C area, 12 are of the "Exclusive" type, 25 are of the "Strong" type, and 10 are of the "Majority" type;
- Out of the 58 WSU allocated in the S area, 20 are of the "Exclusive" type, 23 are of the "Strong" type, and 15 are of the "Majority" type;

Considering the data shown above, it can be said that with regard to the type of composition of the company structure and the management chairs, the WSU with a high technological content in the energy sector in Italy are predominantly of the "Forte" type, with 88 WSU, followed by the "Exclusive" type, with 51 WSU, and, finally, the "Majority" type, with 46 WSU.

The last type of company that remains to be explored in this section dedicated to the business sector of gender startups is being or not in a social vocation.

This particular typology was foreseen within the DL 179/2012, which introduced the innovative tool of startups in the national legal system. Innovative startups with a social vocation are considered all those companies operating in the sectors referred to in art. 2, paragraph 1, of Legislative Decree no.155/2006[4].

---

[4] We refer to the following activities: Social assistance; health; education, education and training; protection of the environment and the ecosystem; enhancement of cultural heritage; social tourism; university and postgraduate education; research and provision of cultural services; extrascholastic training, aimed at preventing early school-leaving and scholastic and educational success; instrumental services to social enterprises, rendered by bodies composed in excess of seventy percent by organizations that carry out a social enterprise.

The table below provides a first analysis of gender startup for this particular sector of activity in the national context (Table 15):

Table 15. Italian startups and Italian woman startups with social vocation.

Startups with Social Vocation (in Italy-cd. Startups a Vocazione Sociale	Italy			
	Italian Startups		Woman Italian Startups	
	unit	%	unit	%
YES	190	2.11%	54	4.53%
NO	8831	97.89%	1137	95.47%
Total	9021	100%	1191	100%

The results extracted from the special section of the Business Register, for the second quarter of 2018, show that socially-driven startups represent a real minority in the Italian economic context—only 190 startups with a social vocation out of 9021 Italian startups. With regard to gender studies, female startups with a social vocation represent, with 54 WSU out of 1191, 4.53% of Italian female startups.

This first analysis allows us to observe, then, how this particular type of business is distributed throughout the country. The table below provides numerical evidence (Table 16).

- In the N/W area: Out of 89 social vocation startups, 26 are female and represent 8.02% of the 324 WSU present;
- In the N/E area: Out of 34 social vocation startups, 9 are female and represent 3.49% of the 258 WSU present;
- In the C area: Out of the 31 social vocation startups, 11 are female and represent 3.85% of the 286 WSU present;
- In the S area: Out of the 36 socially-driven startups, 8 are female and represent 2.48% of the 323 WSU present.

Now that the geographic observation on female startups with a social vocation in the Italian territory is over, we are going to discuss this particular business phenomenon according to its composition, looking at what type of female startups, be it "Exclusive"–"Strong" or "Majority", they belong to.

The following table shows, for each type of gender startup, how many belong to companies with a social vocation (Table 17).

From the reading of the data, it emerges that the prevalent type of female startups with a social vocation is the "Strong" type, with 28 startups, followed by the "Exclusive" one, with 18 startups, and, finally, the "Majority" typology, with 8 startups.

Table 16. Italian startups and Italian woman startups with social vocation for geographical macroarea.

Startups with Social Vocation (in Italy-cd. Startups a Vocazione Sociale)	N/W Area				N/E Area				C Area				S Area			
	Italian Startups		Woman Italian Startups		Italian Startups		Woman Italian Startups		Italian Startups		Woman Italian Startups		Italian Startups		Woman Italian Startups	
	unit	%	unit	%	unit	%	unit	%	unit	%	unit	%	unit	%	unit	%
YES	89	3.14%	26	8.02%	34	1.57%	9	3.49%	31	1.57%	11	3.85%	36	1.76%	8	2.48%
NO	2745	96.86%	298	91.98%	2129	98.43%	249	96.51%	1946	98.43%	275	96.15%	2011	98.24%	315	97.52%
Total	2834	100%	324	100%	2163	100%	258	100%	1977	100%	286	100%	2047	100%	323	100%

Table 17. Type of Italian woman startups (WSU) with or without social vocation to geographical macroarea.

Startups with Social Vocation (in Italy-cd. Startups a vocazione)	Prelevance Exclusive				Prelevance Strong				Prelevance Mayority			
	N/W	N/E	C	S	N/W	N/E	C	S	N/W	N/E	C	S
YES	6	5	3	4	15	4	5	4	5	0	3	0
NO	80	92	100	108	144	106	119	157	74	51	56	50
Total	86	97	103	112	159	110	124	161	79	51	59	50

5. Conclusions

The startups have now become an important vehicle for the development of the Italian economic fabric. Our research, starting from the actual state of international literature on this particular business phenomenon, then developed through the analysis of the Italian economic context. This made it possible to make an important contribution to gender studies, first with the monitoring of the situation of Italian startups and then by centralizing the focus of analysis on an important issue under development: The so-called "woman startups".

From a scientific point of view, the phenomenon of female Startups (RQ1) confirms the lack of contributions to the Corporate Governance of woman startups. Only one contribution (Ebersberger and Pirhofer 2011) deals with company management, identifying the academic approach of women as a success factor for large female startups. In our opinion, the lack of academic contributions to the subjects and the functioning of corporate governance occurs for a structural reason of the startup and not for gender issues. As a rule, startups are SMEs and, as such, do not include integrated governance systems. The absence of complex organizational structures is also demonstrated by the results found in the A2 category, which deals with the different problems encountered by the entrepreneur in doing business. Most of the results (Welsh et al. 2013, 2016; Neill et al. 2015) show that most women who own startups face the difficulties of their business alone, without strong business. In addition, by comparing the results that emerged in Paoloni and Demartini (2016) on female entrepreneurship, and therefore not only on the startup focus, we find the same difficulties common to the entrepreneur in starting up their business. These concern above all the difficulty in facing the startup phase of the company, the undercapitalization of the company, and the difficulties in accessing credit (Dechant and Lamky 2005). In the gender gap and discrimination factors, it is observed that the WSU are discouraged from operating in traditional sectors such as industry (Elam and Terjesen 2010), but rather, very often, they operate in sectors where the business risk is higher. The gender gap phenomenon often emerges from contributions dealing with institutional factors (Itani et al. 2011) listed in the A3 category.

As for the Italian situation of the phenomenon of female startups (RQ2), the second quarter of 2018 registered the presence of 1191 Woman Startups (WSU) out of 9021 Italian startups. The most common type of female startups in Italy, with 554 companies, is the "Strong" type. Woman startups belong to this type when the arithmetic average among the women present in the company's share capital and the percentage of chair ownership in the administrative body exceeds 66%. Followed by that, with 398 companies, is the "Exclusive" type, where the result of the report just described for the determination of the female presence is 100%. Finally, with 239 companies, there is the "Majority" type, where the arithmetic average among the women present in the company's equity and the number of chairs in the administrative body belonging to them is more than 50%.

An important fact of our research is the geographical distribution of Italian WSU that are distributed with minimal differences between north and south. The number of WSU in the north and south cancels the geographical gap, as their presence is almost the same in both Northern and Southern Italy: There are 324 WSU in the N/W area, while there are 323 WSU in the S area. As regards the consistency of the WSU's share capital, our research shows a greater presence of female startups in class 3 (544 units out of 1191 Italian WSU), with a share capital of between 5000 and 10,000 euros.

The data that emerge from our study prove that Italian WSU are structured with very weak equity (equity), an aspect already confirmed in the literature (Muravyev et al. 2009; Robb and Coleman 2010), which often allows the entrepreneur to establish only one company in the form of SRLs (SLLC: Semplified Limied Company) with an equity greater than € 1.00 but less than € 10,000. This type of company allows greater ease of starting up the business activity, but implies a higher business risk related to the responsibilities of the entrepreneur.

A peculiarity related to the study of the consistency of the social capital of Italian female startups is their so-called "bell" trend. Starting from Class 1, they reach the peak in Class 3 and then gradually decrease until they reach Class 9. Moreover, in reaching the highest class in terms of value, there are no vacant classes, so continuity between the capital classes of the WSU is observed.

The 3 WSU in Class 9 all belong to Northeast (N/E) Italy; moreover, two of these are of the "Exclusive" type, while the remaining one is of the "Strong" type.

The undercapitalization of the WSU also implies a further problem related to credit. In Italy, most companies are bank-oriented; therefore, to receive credit capital, they must offer numerous guarantees that, at present, the data of our research show that the WSU do not possess.

As regards the legal form adopted by Italian WSU, our analysis shows a preference, with 941 companies out of 1191, of the legal form of a limited liability company. This is followed, with 205 companies out of 1191, by the form created ad hoc for startups, or the limited-liability one, simplified where a single euro of social capital is sufficient for its establishment. Then, there is the form of a cooperative society with 36 WSU. Finally, with nonsignificant numbers, the types of responsibility are identified with a single shareholder, a consortium with limited liability, and the form of a joint-stock company. There are no European Economic Interest Groups (EEIGs), Companies Established on the basis of the laws of another State, and the so-called European women's predominantly European companies. In our opinion, the data highlight the small size of Italian female startups that choose more and more forms that give a limited responsibility to the social structure to the detriment of all those forms that allow a more widespread corporate base, as well as a simpler international comparison.

What has just been written is then confirmed by the fact that the only 2 WSU constituted in the form of a joint stock company are of the "Strong" type, and the other is of the "Majority" type.

Concluding on the last topic dealt with in this contribution for Italian female startups, we can see how most of these choose the service sector.

The female startups operating in the services sector are 894 and represent 75.06% of the 1191 Italian WSU. Then follow the 197 female companies operating in the Industry/Craft sector and representing 16.54% of the 1191 Italian WSU. Then, there are, in a residual order, the WSU present in the Commerce sector (5.71%), in the Tourism sector (1.68%), and, finally, in the Agriculture sector (0.92%). Only 0.08% of Italian WSU has not declared the sector in which it operates.

In our research, we also deal with the presence, in the Italian economic context, of WSU that operate in particular sectors of activity, such as those with a high technological value in the Energetic field and those in CD social vocation. The first ones, with 185 companies, represent 15.53% of the total of Italian WSU, while the latter, even for their particular business purpose and for their recent introduction into the Italian legal system, with only 54, represent 4.53% of the 1191 Italian female startups.

The limits of our research are undoubtedly traceable in the small dimensions of Italian female startups and in the fact that these are constantly evolving. In addition to this aspect, we must note the absence of good governance systems that allow us to observe the efficiency of their work and operation.

A further limitation is of a territorial nature, as our research is concentrated only on Italian companies.

This contribution aims to be the starting point for future research aimed at the development of female startups over time. First of all, we will present analyses through case studies, then we will analyze some main performance factors and organizational models, and then evolve the study on foreign entities in order to bring to terms a complete comparative analysis on gender startups.

Author Contributions: Conceptualization, P.P.; Data curation, G.M.

Funding: This research received no external funding.

Conflicts of Interest: The authors declare no conflict of interest.

Appendix A

Table A1. Shows the geographical distribution of Italians startups in the second quarter of 2018.

Italian Region	Number of Startups
ABRUZZO	213
BASILICATA	90
CALABRIA	194
CAMPANIA	661
EMILIA-ROMAGNA	889
FRIULI-VENEZIA GIULIA	209
LAZIO	921
LIGURIA	165
LOMBARDIA	2168
MARCHE	370
MOLISE	40
PIEMONTE	482
PUGLIA	342
SARDEGNA	167
SICILIA	469
TOSCANA	402
TRENTINO-ALTO ADIGE	233
UMBRIA	155
VALLE D'AOSTA	19
VENETO	832
ITALY	9021

Table A2. Shows the startups classification to value of production cluster.

Value of Production	Class of Production
0–100.000 euro	A
100.001–500.000 euro	B
500.001–1.000.000 euro	C
1.000.001–2.000.000 euro	D
2.000.001–5.000.000 euro	E
5.000.001–10.000.000 euro	F
10.000.001–50.000.000 euro	G
Over 50.000.000 euro	H
Not Available	

Table A3. Shows the class of Italian startups' number of employees.

Number of Employees	Class of Employees
0–4	A
5–9	B
10–19	C
20–49	D
50–249	E
Over 250	F
Not Available	

Table A4. Shows the class of Italians startups' nominal value of capital.

Nominal Value of Capital	Class of Capital
1 euro	1
From 1 up to 5.000 euro	2
From 5.000 up to 10.000 euro	3
From 10.000 up to 50.000 euro	4
From 50.000 up to 100.000 euro	5
From 100.000 up to 250.000 euro	6
From 250.000 up to 500.000 euro	7
From 500.000 up to 1.000.000 euro	8
From 1.000.000 up to 2.500.000 euro	9
From 2.500.000 up to 5.000.000 euro	10
Over 5.000.000 euro	11

Table A5. Shows the composition of share sapital and of board of directors (or sole director) to consider the orevalence of Italian startups: Majority, Strong, and Exclusive.

Prelevance: Female/Youth/Foreing	Description
NO	[% of (Female or Youth or Foreign) Share Capital+ % (Female or Youth or Foreign) Director]/2 ≤ 50%
Mayority	[% of (Female or Youth or Foreign) Share Capital+ % (Female or Youth or Foreign) Director]/2 > 50%
Strong	[% of (Female or Youth or Foreign) Share Capital+ % (Female or Youth or Foreign) Director]/2 > 66%
Exclusive	[% of (Female or Youth or Foreign) Share Capital+ % (Female or Youth or Foreign) Director]/2 = 100%
Not Available	

References

Alina, Bădulescu. 2011. Start-up financing sources: Does gender matter? Some evidence for EU and Romania. *The Annals of the University of Oradea* 207: 644–9.

Amatucci, Frances M., and Ethné Swartz. 2011. Through a fractured lens: Women entrepreneurs and the private equity negotiation process. *Journal of Developmental Entrepreneurship* 16: 333–50. [CrossRef]

Armstrong, Craig E. 2011. Thinking and slacking or doing and feeling? Gender and the interplay of cognition and affect in new venture planning. *Journal of Developmental Entrepreneurship* 16: 213–26. [CrossRef]

Aziz, Shahnaz, and Jamie Cunningham. 2008. Workaholism, work stress, work-life imbalance: Exploring gender's role. *Gender in Management: An International Journal* 23: 553–66. [CrossRef]

Baines, Donna. 2010. Gender mainstreaming in a development project: Intersectionality in a post-colonial un-doing? *Gender, Work & Organization* 17: 119–49.

Barnir, Anat. 2014. Gender differentials in antecedents of habitual entrepreneurship: Impetus factors and human capital. *Journal of Developmental Entrepreneurship* 19: 1450001. [CrossRef]

Berger, Elisabeth SC, and Andreas Kuckertz. 2016. Female entrepreneurship in startup ecosystems worldwide. *Journal of Business Research* 69: 5163–68. [CrossRef]

Bird, Sharon R. 2011. Unsettling universities' incongruous, gendered bureaucratic structures: A case-study approach. *Gender, Work & Organization* 18: 202–30.

Booysen, Lize AE, and Stella M. Nkomo. 2010. Gender role stereotypes and requisite management characteristics: The case of South Africa. *Gender in Management: An International Journal* 25: 285–300. [CrossRef]

Brana, Sophie. 2013. Microcredit: An answer to the gender problem in funding? *Small Business Economics* 40: 87–100. [CrossRef]

Coleman, Susan, and Alicia Robb. 2009. A comparison of new firm financing by gender: Evidence from the Kauffman Firm Survey data. *Small Business Economics* 33: 397. [CrossRef]

Crump, Barbara J., Keri A. Logan, and Andrea McIlroy. 2007. Does gender still matter? A study of the views of women in the ICT industry in New Zealand. *Gender, Work & Organization* 14: 349–70.

Czarniawska, Barbara, Ulla Eriksson-Zetterquist, and David Renemark. 2013. Women and work in family soap operas. *Gender, Work & Organization* 20: 267–82.

Davey, Kate Mackenzie. 2008. Women's accounts of organizational politics as a gendering process. *Gender, Work & Organization* 15: 650–71.

Dechant, Kathleen, and Asya Al Lamky. 2005. Toward an understanding of Arab women entrepreneurs in Bahrain and Oman. *Journal of Developmental Entrepreneurship* 10: 123–40. [CrossRef]

Derera, Evelyn, Pepukayi Chitakunye, Charles O'Neill, and Amandeep Tarkhar-Lail. 2014. Gendered lending practices: Enabling South African women entrepreneurs to access start-up capital. *Journal of Enterprising Culture* 22: 313–30. [CrossRef]

Dick, Penny, and Rosie Hyde. 2006. Consent as resistance, resistance as consent: Re-reading part-time professionals' acceptance of their marginal positions. *Gender, Work & Organization* 13: 543–64.

Ebersberger, Bernd, and Christine Pirhofer. 2011. Gender, management education and the willingness for academic entrepreneurship. *Applied Economics Letters* 18: 841–44. [CrossRef]

Elam, Amanda, and Siri Terjesen. 2010. Gendered institutions and cross-national patterns of business creation for men and women. *The European Journal of Development Research* 22: 331–48. [CrossRef]

Emslie, Carol, and Kate Hunt. 2009. 'Live to work' or 'work to live'? A qualitative study of gender and work–life balance among men and women in mid-life. *Gender, Work & Organization* 16: 151–72.

Eriksson-Zetterquist, Ulla, and Alexander Styhre. 2008. Overcoming the glass barriers: Reflection and action in the 'Women to the Top' programme. *Gender, Work & Organization* 15: 133–60.

Estrin, Saul, and Tomasz Mickiewicz. 2011. Institutions and female entrepreneurship. *Small Business Economics* 37: 397. [CrossRef]

Ezzedeen, Souha R., and Kristen G. Ritchey. 2009. Career advancement and family balance strategies of executive women. *Gender in Management: An International Journal* 24: 388–411. [CrossRef]

Guillaume, Cécile, and Sophie Pochic. 2009. What would you sacrifice? Access to top management and the work–life balance. *Gender, Work & Organization* 16: 14–36.

Hancock, Amber. 2012. 'It's a macho thing, innit?' Exploring the effects of masculinity on career choice and development. *Gender, Work & Organization* 19: 392–415.

Healy, Geraldine, Harriet Bradley, and Cynthia Forson. 2011. Intersectional sensibilities in analysing inequality regimes in public sector organizations. *Gender, Work & Organization* 18: 467–87.

Holvino, Evangelina. 2010. Intersections: The simultaneity of race, gender and class in organization studies. *Gender, Work & Organization* 17: 248–77.

Itani, Hanifa, Yusuf M. Sidani, and Imad Baalbaki. 2011. United Arab Emirates female entrepreneurs: Motivations and frustrations. *Equality, Diversity and Inclusion: An International Journal* 30: 409–24. [CrossRef]

Jamali, Dima. 2009. Constraints and opportunities facing women entrepreneurs in developing countries: A relational perspective. *Gender in Management: An International Journal* 24: 232–51. [CrossRef]

Joshi, Heather, Gerry Makepeace, and Peter Dolton. 2007. More or less unequal? Evidence on the pay of men and women from the British Birth Cohort Studies. *Gender, Work & Organization* 14: 37–55.

Kelan, Elisabeth K. 2010. Gender logic and (un) doing gender at work. *Gender, Work & Organization* 17: 174–94.

Khan, Muhammad. 2017. Saudi Arabian Female Startups Status Quo. *International Journal of Entrepreneurship* 21: 1–27.

Kirkwood, Jodyanne. 2009. Motivational factors in a push-pull theory of entrepreneurship. *Gender in Management: An International Journal* 24: 346–64. [CrossRef]

Kodama, Naomi, and Kazuhiko Odaki. 2011. Gender difference in the probability of success in starting business turns negligible when controlling for the managerial experience. *Applied Economics Letters* 18: 1237–41. [CrossRef]

Lee, In Hyeock, and Matthew R. Marvel. 2014. Revisiting the entrepreneur gender–performance relationship: A firm perspective. *Small Business Economics* 42: 769–86. [CrossRef]

Lewis, Patricia, and Ruth Simpson. 2010. Meritocracy, difference and choice: Women's experiences of advantage and disadvantage at work. *Gender in Management: An International Journal* 25: 165–69. [CrossRef]

McDonald, Paula, Kerry Brown, and Lisa Bradley. 2005. Explanations for the provision-utilisation gap in work-life policy. *Women in Management Review* 20: 37–55. [CrossRef]

Moswete, Naomi, and Gary Lacey. 2015. "Women cannot lead": Empowering women through cultural tourism in Botswana. *Journal of Sustainable Tourism* 23: 600–17. [CrossRef]

Muravyev, Alexander, Oleksandr Talavera, and Dorothea Schäfer. 2009. Entrepreneurs' gender and financial constraints: Evidence from international data. *Journal of Comparative Economics* 37: 270–86. [CrossRef]

Neill, Stern, Lynn Metcalf, and Jonathan L. York. 2015. Seeing what others miss: A study of women entrepreneurs in high-growth startups. *Entrepreneurship Research Journal* 5: 293–322. [CrossRef]

Paoloni, Paola. 2011. *La Dimensione Relazionale delle Imprese Femminili (trans. The Relationship Dimension of Female Firms)*. Milano Francoangeli.

Paoloni, Paola, and Paola Demartini. 2016. Studi di genere, un'analisi della letteratura, in Paoloni P. (a cura di) I Mondi delle Donne, Edicusano.

Pesonen, Sinikka, Janne Tienari, and Sinikka Vanhala. 2009. The boardroom gender paradox. *Gender in Management: An International Journal* 24: 327–45. [CrossRef]

Powell, Abigail, Barbara Bagilhole, and Andrew Dainty. 2009. How women engineers do and undo gender: Consequences for gender equality. *Gender, Work & Organization* 16: 411–28.

Robb, Alicia M. 2002. Entrepreneurial performance by women and minorities: The case of new firms. *Journal of Developmental Entrepreneurship* 7: 383–97.

Robb, Alicia M., and Susan Coleman. 2010. Financing strategies of new technology-based firms: A comparison of women-and men-owned firms. *Journal of Technology Management & Innovation* 5: 30–50.

Robinson, Sherry, and John Finley. 2007. Rural Women's Self-Employment: A Look at Pennsylvania. *Academy of Entrepreneurship Journal* 13: 21–30.

Sequeira, Jennifer M., Zhengjun Wang, and Joseph Peyrefitte. 2016. Challenges to New Venture Creation and Paths to Venture Success: Stories from Japanese and Chinese Women Entrepreneurs. *Journal of Business Diversity* 16: 42–59.

Swan, Elaine. 2010. "A testing time, full of potential?" Gender in management, histories and futures. *Gender in Management: An International Journal* 25: 661–75. [CrossRef]

Tienari, Janne, Charlotte Holgersson, Susan Meriläinen, and Pia Höök. 2009. Gender, management and market discourse: The case of gender quotas in the Swedish and Finnish media. *Gender, Work & Organization* 16: 501–21.

Tlaiss, Hayfaa, and Saleema Kauser. 2011. The impact of gender, family, and work on the career advancement of Lebanese women managers. *Gender in Management: An International Journal* 26: 8–36. [CrossRef]

Tyler, Melissa, and Laurie Cohen. 2008. Management in/as comic relief: Queer theory and gender performativity in The Office. *Gender, Work & Organization* 15: 113–32.

Van den Brink, Marieke, and Yvonne Benschop. 2012. Gender practices in the construction of academic excellence: Sheep with five legs. *Organization* 19: 507–24. [CrossRef]

Van den Brink, Marieke, and Lineke Stobbe. 2009. Doing gender in academic education: The paradox of visibility. *Gender, Work & Organization* 16: 451–70.

Welsh, Dianne HB, Esra Memili, Eugene Kaciak, and Saddiga Ahmed. 2013. Sudanese women entrepreneurs. *Journal of Developmental Entrepreneurship* 18: 1350013. [CrossRef]

Welsh, Dianne HB, Eugene Kaciak, and Narongsak Thongpapanl. 2016. Influence of stages of economic development on women entrepreneurs' startups. *Journal of Business Research* 69: 4933–40. [CrossRef]

Wood, Glenice J., and Janice Newton. 2006. Childlessness and women managers: 'choice', context and discourses. *Gender, Work & Organization* 13: 338–58.

Zartaloudis, Sotirios. 2015. Money, Empowerment and Neglect–The E uropeanization of Gender Equality Promotion in G reek and Portuguese E mployment Policies. *Social Policy & Administration* 49: 530–47.

*administrative
sciences*

MDPI

Article

Women Founders in the Technology Industry: The Startup-Relatedness of the Decision to Become a Mother

Katherina Kuschel

Dirección de Investigación y Desarrollo Académico, Universidad Tecnológica Metropolitana, Santiago 8330378, Chile; kkuschel@utem.cl; Tel.: +56-9-525-800-35

Received: 5 March 2019; Accepted: 28 March 2019; Published: 1 April 2019

Abstract: This paper explores the decision to become a mother among women in the technology industry, particularly if there is an "optimal context" regarding startup development (business stage and size). Eighteen interviews were conducted with an international sample of women founders and analyzed using a grounded theory approach. Findings suggest two sources of "mumpreneurs" in technology ventures: (1) women who created a startup while young and childless, postponing maternity until the business is "stable"; and (2) mothers who created a technology venture as a strategy to gain higher levels of flexibility and autonomy than they experienced in the corporate world. The first group is highly work-role salient, while the second is highly family-role salient. The results of this work contribute to theory development by revealing the "startup-relatedness" of family decisions by women founders in the technology industry. I offer recommendations of how accelerators can improve mentorship for women in high-growth technology ventures and unleash women's potential.

Keywords: entrepreneurship; new high-technology ventures; women founders; motherhood; decision-making; role salience; mumpreneurs; startups

---

With the introduction of the Internet and related technologies into the market, the industry of startups arose. A startup is a short-term—and often informal—organization that seeks to create a product under conditions of high uncertainty. Globally, national public policy, many business schools and corporations, and some industries have embraced this type of organization. It has been documented that high rates of entrepreneurship with an innovation component play a critical role in the wealth of nations, economic dynamism (Decker et al. 2014), and job creation (Kuschel et al. 2018).

Moreover, and parallel with the increased number of women in science, technology, engineering, and mathematics (STEM), more startups are being led by women. Still, according to the estimations of Robb and Coleman (2009), only 5–6% of high-technology entrepreneurs are women, and about 3–5% of incubated and accelerated projects are led by women. Start-Up Chile, a public accelerator in South America, bucks that trend, with around 20% women founders and 8.9%[1] women-led startups (Kuschel and Labra 2018). In general, though, women are poorly represented in these spaces. Uncertainty, competitiveness, aggressiveness, and fast pace are characteristics of the high-growth technology industry.

The "masculine" and "male-dominated" features of the environment raises the question of whether the technology industry is welcoming to women who expect to become mothers.

---

[1] Number calculated by Kuschel and Labra (2018) with data provided by Start-Up Chile accelerator, since the 1st generation to the 11th (2173 founders, and 972 startups supported by the program), as of March 2015.

The motherhood decision is defined as the choice to forego, start, or enlarge a family (Prunty et al. 2008). Also, some investors (e.g., public funds, business angels, venture capitalists) might not fund women-led startups because of the potential for the leader to get pregnant and leave the startup a lower priority, at least temporarily (Kuschel and Lepeley 2016b).

This article does not directly examine women's participation in tech. The aim of this study is to explore the conditions under which women decide to have children in one extreme case—women leading a startup in the technology industry. Do women postpone maternity in the technology industry?

First, this study provides a literature review on startups functioning, the profile of women in the technology industry, and the decision to become a mother for those involved as business founders in the technology industry. After the theoretical and methodological sections, the findings are presented. Two main paths into being "mumpreneurs" are found, those entering business ownership before having children and those entering business ownership because of their mothership. Within the study, the authors find that the former group can be further broken down into subgroups depending on the development stage of their business. Finally, suggestions are proposed for support of such entrepreneurs and also future directions for research.

1. Literature Review

1.1. Business Stages at a Technology Startup

A new high-technology venture (NHTV) or startup is defined as a business model (Blank 2010) that is profitable, repeatable, and scalable[2]. At its beginning, a startup is an informal business with a small team. The goal of the startup is to create technology or to leverage a business model based on technology to make money. There are three broad business stages for startups: product development, growth, and heavyweights. First, the "product development" stage includes the ideation, working prototype in development and prototype validation, functional product with users, and business model validation (also known as the search for market fit). Founders in the product development stage are searching for seed funding because the companies are not yet economically sustainable. Early-stage investors respond strongly to information about the founding team rather than to traction or previous investors (Bernstein et al. 2017), which is a critical factor for women founders (Kuschel et al. 2017). Second, the "growth stage" of a tech startup includes scaling sales and raising capital. Normally, entrepreneurs "pitch"[3] to investors, trying to attract interest by exhibiting their startup's "traction"[4]. In this stage, startups raising venture capital (VC) must incorporate to receive funding from private investors. Investors also give access to a significant network, mentorship, board, and assistance in decision-making in exchange for equity (business participation) and/or return on investment. Third, "heavyweights" sell the company (exit strategy), acquire other startups, or make an initial public offering (IPO). The dynamic environments in which these companies are inserted make most traditional management methods obsolete (Ries 2011). The participants in this study are leading startups in the product development and growth stages.

1.2. Women in New High-Technology Ventures

For many years, women's spectacular progress in business ownership has been virtually invisible in mass media and academic journals in the U.S. (Baker et al. 1997). A recent review of the literature on startups and gender (Kuschel and Lepeley 2016a) identified that most studies were concentrated

---

[2] Coaching, consulting, and freelancing are not considered startups—although they may use technology—because they do not have the potential for scaling. They are self-employed.
[3] The pitch is a short (2–3 min) presentation of the business plan.
[4] The traction is the validation of the product or business model. It consists in metrics of market demand (i.e., profit, revenues, active users, registered users, engagement, partnerships/clients, traffic) used to convince investors of the startup potential.

in the U.S., and there is little knowledge of startups in Europe and emerging economies [such as Latin America, BRIC (Brazil, Russia, India, China), and MENA (Middle Eastern and North African countries[5]]. In most of those studies, startup performance was compared without reference to the perspectives of women entrepreneurs in technology (Singh Cassidy 2015).

Lately, new evidence has shown that women leading tech ventures face gender-based stereotypes. This affects how these women design their teams, raise capital, and grow their businesses. Women normally build their teams based on trust, partnering with their romantic partners or close friends (Kuschel and Lepeley 2016b). Therefore, these teams are smaller, less diverse, have less credibility with potential investors, and grow more slowly than male-led teams (Kuschel and Labra 2018; Kuschel and Lepeley 2016b; Kuschel et al. 2017). However, women-led startup teams contribute to job creation (Kuschel et al. 2018), and a third of women-led startups keep raising funds after acceleration (Kuschel et al. 2017).

Women must surmount several obstacles to be part of the growth of women's business ownership. The masculinization of entrepreneurship—including stereotypical masculine behaviors such as aggressiveness, assertiveness, independence, and self-confidence—generates serious difficulties for women who wish to engage in entrepreneurial activities (Ahl 2002; Bird and Brush 2002; Eagly and Johannesen-Schmidt 2001). Moreover, women's perceived capabilities (a type of human capital) and economic participation both play roles in influencing the start-up rates of women entrepreneurs (Brush et al. 2017). The constant comparison also ends up becoming a trap. Researchers and society both tend to overlook the complexity and variety of women entrepreneurs, and women become "victims of the male norm" (Billing 2011).

Historically, self-employed women were less likely than men to become small business owners due to societal and patriarchal pressures (Marlow 1997) that acted as discriminatory barriers at all business stages. A proven barrier for women's small business growth has been limited access to financial resources (Carter and Allen 1997; Brush et al. 2004), and this is true for women founders of technology ventures as well (Demartini 2018; Demartini and Marchegiani 2018).

Women who *do* participate in business incubator or startup acceleration programs are often exhibited as "tokens" to illustrate gender diversity. This visibility may have negative consequences for the founder. Tokenism affects women's "sense of fit" and draws attention away from their businesses (Marlow and McAdam 2012).

Nevertheless, there are some successes specific to women in tech startups. Unlike gender discrimination in traditional investment settings, crowdfunding has been found to be a great tool for women in the early stages of raising capital (Gorbatai and Nelson 2015). According to Gorbatai and Nelson (2015), donation-based crowdfunding sites offer a completely different institutional setting in which to obtain funding for new small businesses or products, bypassing many risks and difficulties inherent in traditional methods of fundraising, as success depends much more on written language rather than visual and verbal cues.

Nowadays, research on women's entrepreneurship is growing (Jennings and Brush 2013), but there are still some gaps, particularly regarding women-led startups (Kuschel and Lepeley 2016a) in developing countries (Bullough 2013) and from a feminist perspective (Marlow and McAdam 2012, 2015).

1.3. The Decision to Become a Mother

Previous studies explore how dominant discourses of mothering influence women in their life decisions about children. Most evidence indicates that all women negotiate dominant

---

[5]   Brazil, Russia, India and China (BRIC) show a similar stage of development. Middle East and North African (MENA) region has 60% of the world's oil reserves and 45% of the world's natural gas reserves. MENA region shows newly advanced economic development yet some areas are still in conflict.

ideals of a "good mother" and a "self-sacrificing mother" (Knaak 2010). However, as noted by Maher and Saugeres (2007) after analyzing the fertility decision-making of 100 Australian women, such stereotypes need to be further broken down, since women with and without children respond to different aspects of such ideals. For women who have children, images of the "good mother" are less prevalent than pragmatic concerns about how to manage mothering. In contrast, childless women understand mothering as all-encompassing and potentially overwhelming. Nevertheless, fertility decision-making is often situational and affected by social expectations and employment conditions (Maher and Dever 2004) instead of influenced by specific policies.

Despite significant changes to women's involvement in the public sphere, cultural discourses of femininity still highlight motherhood, which has been perceived as "natural" for women. Consequently, women who choose not to have children are viewed as abnormal or deviant (Gillespie 2000). Nowadays, postfeminist approaches or "choice" feminism is installing a new gender order of "self-determining, individuated, and empowered" women (Budgeon 2015), which, blended with the previous feminist perspectives, presents "disparate discourses around contemporary mothering" (Vincent et al. 2004). This has led to both an entrepreneurialization of motherhood (Thornton 2011) and new forms of entrepreneurial feminities (Byrne et al. 2019; Lewis 2014).

On average, Latin American women in the technology sector have higher levels of education and represent upper-middle socioeconomic status (Kuschel and Labra 2018), are a cohort with lower fertility rates (Adsera and Menendez 2011), and may be less influenced by Latino and macho culture (Susaeta et al. 2013) than Latina women not in the tech sector.

When is the optimal time to become an entrepreneur? Motherhood can also serve as a trigger to start a business, as women seek greater autonomy and time flexibility via self-employment (Annink and Dulk 2012; Loscocco 1997). Greene et al. (2013) explore how stereotypes and role expectations influence women's propensity toward entrepreneurial activity: "Maternal self-employment has a counter-stereotypical effect, and so positively influences daughters to become self-employed."

1.4. Theoretical Framework: Testing the Family Embeddedness Theory

This study combines two frameworks; role salience within social identity theory and family embeddedness. First, the importance of a role or "role salience" is "determined by commitment to the role, which includes attitudes and emotions, participation in the role, and knowledge about the role. An important issue in career development is how individuals integrate the various life roles" (Matzeder and Krieshok 1995, p. 333). According to social identity theory, whether or not men and women report key roles as similarly salient, and how they define, enact, and manage these roles, may differ substantially (Cook 1994). These individual ways of "doing gender" (West and Zimmerman 1987) significantly impact women's success.

Some studies find relations between family factors and starting a new business (Boden 1996, 1999; Brown et al. 2006; Green and Cohen 1995) or becoming self-employed (Carr 1996). Loscocco (1997) argues that women may make the decision to start their own businesses because they need more flexibility to meet family demands and responsibilities.

The family embeddedness perspective of entrepreneurship (Aldrich and Cliff 2003) portrays entrepreneurs' family and business domains as highly interrelated. Business owners can structure their work according to personal preferences (Bird and Brush 2002), whereas organizational employees have less control over flexibility and autonomy. Moreover, entrepreneurs may more easily transfer human, social, and financial resources between their family and business domains (Danes et al. 2009).

Similarly, Greenhaus and Powell (2012) suggest that individuals may have family considerations that influence work decisions, such as job relocation, whether to quit a job, pursue a new job opportunity, seek part-time employment, interrupt paid employment, or start a new business. They call this the "family-relatedness of work decisions." However, further research is still needed to understand how the decision-making process is different according to work, industry, individual, family, and social variables (Powell and Greenhaus 2012).

This study tests the "family-relatedness of work decisions" by exploring the extreme case of women in a very demanding environment with economic constraints, long working hours, and high time pressure for developing a product and getting users. The results of this work expand the family-embeddedness perspective and contribute to theory development by revealing the decision of women founders to become a mother while working in the technology industry.

2. Methodology

The current study was designed with a qualitative, inductive, and constructive approach. In 2014 and 2015, I explored the experiences of an international sample of women entrepreneurs in technology; most of the participants were beneficiaries of Start-Up Chile.

2.1. Sample

Participant selection criteria: This study gathered data from women founders of startups. Most of the participants of the study were benefited by Start-Up Chile (SUP), an international acceleration program located in Santiago de Chile. A snowball technique was used to find mothers. I initially found six mothers leading startups, only two of whom were from Chile originally. Therefore, I decided to expand the sample by interviewing women founders without children on their decision to become mothers; these participants are included in the sample. SUP has an international focus, which is reflected in the mixed-country sample. Table 1 presents both the business and founder's characteristics. As shown in Table 1, I conducted 18 interviews, including with women that were solo founders ($n = 4$) or members of the founding team ($n = 14$). Six founders (33%) had no employees or freelancers, either because of the early stage of the startup (product development stage) or because of an eventual pivot or exit. Of the participants, 50% ($n = 9$) of this study were leading startups in the growth stage. They were from nine different countries of origin, yet most were contacted while being accelerated and therefore located in Santiago, with ages ranging from 26 to 40; 28% ($n = 5$) had a STEM educational background and 50% ($n = 9$) had studied business. Finally, 41% ($n = 6$) of them were mothers.

Interview design considerations: I incorporated work-family (WF) scholars' suggestions to capture heterogeneity, including single people, those with and without children, single-parent families, and dual earners in the sample (Greenhaus et al. 2000; Parasuraman et al. 1997; Voydanoff 1988; Watkins and Subich 1995). Moreover, I included women who have participated in startup accelerators (in Start-Up Chile, Wayra Chile, or other accelerators abroad) as well as women who have not, from both Latin America and abroad. The sample includes women engaged in various stages of the decision-making process of motherhood and startups from a variety of industries and stages.

Procedure: Each participant was contacted by e-mail and invited to an online interview (via Skype) in Spanish. Four interviews were conducted in English. The researcher explained the consent form verbally. The form was then signed, and a copy was delivered to the participant. All participants agreed to be audio-recorded. Each interview was transcribed semi-verbatim, excluding identifying information. The transcriptions were entered into ATLAS.ti v.7.0 software for qualitative analysis. The questions cover the topics of motivation to startup a technology venture, team composition, and motherhood expectations. A few sample questions: What are your future growth expectations for this venture? Do you see yourself as a mother? What are the pros and cons that this industry offers mothers? As a women startup founder, did you confront special challenges when becoming a mother (if you did)?

Table 1. Sample characteristics.

Founder ID	Country	Industry	Cofounders	Employees	Work Role	Team Gender Diversity	Accelerated	Business Stage	Age	Educational Background	Marital Status	N° of Children
				Business Characteristics						Founder Characteristics		
CA	Chile	Biotechnology	1	0	COO	Mixed	Wayra	Product development	28	STEM	Single	0
AS	Venezuela	Health	5	0	CEO	Mixed	SUP	Product development	26	Industrial Design	Single	0
LF	USA	Energy	2	0	COO	Mixed	SUP	Product development	31	Communications	Single	0
MA	Pakistan-UK	MarketPlace	1	0	CEO	Female	SUP	Product development	29	Business	Single	0
AM	USA	Services	3	1	CEO	Mixed	SUP	Product development	26	Business	Single	0
CM	Argentina	eCommerce	2	8	CEO	Mixed	SUP	Growth stage	32	Business	Married	0
PC	Chile	Education	2	4	CEO	Mixed	-	Growth stage	31	STEM	Married	0
DG	Chile	eCommerce	3	35	CMO	Mixed	SUP	Growth stage	30	Communications	Married	1
SC	Argentina	Software	4	6	COO	Female	SUP	Growth stage	32	Business	Married	1
VK	Argentina	Services	3	2	CEO	Mixed	-	Product development	40	Business	Divorced	1
CA	Chile	Software	3	4	CEO	Mixed	SUP	Growth stage	36	STEM	Single	0
CN	Mexico	Services	3	0	CEO	Mixed	SUP	Exit strategy	33	Business	Single	0
GV	Estonia	MarketPlace	3	2	COO	Mixed	-	Growth stage	29	Business	Single	0
KD	Chile	Biotechnology	4	6	CEO	Mixed	SUP	Growth stage	26	STEM	Single	0
LC	Argentina	Software	1	6	CEO	Female	SUP	Growth stage	32	Business	Cohabit	0
FH	Morocco-Chile	MarketPlace	2	0	CEO	Mixed	SUP	Product development	32	STEM	Married	2
VH	Brazil	Services	1	5	CEO	Mixed	-	Product development	28	Business	Married	1
VM	Venezuela	MarketPlace	1	6	CEO	Female	Other	Growth stage	32	Communications	Single	1

2.2. Analysis

The analysis of data used a grounded theory approach (Glaser and Strauss 1967) as a way of arriving at a theory when there were no (or few) previous theoretical frameworks. The theory provided explanatory power by including controllable and access variables if they did not emerge by themselves. In addition, a particular interest was to find the "hidden assumptions" of various participants (Charmaz 2006). I conducted a first open coding, inductively, trying to identify emerging topics. Significant paragraphs (quotes) were selected and categorized into codes. Then, selected coding inductively identified the central category.

Figure A1 shows the emergent topics that were coded. The tag cloud is a visual depiction of content tags used in the hermeneutic unit. More frequently used tags are depicted in a larger font, and the display order is alphabetical. The tag cloud allowed me to find a tag both by alphabet and by frequency. After this process, axial coding was conducted to seek the relationship between categories and sub-categories. Families of codes were built with related codes.

The "network of codes" in Figure A2 is a visual representation of the type of link (axial coding) relating significant codes. Then, selected coding identified the central category, which interpreted the studied phenomena. The co-occurrent and neighbor codes were explored around the central category.

Lastly, a discriminant analysis was conducted to test if this theory fit a different sample. Constant comparative analysis (Corbin and Strauss 2008) was conducted to determine consistency between codes and the data. The goal was to gather the women founders into categories that shared similar characteristics, and it can be read as a time line from the left to the right. The analysis revealed that motherhood-related expectations often co-occur and overlap with their business stage.

3. Findings

Two configurable patterns were found that led to the outcome of entrepreneurs in technology who were mothers: (1) women who created a startup while young and childless, and (2) women who created a technology venture while a mother. Table 2 summarizes the particular characteristics that distinguish each category.

Table 2. Emerging categories and its characteristics.

Category	1. Women Creating a Startup While Young and Childless				2. Women Creating a Tech Venture While a Mother
Subcategory	1.1	1.2	1.3	1.4	2
Motherhood Expectations	Not thinking about motherhood	Wishing to be a mother	Mother	Women with conditions to be a mother	Women who create a technology venture while being a mother
Business Stage	Product Development	Growth	incorporated, raising capital, scaling	Growth	Any
Team Size	1 to 5	1–2 cofounders, some freelancers (as employees)	3–4 cofounders with employees	3–5 cofounders with employees	1–2 cofounders, some freelancers (as employees)
Team Gender	Mixed	Mixed	Mixed	Mixed	Mixed
Avg. Age	28	31.5	· 34	31	31
Work Role	CEO, COO	CEO	CEO, CMO, COO	CEO, COO	CEO

3.1. Women Creating a Startup While Young and Childless

Four subcategories divide this main category and can be conceived as continuous stages. The axial and selected coding revealed that motherhood expectations of women entrepreneurs in tech are: "not thinking about motherhood," "wishing to be a mother," "mother," and "women with conditions to become mothers", and that those codes are associated with the business stage of the startup.

3.2. Not Thinking about Motherhood

Young and single is the common profile of women founders. For them, motherhood is not an issue. They are young (average age 28) and ambitious. As their startups are still in the product development stage, they do not have employees. Their work role is highly salient, and they prioritize traveling and personal development.

> "Yes, I can see myself being a mother in the future, but I feel like right now is a very freeing moment." AS, 26, single, childless, chief executive officer (CEO), health devices

> "Yes. I can see myself as a mother. Well, I'm already 31 years old . . . (Laughter). Umm . . . I think I'm scared of it, but mainly because of my lifestyle. I travel a lot and I have a roommate . . . " LF, 31, single, childless, chief operating officer (COO), energy

3.3. Wishing to Be a Mother

These are women (average age 31.5) in romantic relationships. They have great expectations for being mothers. As they are hiring employees and raising capital from investors, they are postponing maternity and hiding their true family expectations from them.

> "I'm a woman, I'm 32 years old, I've been married for two years, and of course I think about having children. I still don't know how I will make the pieces fit (. . .) I feel like I'm postponing it. If it weren't at [the startup] I probably would already have had a child. I did delay it a bit, but I'm not going to abandon it (. . .) During the first investment round they asked me about it. They said, 'Are you thinking about having children?' I didn't take it very well. (. . .) All the investors at the moment (three) were men, and they said they wouldn't invest if it were the case. I didn't like that comment at all, I took it poorly and I said, 'Look, I can't promise anything. I'm 31 years old. What I can promise, however, is that I won't have any children a year from now.' It wasn't in my interest to have a baby, but that doesn't mean I could have one in two years. And the truth is I want to have a family, and I know I will. What I'm trying to do is build a good, profitable business. I believe things will shape up eventually." CM, 32, married, childless CEO, eCommerce

3.4. Mother

When the business is incorporated, "stable", and the team is growing (has fixed employees), women (average age 34) take the next step toward motherhood and get pregnant. Particularly for women in this category, teams are bigger and more diverse in gender. The interviewer asked whether it was possible to have a baby at the early stage of her startup.

> "No, impossible, no. We work there 24/7. (. . .) What we did was look for people to cover for us in these two key areas. We hired a CEO and a COO to lighten up work and so I could spend more time with my baby. (. . .) You never should have a child during your first year of launching a startup unless your parents live very close or you hire external help." DG, 30, married, mother, chief marketing officer (CMO), eCommerce

They work "until the last day" before giving birth.

> "At first it was very tough. I got pregnant last summer and worked until the last day. Prenatal leave does not exist . . . I worked until a week before I gave birth." DG, 30, married, mother, CMO, eCommerce

> "I worked until I had my C-section (. . .). I almost had to drive to my own C-section." VK, 40, divorced mother, CEO, investment

They take a short maternity leave (one to three months).

> "I used to say, 'I'll have the baby and return to work in a month,' but you never know how important work is and how it changes your life. (. . .) It was very hard for me; I had to go back to work as soon as possible. And you pressure yourself that way, and with a baby . . . " DG, 30, married, mother, CMO, eCommerce

> "I went back to work three months after having my son." VK, 40, divorced, CEO investment

3.5. Women with Conditions Placed on Being a Mother

The discriminant analysis resulted in a fourth group (1.4). This group did not fit in any category above, although they did share the same business characteristics (business stage, team size, team gender) as the group of mothers (1.3)—they were single or cohabiting for a short period, and they did not have children. Their average age was 31 years old.

> *"Now it's a problem. I do want to have children now, but it's complicated because I'm single. But it is a problem for me, and a constant worry. For example, I want to travel to the U.S. for some time, to open a new office. And I think, 'It has to be really quick,' because I want to be a mother and I'm already 35. So I'm running out of time."* CA, 35, single, childless, CEO, software as a service

3.6. Women Who Create a Technology Venture While Already a Mother

Another discriminant analysis showed the second path—women who create a technology venture while already a mother. Most have become first-time mothers and are creating a startup because of the time flexibility and autonomy it affords them with the ability to work anywhere. These factors are valued as great benefits that facilitate the meeting of demands from the startup and the home. All of the participants in this category were well-educated women with long work experiences in the corporate world. They left their jobs with a deep knowledge of the industry. Their average age was 30.6 years old.

> *"I worked as a Communications Director at a multinational company. I got pregnant while I was there. I took my pre- and post-natal maternity leave and returned to the company. I left someone taking care for my baby, along with my mother. It was very tough, since I had long work hours. I was home late and the baby would be sleeping, so I decided to become an entrepreneur."* VM, 32, single, mother, CEO, marketplace

3.7. Flexibility and Autonomy

Women with and without children value flexibility and autonomy as working conditions that allow them to balance family life and a startup. Particularly, among women who worked in the corporate world, there was a desire for independence that strengthens the argument for autonomy.

> *"One of the advantages of being an entrepreneur is the flexible schedule. It was one of the reasons I decided to start my own company."* PM, 30, married, childless, CEO, education platform

> *"It's very hard to balance maternity and startups . . . it has its pros and cons. The good part is that I can get home by 2 pm and then spend the afternoon with him [the baby]. (. . .) I went back to work after two months . . . my friends are mothers too, and they would tell me I was crazy. But now they return to work after six months of maternity leave and they [her girlfriends who are employees] feel terrible because they work until 7 pm and they have to leave their babies at home. At least I can manage my schedule; if I want to take him to the pediatrician, I can. At this stage, now the baby is six months, I feel like I'm at the best work-family situation. Four months ago, I was in the worst."* DG, 30, married, mother, CMO, eCommerce

> *"Irony lies in the fact that you can find something in technology that you might not be able to find in any other type of business. It's not physical labor. It's true that you work for many hours, but those are hours that can be spread out. My cellphone is my main tool for work. I can be waiting in line to pick up my daughter [from school] and take that time to answer emails and listen to things. You can take advantage of those moments, and that is all thanks to technology. So it is ironic [that] there aren't more women and mothers in technological entrepreneurship."* VM, 32, single, mother, CEO, marketplace

3.8. Family Sacrifices

Nevertheless, sacrifices must be made to achieve company success. An example of such sacrifice is offered by one women founder who had to leave her baby back in Argentina—her home country—in order to raise venture capital in the U.S.

> *"Yes, it was tough because they grow up so much in a couple of months! When I left, she slept in a crib and didn't speak. After four months she spoke, she slept in a bed; she wasn't a baby anymore. She still calls me 'Dad' (laughter). (. . .) For me, leaving for four months wasn't cheap, and I'm not speaking in terms of money. Coming back and her calling me 'Dad,' I don't know. Going back to that routine of waking up at night when she cried. Obviously, I'm responsible for the decisions I make, but there are sacrifices you make, and you have to pay for them. At a moment I decided that she wouldn't have a mom for four months, but not for her entire life, and I wouldn't tell her, 'I stopped doing something for you.' Let her carry that guilt around the rest of her life, because it was a great opportunity for me; you don't always get invited to programs at Silicon Valley. So instead I preferred to say, 'Nothing will happen to her in four months.'"* SC, 32, married, one child, COO, software as a service

This case illustrates the pervasive effects of the startup on the family, and in this sense, it directly challenges Aldrich and Cliff's family embeddedness perspective (2003).

3.9. Productivity

These family sacrifices have embedded a great opportunity cost. The resistance of the team, the couple, and the entrepreneur have been tested. Recent mothers in technology ventures acknowledge the value of quality time with their children; therefore, they try to ensure that the work done is as efficiently as possible.

> *"Being out of your comfort zone makes you move around, and you're constantly trying to get the best out of the situation, since you're risking a lot. In my case it was being with my daughter."* SC, 32, married, one child, COO, software as a service

> *"I now prefer to have lunch at my desk and leave work two hours earlier in order to be with my baby."* DG, 30, married, one child, CMO, eCommerce

> *"Having children is time-consuming and leaves you out of focus, but at the same time, it helps you clear out your mind and helps you realize what is not important. It brings you to reality, and what really matters."* VK, 40, divorced, mother, CEO, investment

4. Discussion

We can see that among women who created a startup while young and childless (Category 1), the role salience is not a fixed category. The value placed on work and family changes through the course of life (Carlson and Kacmar 2000).

For the vast majority of the women founders, it seemed as though there was nothing more important than having a career first and postponing motherhood for as long as possible. Identity-based perspectives may provide a solid framework to understand this decision-making process. The participants who created a startup while young and childless behave consistently with the socially constructed identity (Hastie 2001) of a founder, rather than of a women founder or a potential mother.

According to social identity theory, individuals tend to invest more of themselves in roles that are highly salient (Burke and Reitzes 1991; Lobel 1991; Rothbard and Edwards 2003; Stryker and Serpe 1994). The reason is that positive experiences in highly salient roles reinforce their self-identity (Thoits 1991). Therefore, it may be argued that a strong work-role salience exists for women founders postponing maternity and taking advantage of an accelerator program (and, for instance, leaving the baby back in their home country), while a strong family-role salience exists for mothers who decided to leave the organizational job to create a startup.

In the second category, the motivation to start up a business is the need for flexibility and autonomy that will serve the family (Annink and Dulk 2012; Loscocco 1997). The case of Category 2 supports a family-embeddedness perspective on new venture creation (Aldrich and Cliff 2003). However, the first group of participants shows a business-relatedness of family decisions rather than a family-relatedness of work decisions (Greenhaus and Powell 2012; Powell and Greenhaus 2012). Women in both main categories have postponed maternity in pursuit of career success, defined as stability or growth. The business-relatedness of postponing maternity among women founders in the technology industry implies the use of a different lens to approach the entrepreneurial career. Particularly, mothers in group 2 are part of the less-common category, although there is a general belief that women with advanced knowledge of the industry will leave the corporate world to start a tech venture. For this group, becoming a tech entrepreneur seems to be a "career renewal," defined as "a period of doubt and self-examination that could be followed by a renewed commitment to career issues" (Bejian and Salomone 1995, p. 53). This process contributes to a richer understanding of individuals with interrupted career paths (Sullivan 1999).

Women's underrepresentation in the high-tech sector is strongly associated with their under-participation in executive boards and their exclusion from corporate management and strategy-based company and association boards (Kariv 2013, p. 493). This affirmation is true for group 2—mothers who have left jobs in organizations and set up their startups—which was represented by a smaller group of women in startups, as seen in our study. Mothers in Category 1.3 and mothers in Category 2 have followed different paths. Therefore, their team compositions and business development are radically different.

Finally, this study provides further evidence rebutting myths related to the advancement of women in STEM fields. While the author acknowledges the importance of STEM, it is possible for women who do not come from a STEM background to individually or collectively start a technology venture. Notably, in this sample, only 28% (*n* = 5) of the participants had a STEM educational background.

5. Conclusions

In summary, the findings of this study showed two different configural patterns that led to the outcome of "mumpreneur" in technology: (1) women who created a startup while young and childless, becoming mothers after postponing maternity until the startup is "stable," and (2) women who created a technology venture while a mother. The first group is more work-role salient, while the second is highly family-role salient.

Three subgroups divide the first category and can be conceived of as continuous stages: "not thinking about motherhood," "wishing to be a mother," and "mother," and those stages are associated with the business stage of the startup.

All participants acknowledged flexibility and autonomy as key working conditions that allow work-family balance, although mothers acknowledge a huge family sacrifice for achieving business success, contrary to evidence from the work–family literature from the corporate or traditional entrepreneurship context.

5.1. Theoretical Contribution to the Work–Family Field

This study contributes to the examination of characteristics among women entrepreneurs in technology, a sample that has been generally overlooked in the work–family field. The grounded theory emerging from the data is the main contribution of this study. The data revealed that the type of mumpreneur in technology appears to determine her work or family role salience. The role salience associated with the business stage and personal development explains the decision to postpone maternity in the technology industry, while a separate cohort of mothers left the corporate world and created a tech venture.

The results of this work contribute to theory development by revealing a "startup-relatedness of family decisions" of women founders in the technology industry.

5.2. Limitations and Directions for Future Research

Because of the low number of women and mothers participating in acceleration programs, the design of this study included a mixed-country sample. This decision entails advantages and disadvantages. As an advantage, the common themes emerging from the analysis was more likely to be universal for women techpreneurs rather than simply outcomes specific to a particular situation. Future studies should address cultural and regulatory influences from the host country and/or home culture among these women and examine whether they face similar gender-related constraints. Future research might explore changes in role salience and what factors promote identity change among women founders in technology.

Do investors perceive founder role salience? How can it impact the fundraising process? As this environment might seem hostile to motherhood, research must be conducted to explore the length of time mothers maintain their entrepreneurial activity, the sustainability of being a mumpreneur in the technology industry, as well as the implications it has for their children (Schindehutte et al. 2003).

A new line of research that emerged in this study is related to the literature of success and failure—how flexibility, autonomy, wellbeing, reputation, visibility, and growth are measures of success for women "techpreneurs", as well as how work and family management styles may affect their own wellbeing differently. How do these "startuppers" manage the spillover effect to their children and the romantic and business partners? Finally, how is techpreneurship being presented as an attractive choice for mothers (Byrne et al. 2019)? Work–family issues and wellbeing is a key emerging area of research among women in entrepreneurship (Lepeley et al. 2019) and mothers in technology.

5.3. Implications for Career Development

Mothers categorized in the second group have left the corporate world seeking flexibility and autonomy. There is a huge opportunity for corporations to offer new "intrapreneurial career paths" for new mothers (Kuschel and Salvaj 2018). After several months, the new venture may create a spin-off and become a profitable business. This process may be supported by alliances with university accelerators and external mentors, and there is no need to add organizational institutions to support spin-offs.

5.4. Recommendations for Policymakers and Managers of Accelerator Programs

These results indicating that women postpone maternity until their startup is growing may give rise to contradictory interpretations. On one hand, people may assume that single and childless women are more suitable as founders. On the other, the low participation of mothers in the technology sector reflects a highly competitive and hostile environment for both women and mothers. The findings should be carefully analyzed. The solution of a cultural change towards a shared responsibility of family roles, family leave, paternity leave, and flexi-time to both men and women in the workforce may help them decide to accelerate their family decisions. Yet, the profile of highly educated women, such as the ones of this sample, have many resources, and contrary to women with low levels of education, they tend to postpone maternity (Gustafsson and Kalwij 2006).

My suggestion is to create a group of mentors as part of the other resources provided by the accelerator who can serve as role models and offer advice to founders with motherhood expectations. Mentorship is a key element of an enabling entrepreneurship ecosystem for women (Kuschel 2019). This will help women who are struggling with gaining legitimacy when starting STEM ventures (Eddleston et al. 2016). Concerted efforts to increase business sustainability and the participation of women in startups offer a chance to increase the personal and collective wellbeing of women around the world.

Funding: This research received no external funding.

Conflicts of Interest: The author declares no conflict of interest.

Appendix A

Figure A1. Open coding in a tag cloud.

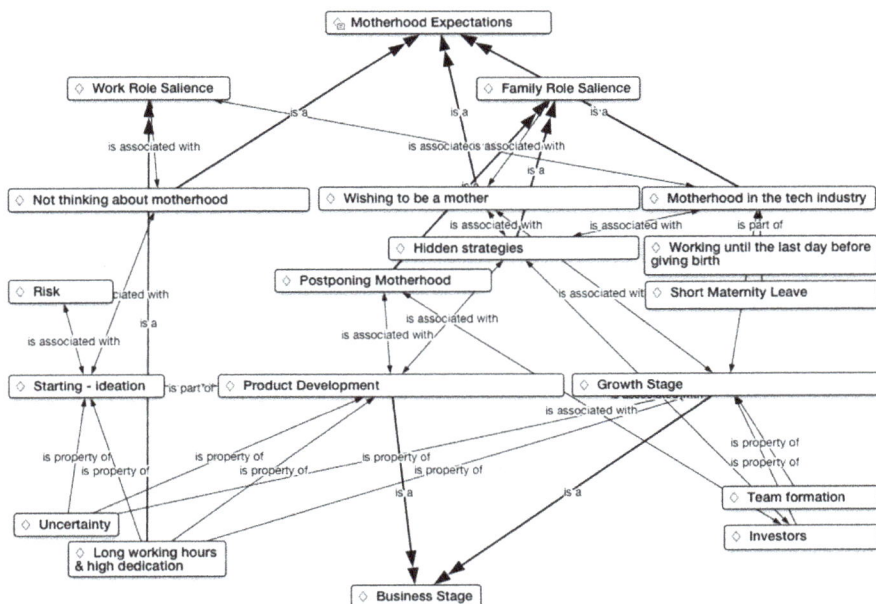

Figure A2. Axial and selected coding.

References

Adsera, Alicia, and Alicia Menendez. 2011. Fertility changes in Latin America in periods of economic uncertainty. *Population Studies* 65: 37–56. [CrossRef] [PubMed]

Ahl, Helene J. 2002. *The Making of the Female Entrepreneur: A Discourse Analysis of Research Texts on Women's Entrepreneurship.* Jönköping: Jönköping University.

Aldrich, Howard E., and Jennifer E. Cliff. 2003. The pervasive effects of family on entrepreneurship: Toward a family embeddedness perspective. *Journal of Business Venturing* 18: 573–96. [CrossRef]

Annink, Anne, and Laura den Dulk. 2012. Autonomy: The panacea for self-employed women's work-life balance? *Community Work & Family* 15: 383–402.

Baker, Ted, Howard E. Aldrich, and Liou Nina. 1997. Invisible entrepreneurs: The neglect of women business owners by mass media and scholarly journals in the USA. *Entrepreneurship & Regional Development* 9: 221–38.

Bejian, Donna V., and Paul R. Salomone. 1995. Understanding Midlife Career Renewal: Implications for Counseling. *The Career Development Quarterly* 44: 52–63. [CrossRef]

Bernstein, Shai, Arthur Korteweg, and Kevin Laws. 2017. Attracting Early-Stage Investors: Evidence from a Randomized Field Experiment. *The Journal of Finance* 72: 509–38. [CrossRef]

Billing, Yvonne D. 2011. Are women in management victims of the phantom of the male norm? *Gender, Work & Organization* 18: 298–317.

Bird, Barbara, and Candida G. Brush. 2002. A gendered perspective on organizational creation. *Entrepreneurship Theory and Practice* 26: 41–65. [CrossRef]

Blank, Steven. 2010. What's A Startup? First Principles. Available online: http://steveblank.com/2010/01/25/whats-a-startup-first-principles/ (accessed on 31 March 2019).

Boden, Richard J., Jr. 1996. Gender and self-employment selection: An empirical assessment. *Journal of Socio-Economics* 25: 671–82. [CrossRef]

Boden, R. J., Jr. 1999. Flexible working hours, family responsibilities, and female self-employment. *American Journal of Economics and Sociology* 58: 71–83. [CrossRef]

Brown, Sarah, Lisa Farrel, and John G. Sessions. 2006. Self-employment matching: An analysis of dual earner couples and working households. *Small Business Economics* 26: 155–72. [CrossRef]

Brush, Candida G., Nancy M. Carter, Elizabeth J. Gatewood, Patricia G. Greene, and Myra Hart. 2004. Gatekeepers of Venture Growth: A Diana Project Report on the Role and Participation of Women in the Venture Capital Industry. Available online: http://ssrn.com/abstract=1260385 (accessed on 31 March 2019).

Brush, Candida G., Abdul Ali, Donna Kelley, and Patricia Greene. 2017. The influence of human capital factors and context on women's entrepreneurship: Which matters more? *Journal of Business Venturing Insights* 8: 105–13. [CrossRef]

Budgeon, Shelley. 2015. Individualized Femininity and Feminist Politics of Choice. *European Journal of Women's Studies* 22: 303–18. [CrossRef]

Bullough, Amanda. 2013. Perceptions of Women Entrepreneurs in Male-Dominated Leadership Cultures: More Positive Support for Women than Many Thought. *Journal of Enterprising Culture* 21: 359–74. [CrossRef]

Burke, Peter J., and Donald C. Reitzes. 1991. An identity approach to commitment. *Social Psychology Quarterly* 54: 239–51. [CrossRef]

Byrne, Janice, Salma Fattoum, and María Cristina Diaz-García. 2019. Role models and women entrepreneurs: Entrepreneurial superwoman has her say. *Journal of Small Business Management* 57: 154–84. [CrossRef]

Carlson, Dawn S., and K. Michele Kacmar. 2000. Work–family conflict in the organization: Do life role values make a difference? *Journal of Management* 26: 1031–54. [CrossRef]

Carr, Deborah. 1996. Two paths to self-employment? Women's and men's self-employment in the United States, 1980. *Work and Occupations* 23: 26–53. [CrossRef]

Carter, Nancy M., and Kathleen R. Allen. 1997. Size determinants of women-owned businesses: Choice or barriers to resources? *Entrepreneurship & Regional Development* 9: 211–20.

Charmaz, Kathy. 2006. *Constructing Grounded Theory.* Thousand Oaks: Sage Publications.

Cook, Ellen P. 1994. Role salience and multiple roles: A gender perspective. *The Career Development Quarterly* 43: 85–95. [CrossRef]

Corbin, Juliet, and Anselm Strauss. 2008. *Basics of Qualitative Research*, 3rd ed. Los Angeles: Sage.

Danes, Sharon M., Kathryn Stafford, George Haynes, and Sayali S. Amarapurkar. 2009. Family capital of family firms: Bridging human, social, and financial capital. *Family Business Review* 22: 199–216. [CrossRef]

Decker, Ryan, John Haltiwanger, Ron Jarmin, and Javier Miranda. 2014. The Role of Entrepreneurship in US Job Creation and Economic Dynamism. *The Journal of Economic Perspectives* 28: 3–24. [CrossRef]

Demartini, Paola. 2018. Innovative Female-Led Startups. Do Women in Business Underperform? *Administrative Sciences* 8: 70. [CrossRef]

Demartini, Paola, and Lucia Marchegiani. 2018. Born to Be Alive? Female Entrepreneurship and Innovative Start-Ups. In *Advances in Gender and Cultural Research in Business and Economics*. Edited by Paola Paoloni and Rosa Lombardi. Cham: Springer, pp. 219–35.

Eagly, Alice H., and Mary C. Johannesen-Schmidt. 2001. The leadership styles of women and men. *Journal of Social Issues* 57: 781–97. [CrossRef]

Eddleston, Kimberly A., Jamie J. Ladge, Cheryl Mitteness, and Lakshmi Balachandra. 2016. Do you see what I See? Signaling effects of gender and firm characteristics on financing entrepreneurial ventures. *Entrepreneurship Theory and Practice* 8: 489–514. [CrossRef]

Gillespie, Rosemary. 2000. Disbelief, Disregard and Deviance as Discourses of Voluntary Childlessness. *Women's Studies International Forum* 23: 223–34. [CrossRef]

Glaser, Barney G., and Anslem L. Strauss. 1967. *The Discovery of Grounded Theory: Strategies for Qualitative Research*, 8th ed. New Brunswick: Transaction Publishers.

Gorbatai, Andreea, and Laura Nelson. 2015. *The Narrative Advantage: Gender and the Language of Crowdfunding*. Research Papers. Berkeley: Haas School of Business UC Berkeley.

Green, Eileen, and Laurie Cohen. 1995. 'Women's business': Are women entrepreneurs breaking new ground or simply balancing the demands of women's work' in a new way? *Journal of Gender Studies* 4: 297–314. [CrossRef]

Greene, Francis J., Liang Han, and Susan Marlow. 2013. Like mother, like daughter? Analyzing maternal influences upon women's entrepreneurial propensity. *Entrepreneurship Theory and Practice* 37: 687–711. [CrossRef]

Greenhaus, Jeffrey H., and Gary N. Powell. 2012. The family-relatedness of work decisions: A framework and agenda for theory and research. *Journal of Vocational Behavior* 80: 246–55. [CrossRef]

Greenhaus, Jeffrey H., Gerard. A. Callanan, and Veronica M. Godshalk. 2000. *Career Management*, 3rd ed. Fort Worth: Dryden Press.

Gustafsson, Siv, and Adriaan Kalwij, eds. 2006. *Education and Postponement of Maternity: Economic Analyses for Industrialized Countries*. Berlin: Springer Science & Business Media, vol. 15.

Hastie, Reid. 2001. Problems for judgment and decision making. *Annual Review of Psychology* 52: 653–83. [CrossRef] [PubMed]

Jennings, Jennifer E., and Candida G. Brush. 2013. Research on Women Entrepreneurs: Challenges to (and from) the Broader Entrepreneurship Literature? *The Academy of Management Annals* 7: 663–715. [CrossRef]

Kariv, Dafna. 2013. *Female Entrepreneurship and the New Venture Creation: An International Overview*. London: Routledge.

Knaak, Stephanie J. 2010. Contextualising risk, constructing choice: Breastfeeding and good mothering in risk society. *Health Risk & Society* 12: 345–55.

Kuschel, Katherina, and Juan Pablo Labra. 2018. Developing Entrepreneurial Identity among Start-ups' Female Founders in High-Tech: Policy Implications from the Chilean Case. In *A Research Agenda for Women and Entrepreneurship: Identity through Aspirations, Behaviors, and Confidence*. Edited by Patricia G. Greene and Candida G. Brush. Boston: Edward Elgar, pp. 27–44.

Kuschel, Katherina. 2019. Ecosystems enabling women entrepreneurs—Santiago, Chile. In *The Wellbeing of Women in Entrepreneurship: A Global Perspective*. Edited by María Teresa Lepeley, Katherina Kuschel, Nicholas Beutell, Nicky Pow and Emiel Eijdenberg. London: Routledge.

Kuschel, Katherina, and María Teresa Lepeley. 2016a. Women start-ups in technology: Literature review and research agenda to improve participation. *International Journal of Entrepreneurship and Small Business* 27: 333–46. [CrossRef]

Kuschel, Katherina, and María Teresa Lepeley. 2016b. Copreneurial Women in start-ups: Growth-oriented or lifestyle? An aid for technology industry investors. *Academia Revista Latinoamericana de Administración* 29: 1–19. [CrossRef]

Kuschel, Katherina, and Erica Salvaj. 2018. Opening the "Black Box". Factors Affecting Women's Journey to Top Management Positions: A Framework Applied to Chile. *Administrative Sciences* 8: 63. [CrossRef]

Kuschel, Katherina, María Teresa Lepeley, Fernanda Espinosa, and Sebastián Gutiérrez. 2017. Funding Challenges of Latin American Women Start-up Founders in the Technology Industry. *Cross Cultural & Strategic Management* 24: 310–31.

Kuschel, Katherina, Juan Pablo Labra, and Gonzalo Diaz. 2018. Women-led startups and their contribution to job creation. In *Technology Entrepreneurship—Insights in New Technology-Based Firms, Research Spin-Offs and Corporate Environments*. Edited by Orestis Terzidis and André Presse. Cham: Springer.

Lepeley, María Teresa, Katherina Kuschel, Nicholas J. Beutell, Nicky Pouw, and Emiel Eijdenberg. 2019. *The Wellbeing of Women in Entrepreneurship. A Global Perspective*. London: Routledge.

Lewis, Patricia. 2014. Postfeminism, femininities and organization studies: Exploring a new agenda. *Organization Studies* 35: 1845–66. [CrossRef]

Lobel, Sharon A. 1991. Allocation of investment in work and family roles: Alternative theories and implications for research. *Academy of Management Review* 16: 507–21. [CrossRef]

Loscocco, Karyn A. 1997. Work–family linkages among self-employed women and men. *Journal of Vocational Behavior* 50: 204–26. [CrossRef]

Maher, JaneMaree, and Maryanne Dever. 2004. What Matters to Women: Beyond Reproductive Stereotypes. *People and Place* 12: 7–12.

Maher, JaneMaree, and Lise Saugeres. 2007. To be or not to be a mother? Women negotiating cultural representations of mothering. *Journal of Sociology* 43: 5–21. [CrossRef]

Marlow, Susan. 1997. Self–employed women—New opportunities, old challenges? *Entrepreneurship & Regional Development* 9: 199–210.

Marlow, Susan, and Maura McAdam. 2012. Analyzing the Influence of Gender upon High–Technology Venturing within the Context of Business Incubation. *Entrepreneurship Theory and Practice* 36: 655–76. [CrossRef]

Marlow, Susan, and Maura McAdam. 2015. Incubation or induction? Gendered identity work in the context of technology business incubation. *Entrepreneurship Theory and Practice* 39: 791–816. [CrossRef]

Matzeder, Mary E., and Thomas S. Krieshok. 1995. Career self-efficacy and the prediction of work and home role salience. *Journal of Career Assessment* 3: 331–40. [CrossRef]

Parasuraman, Saroj, Romila Singh, and Jeffrey H. Greenhaus. 1997. The influence of self and partner family variables on career development opportunities of professional women and men. In *Australian Industrial and Organizational Psychology Conference*. Edited by P. Tharenou. Melbourne: Australian Psychological Society, pp. 125–29.

Powell, Gary N., and Jeffrey H. Greenhaus. 2012. When family considerations influence work decisions: Decision-making processes. *Journal of Vocational Behavior* 81: 322–29. [CrossRef]

Prunty, Martine C., Louise Sharpe, Phyllis Butow, and Gary Fulcher. 2008. The motherhood choice: A decision aid for women with multiple sclerosis. *Patient Education and Counseling* 71: 108–15. [CrossRef] [PubMed]

Ries, Eric. 2011. *The Lean Startup: How Today's Entrepreneurs Use Continuous Innovation to Create Radically Successful Businesses*. New York: Crown Business.

Robb, Alicia, and Susan Coleman. 2009. Characteristics of New Firms: A Comparison by Gender. Available online: http://ssrn.com/abstract=1352601 (accessed on 31 March 2019).

Rothbard, Nancy P., and Jeffrey R. Edwards. 2003. Investment in work and family roles: A test of identity and utilitarian motives. *Personnel Psychology* 56: 699–730. [CrossRef]

Schindehutte, Minet, Michael Morris, and Catriona Brennan. 2003. Entrepreneurs and Motherhood: Impacts on Their Children in South Africa and the United States. *Journal of Small Business Management* 41: 94–107. [CrossRef]

Singh Cassidy, Sukhinder. 2015. Tech Women Choose Possibility. Available online: http://recode.net/2015/05/13/tech-women-choose-possibility/ (accessed on 31 March 2019).

Stryker, Sheldon, and Richard T. Serpe. 1994. Identity salience and psychological centrality: Equivalent, overlapping, or complementary concepts? *Social Psychology Quarterly* 57: 16–35. [CrossRef]

Sullivan, Sherry. E. 1999. The Changing Nature of Careers: A Review and Research Agenda. *Journal of Management* 25: 457–84. [CrossRef]

Susaeta, Lourdes, José Ramon Pin, Sandra Idrovo, Alvaro Espejo, María Belizón, Angela Gallifa, Marisa Aguirre, and Eugenio Avila-Pedrozo. 2013. Generation or culture? Work attitude drivers: An analysis in Latin America and Iberian countries. *Cross Cultural Management: An International Journal* 20: 321–60. [CrossRef]

Thoits, Peggy A. 1991. On merging identity theory and stress research. *Social Psychology Quarterly* 54: 101–12. [CrossRef]

Thornton, Davi J. 2011. Neuroscience, affect, and the entrepreneurialization of motherhood. *Communication and Critical/Cultural Studies* 8: 399–424. [CrossRef]

Vincent, Carol, Stephen J. Ball, and Soile Pietikainen. 2004. Metropolitan Mothers: Mothers, Mothering and Paid Work. *Women's Studies International Forum* 27: 571–87. [CrossRef]

Voydanoff, Patricia. 1988. Work and family: A review and expanded conceptualization. In *Work and family: Theory, Research, and Applications*. Edited by Elizabeth B. Goldsmith. Newbury Park: Sage.

Watkins, C. Edward, and Linda Mezydylo Subich. 1995. Annual review, 1992–94: Career development, reciprocal work/non-work interaction, and women's workforce participation. *Journal of Vocational Behavior* 47: 109–63. [CrossRef]

West, Candace, and Don H. Zimmerman. 1987. Doing Gender. *Gender and Society* 1: 125–51. [CrossRef]

administrative
sciences

MDPI

Article

It's Always a Women's Problem! Micro-Entrepreneurs, Work-Family Balance and Economic Crisis

Francesca Maria Cesaroni [†], Maria Gabriella Pediconi [†] and Annalisa Sentuti [*,†]

Department of Economics, Society, Politics, University of Urbino Carlo Bo, 61029 Urbino, Italy;
francesca.cesaroni@uniurb.it (F.M.C.); maria.pediconi@uniurb.it (M.G.P.)
* Correspondence: annalisa.sentuti@uniurb.it; Tel.: +39-0722-305528
† These authors contributed equally to this work.

Received: 8 October 2018; Accepted: 13 November 2018; Published: 24 November 2018

Abstract: Gender inequality in the division of family work is vastly corroborated and work–family balance is an important topic in the female entrepreneurship field of research. Even if work–family balance should be a necessity indiscriminately perceived by all women and men who have a paid job, it is a particularly pertinent issue for women, called to find equilibrium between work and family. This study analyses the situation of men and women entrepreneurs in order to investigate how the economic crisis affected the work–family balance. A survey was conducted on a sample of 218 men and women sole-proprietors. Findings show that the work–family balance of women entrepreneurs does not seem to have been particularly affected by the crisis. However, some differences between men and women remain. Concerning balance, as expected, only women stated that they personally take care of the house and family. Different perceptions of the crisis between men and women also emerged, as a consequence of gender stereotypes. Women entrepreneurs have greater difficulty in having an internal psychological balance of the double role than men, who are more involved in the implementation of external balance and focus on corporate and social provisions.

Keywords: work–family balance; female entrepreneurship; gender stereotypes; economic crisis; Italy

---

1. Introduction

Work–family balance is an interrole phenomenon (Marks and MacDermid 1996) as it refers to as "the extent to which an individual is equally engaged in—and equally satisfied with—his or her work role and family role" (Greenhaus et al. 2003, p. 513). Work–family balance is an issue for many men and women who have a paid work and have to deal with stressors related to work (time pressure, and work responsibilities) and family characteristics (childcare, household duties and family obligations) (Kim and Ling 2001). However, the issue of work–family balance mainly concerns women, despite the important changes that have occurred both in the family and in the labour market (Poggesi et al. 2017). In recent years, women's participation in the workforce has increased significantly in many countries (ILO 2017), the implication being important changes in family composition and organization. Available data show that women are having fewer children and later in life (Eurostat[1]). Moreover, the "male-breadwinner" model is gradually declining, due to a greater involvement of men with family duties and responsibilities. Nonetheless despite these changes, gendered role stereotypes are still very common, and the role of women within the family has only partially changed.

The recent economic crisis has apparently made the situation even worse by exacerbating conflicts between work and family. Such conflicts, in fact, occur when the same person holds two roles, and the

---

[1] Data available at https://ec.europa.eu/eurostat/data/database.

responsibilities and obligations of one role are incompatible with those of the other role. Previous studies on work–family conflicts show that, for women entrepreneurs, they can be related to job–parent conflicts, job–homemaker conflicts and job–spouse conflicts (Kim and Ling 2001). In such situations during the recent economic crisis:

(1) work–family conflicts (work demands that are in contrast with family responsibilities) may have worsened because the crisis may have placed an increased pressure on women entrepreneurs with regard to the survival of their business, relating to a desire to self-insure. This may have forced women entrepreneurs to devote more time to their businesses (Kirkwood and Tootell 2008), to try to avoid failure, thus reducing time and energies available for the family and the household. Moreover, the crisis may have created more psychological stress that has spilled over into other dimensions of life (Cardon and Patel 2015; Kollmann et al. 2018) and women entrepreneurs' sense of guilt may have increased, as they feel they have neglected their role as mothers and wives (McGowan et al. 2012;)

(2) family–work conflicts (family responsibilities that interfere with work) may have worsened because the crisis have reduced family income. Therefore, families may have had problems in bearing costs for family and domestic services and the burden of taking on such services have fallen mostly on women. On the other hand, the crisis may have reduced the supply of such services, or increased their cost, given the difficulty of national governments to maintain the same levels of welfare.

Italy is a country already known for its poor consideration for family support. However public services for children and family have recently undergone substantial cuts due to the economic recession. According to Eurostat data, in 2013, Italy spent only 1% of GDP for the family, in contrast to a European average of 1.7%. In the EU ranking, led by Denmark with 5% of GDP, Italy is the 22nd[2].

With such premises, this study analyses the situation of men and women entrepreneurs in order to investigate how the crisis affected the work–family balance. The study is structured as follows. The next section presents a literature review on what work–family balance means, what the relationship between work–family balance and women entrepreneurs is and why it is credible to speculate that the crisis has affected the work–family balance. In the following section, the research methodology is described and then the main results are presented. Finally, the conclusions, the limitations and the implications of the study are presented.

2. Work–Family Balance, Entrepreneurship and Economic Crisis

2.1. Women Entrepreneurs between Work and Family

The term work–family balance implies the ability to find equilibrium between the commitment, the time and the energy dedicated to remunerated work and the care of family members and the house. Principally, due to the unbalanced division of family responsibilities between men and women, work–family balance is one of the central issues in gender studies. Gender inequality in the division of family work is vastly corroborated (Shelton 1992; Milkie and Peltola 1999; Ocse 2013). This unbalance in the division of family work implies greater barriers in career progress and professional achievements for many women (Cross and Linehan 2006) and partially explains their lower employment rates, their prevalent involvement in under-paid and/or part-time jobs and their quasi-absence in senior management roles. As observed by Rehman and Roomi (2012), the trade-off between family and professional roles has been extensively analysed in literature, mostly to reveal the difficulties that working women particularly encounter if they aspire to a management career. Studies referring to

---

[2] Data available at http://www.confartigianato.it/2015/11/donne-impresa-occupazione-femminile-penalizzata-da-bassa-spesa-pubblica-per-la-famiglia-solo-1-del-pil/.

women entrepreneurs and the way they face problems connected to the work–family balance are less numerous (Parasuraman et al. 1996; Kim and Ling 2001; Shelton 2006; Jennings and McDougald 2007; Kirkwood and Tootell 2008; Walker et al. 2008; Rehman and Roomi 2012; Poggesi et al. 2017). From both the managerial and entrepreneurship perspectives, researchers have explained and described the interdependences between work and family differently, up to the definition of two opposing perspectives: the conflict perspective and the enrichment perspective (Greenhaus and Powell 2006; Shelton 2006; Jennings and McDougald 2007).

The conflict perspective is the dominant one and is based on the assumption that individual resources (time, energy, attention, etc.) are scarce and unrepeatable, so that anyone willing to undertake multiple roles at the same time has to face a conflict situation that will exacerbate the quality of his/her life (Greenhaus and Powell 2006). Work and family are the two incompatible spheres par excellence because the first subtracts resources from the second and vice versa. The conflict is harsher when the requirements of one role are not compatible with the needs of the other (Greenhaus and Beutell 1985). Therefore, balancing work and family is perceived as a complex and difficult problem to solve, which causes anxiety, dissatisfaction, stress and lower performances (Higgins and Duxbury 1992; Martins et al. 2002). In particular, three conflict types have been identified (Greenhaus and Beutell 1985): (1) the time conflict, the necessity to dedicate oneself to both work and family (husband, children, aging parents, and house) with a limited amount of hours in a day; (2) the anxiety conflict, when stress generated within the family negatively affects the professional sphere and vice versa; (3) the behavioural conflict, when behaviours required in one sphere are not compatible with those suitable in the other. Moreover, some studies affirm that the work–family conflict tends to be "bi-directional" for men and "uni-directional" for women (Posig and Kickul 2004). In fact, a man living in a trade-off situation between the two spheres usually manages to "adjust one sphere to compensate for the other" more easily and indifferently, while for a woman, it is more difficult because her commitment to the family is inflexible and is often considered independent from her work commitment (Posig and Kickul 2004). In other words, in any case, a working woman must take care of the family, so the work sphere must conform to family needs, while the opposite is a very rare occurrence.

The theory of work–family enrichment (Greenhaus and Powell 2006) is less known and is based on the assumption that time and energy can be shared, integrated and extended between these different life spheres (Shelton 2006). From this perspective, adopting different roles can generate positive consequences. In particular, emotions, experiences and behaviours that enrich the person and improve professional contribution can arise from the alliance between family and work. Within this theory, the concept of work–family balance merges with the concept of work–family enrichment, which occurs when the experience in one role improves the quality of life in other roles. In particular, work-to-family enrichment occurs when the work experience improves the quality of family life, while the family-to-work enrichment occurs when the experience in the family context improves the quality of life at work (Greenhaus and Powell 2006). The supporters of this theory, based on the results of many studies on this subject, also affirm that the adoption of multiple roles generates positive effects on the person because: (1) the double participation in work and family can be a source of physical and psychological wellness; (2) the family can help relieve tension and stress accumulated at work and vice versa; (3) the experience in one role can positively influence the other. For example, the flexibility and organizational skills developed in the family role to manage the needs of all family members can be successfully employed in the professional activity to carry out managing tasks more efficiently. In turn, such positive mutual influence between different roles and settings derive from the possibility to activate essential resources, such as individual capabilities (for example, multitasking), psychological and physical resources (for example, self-esteem, optimism, and health), flexibility (intended as the opportunity to define, at least in part, the time, pace and location of the different roles), and material resources (mainly economic) (Greenhaus and Powell 2006).

In the literature dedicated to women entrepreneurship, work–family balance issues have gained increasing attention from scholars. As highlighted by Ahl (2006), some researchers (in agreement with the theory of conflict) affirm that family can be an obstacle for a woman willing to start and manage a business, while others (aligned with the work–family enrichment theory) affirm that family is an inspirational source for women entrepreneurs, because it is precisely in the family environment that they develop their peculiar skills of democratic leadership, networking and relational marketing. As a matter of fact, many studies demonstrate that, for many women (more frequently than for men), the decision to start a business comes from the need to find a balance between their desire to have a job that satisfies their self-realisation and their ambition for independence and the will and/or the necessity to take care of the family (Boden 1999; DeMartino and Barbato 2003; Heilman and Chen 2003; Hughes 2003; Marlow 1997; Walker and Webster 2006; Walker et al. 2008; Kirkwood and Tootell 2008). However, if self-entrepreneurship implies a greater flexibility in work organization, compared to being an employee, it also implies the assumption of responsibilities and commitments that continuously increase with business size and complexity. Some studies (Parasuraman et al. 1996; Kim and Ling 2001; Walker et al. 2008; Rehman and Roomi 2012) demonstrate that the work–family conflict is far from being resolved for women entrepreneurs, but it is rather the opposite. In general, a woman entrepreneur works more hours and has more responsibilities with respect to an employee, and the more time she devotes to the business, the less she will be available for the family (Kim and Ling 2001; DeMartino et al. 2006). Therefore, self-entrepreneurship favours women's work–family balance as it provides greater flexibility for work time and organisation, provided that the business does not take over. In fact, statistical and empirical data demonstrate that women entrepreneurs very often start micro or small businesses; these business run by women entrepreneurs prefer to stay small and obtain lower financial performances than businesses managed by men (Hisrich and Brush 1984; Fischer et al. 1993; Cliff 1998; Bates 2002; Watson and Robinson 2003; Collins-Dodd et al. 2004; Fairlie and Robb 2009). For some scholars, these results are due to the fact that women: (1) have less capital for start-ups (Fairlie and Robb 2009) and are discriminated against when requesting credit (Alesina et al. 2013); (2) have less entrepreneurial experience (Hisrich and Brush 1984; Boden and Nucci 2000); (3) have limited managerial training and fewer managerial competences (Hisrich and Brush 1984; Boden and Nucci 2000; Kickul et al. 2007; Carter et al. 2015); (4) are less risk and innovation-oriented; and (5) have a lower social capital, formal and informal, than men (Kickul et al. 2007). However, research on this topic often shows contradictory results and does not unequivocally explain the reasons behind size differences between businesses owned by women and men.

Other scholars maintain that the smaller size and lower performances of female businesses can also be explained as a result of work–family balance, which is the compromise women are forced to make in order to have a satisfying work life and not to subtract too much time and energy from the family (Jennings and McDougald 2007). In other words, some women entrepreneurs choose to "limit" the size of their business, preferring a size that is easier to manage and that allows them to better manage their work–family balance (Shelton 2006; Cliff 1998). In this way, factors that initially guide women towards entrepreneurship are then the same that restrict profitability, growth and the development of their businesses (Walker et al. 2008). Furthermore, several scholars have shown that the profitability of female small businesses is negatively influenced by the role of women entrepreneurs in their family (Loscocco et al. 1991), and the time women entrepreneurs spend taking care of their children significantly reduces the business's life span (Williams 2004). It is further demonstrated that high conflict levels between work and family have a negative impact on business performance, because the work–family balance issues reduce women entrepreneurs' well-being and quality of life, and as a consequence, impede their work (Shelton 2006).

Finally, some scholars focus on the gender differences by comparing the work–family balance of men and women entrepreneurs. Eddleston and Powell (2012) analysed the gender relationship, family-to-business enrichment, family-to-business support and satisfaction in relation to the personal work–family balance. Their results highlight that, while the work–family balance satisfaction for women entrepreneurs is mainly fostered by family-to-business enrichment, for men, it is family support that makes a difference. Women entrepreneurs tend to adopt a holistic approach toward work and family, creating and capitalising synergies among the different roles that enrich their entrepreneurial experience and increase their satisfaction with respect to work–family balance. Entrepreneur men, on the other hand, prefer the segmentation approach, that is, they tend to separate their work role from their family, and they obtain their satisfaction with respect to work–family balance from family support, in particular, emotional support and alleviation from family responsibilities. Instead, Johansson Sevä and Öun (2015) analysed self-employment as a strategy for the improvement of work–family balance and demonstrate that this is the best choice only for autonomous working women without employees, who appear to have less work–family balance problems than male colleagues. Such a difference, however, vanishes by increasing the number of collaborators.

2.2. Subjective Work–Family Balance as a Psychological Challenge

Research that emphasises psychological aspects that characterise the work–family balance of both men and women are more and more numerous. The need to balance family and work is a challenge, first of all for the person, and then for the company and the production system as a whole. It is a challenge that, above all, reveals the strong competition between women's participation in the labour market and their maternal role. Women's double workload is often disputed, as they are forced to divide their time and dedication between their home and their business. For centuries, the traditional social organization has entrusted women with the task of caring for and raising children, so much so that the dual role was only conceived for working women. It is a stereotype that is far from over, considering that the studies continue to show that family and domestic activities remain a prerogative of women. Indeed, the increase in female participation in the labour market did not correspond to male participation in domestic activities. Furthermore, maternity continues to be perceived as a strong limitation on career opportunities for women, as it is considered irreconcilable with a qualified and professional work (Girelli and Mapelli 2016).

Stereotypes are subtle psychological structures that transversely affect both stigmatised and stigmatizing individuals. They influence the behaviours and attitudes of bosses and colleagues of the working women in a double direction. On the one hand, working mothers are considered less competent and less attached to work (Bornstein et al. 2012), and, on the other hand, those who work with a strong mental and time commitment are portrayed as cold, false and a careerist (Heilman 2001). The experience of becoming mothers and fathers reveals that a mental balance must be developed before an organizational and logistic one; it is not simply a matter of allocating time or negotiating spaces. The work–family balance is a slow process that, in keeping the parties together, has to deal with the alternation of conflicting effects to be able to compose often-antithetical affective and professional aspirations. Corporate tools can be crucial to effectively manage the work–family balance. However, the mere availability of organizational measures will not guarantee its use by those in difficulty (Girelli and Mapelli 2016). A good external, practical and operational work–family balance will only be achieved by starting with an internal, subjective and personal equilibrium. Indeed, Eisler (2015) argues that work–family balance is not a "universal formula" but an "individual model" developed by each worker.

A few qualitative studies have compared men and women to understand how they perceive the intersection of work and home and family life, paying attention to psychological issues. Loscocco (1997) study of small business owners in the USA found that men perceive the flexibility of work hours as a symbol of control over their life and work, and women use flexibility as a key resource in trying to achieve a work–family balance. If women accommodate work to family life, men will continue to put their business first. The lack of work–family balance is a problem for men as well as for women, overall in relation with the presence of children in the household. These difficulties take more complicated forms for women, as they perceive themselves as responsible for maintaining, at a minimum, the transitions between home and work life. Men who say that they "work to live" or "live to work" maintain a more traditional version of masculinity. On the contrary, women construct a range of femininities through their different narratives, emphasising their close family ties or underscoring their independence from partners (Emslie and Hunt 2009).

2.3. Work–Family Balance and Economic Crisis

The recent economic crisis appears to have per se further complicated an already problematic and complex picture, reducing access to external services, both because of reduced family incomes and the cuts to family support services. Istat data highlight that, during the crisis period, accessibility to childhood services (Istat 2014a) decreased (after years of constant growth), and the number of working women with young children that denounced difficulties in balancing work and family increased (from 38.6% in 2005 to 42.7% in 2012) (Istat 2014b). At the same time, the number of beds in the social-assistance districts decreased (from 7.1% in 2009 to 6.5% in 2011), while the needs for Integrated Home Assistance remained constant at four beneficiaries for every 100 elderly (Istat 2014a). In this context, families, and women, in particular, continue to have "a principal role, in many cases unique, as social regulators" (Macchioni 2012), which often impedes the participation of women in the country's economy. It is no coincidence that, in the Global Gender Report 2015 (WEF 2015), Italy ranks 111th (out of a total of 145 world countries) concerning the participation of women in the labour market. Considering the European situation, ahead of us are all the Northern European countries (also known to have both a high birth rate and a high women employment rate), including countries like Greece (ranking 87th), Croatia (78th), Spain (67th), France (56th) and Germany (38th).

In conclusion, work–family balance seems to have worsened during the crisis. Due to the above-mentioned reasons, women entrepreneurs could have been affected more than their male colleagues. In this context, the aim of this study is to answer the following research questions:

1.   How did entrepreneurs' ability to balance work and family change during the economic crisis?
2.   Did these changes affect men and women entrepreneurs in the same way?

In addition to our contribution to the literature on work–family balance and women entrepreneurs, the in-depth analysis of these aspects can be useful to highlight whether gender differences persist and have been accentuated by the crisis. Such analysis can further provide useful indications for the policy makers that, for various purposes, deal with gender equality and policies to support the work–family balance of men and women entrepreneurs.

3. Methodology

In order to answer our research questions, a survey was carried out among a sample of Italian sole-proprietors, owners of micro-enterprises located in the Marche region, in Central Italy. The survey aims to compare men and women's work–family balance during the economic crisis and identify possible similarities or differences.

The Marche region has one of the highest concentrations of micro and small enterprises in Italy. The impact of the economic crisis has been particularly harsh. For instance, in 2009, the regional GDP declined by 5.4% (Istat 2014b), the joint-stock companies' mortality rate was the highest in Italy and between 2008 and 2012, the number of artisan enterprises decreased by 5.1%. With respect to entrepreneurs' gender, the regional feminisation rate (22.9%) is slightly higher than the national percentage of women-owned businesses (21.6%) (Unioncamere 2016). However, despite this encouraging data, the Marche region is characterised by a cultural background based on a traditional division of roles between men and women, who have historical origins, and continues to show its effects (Farina 2012; Cesaroni and Sentuti 2014), often still affecting the sharing of family responsibilities and obligations between men and women. For all these reasons, the Marche region is ideally suited to such a study.

The decision to involve only sole-proprietors in the survey was motivated by two main reasons. First, despite the presence of many female companies and partnerships, in Italy, sole proprietorships represent a very high percentage of the total number of women-owned businesses (65% in 2014, according to data from Girelli and Mapelli (2016)). Second, the decision to limit the analysis to sole proprietorships resolves the problem of the correct identification of the person who runs the business. A micro-entrepreneur is directly involved in all business functions and activities, without regard to gender.

A non-proportional stratified sample, with the same number of men and women, was selected using the list of members in one of the main regional business associations. The purpose of the survey was to understand how the onset of the crisis changed men and women micro-entrepreneurs' work–family balance. For this reason, businesses set up after autumn 2008 were excluded. In fact, changes in their usual work–family balance could have been caused by the establishment of a new business and not necessarily by the economic crisis. This also means that the sample clearly has an element of survivor bias, as we were only able to analyze businesses that were present before the crisis and did not close due to pressures caused by difficulties connected to the crisis, including work–family balance issues. Starting from a list of 1627 sole-proprietors (429 women and 1198 men), a sample of 300 sole-proprietors (150 men and 150 women) was randomly extracted. Entrepreneurs selected this way took part in a telephone questionnaire in October and November 2013 and were asked questions regarding their personal and familiar situation (age, marital status, family composition, and age of children), their work–family balance and if/how it was affected by the economic crisis. In particular, efforts were made to figure out:

- Whether the interviewee's ability to balance work and family changed during the economic crisis and, if so, how (improved or worsened);
- What the reasons for any possible change were. In particular, those who said they noticed an improvement in their work–family balance were asked to describe the reasons, and those who said it worsened were given a list of eight possible reasons, asking them to give a point according to the Likert 5 point scale, in which 1 = Absolutely irrelevant and 5 = Extremely important;
- How the costs related to keeping a work–family balance changed; that is, whether the costs incurred by the interviewee for schools, domestic help, caregivers, nannies and other services in support of the family and household increased, decreased or remained stable during the crisis.

Questions refer to the previous 5 years. The survey enabled us to obtain 218 fully completed questionnaires. Women compiled 110 and men provided 108 questionnaires. The response rate was particularly high, standing at 73% and substantially similar for entrepreneurs of both genders (men: 72%; women: 73.3%). With regard to the features of the sample, most of entrepreneurs (67.4%) are middle-aged (36–55 years), and 19.7% are in a medium-high range (56–65 years), while the younger and the older entrepreneurs are very few (only 7.3% of entrepreneurs are under 35 and 5.5% are over sixty). A greater representation of women emerged in the lower age bracket (26–35 years), where no men at this age range were included. Regarding marital status, the percentage of married entrepreneurs is dominant (66.5% of the sample), 8.7% of the interviewees are life partners, while singles represent 13.8% of the sample and the remaining 11% are separated/divorced or widowed. No noteworthy differences between women and men emerged. Finally, concerning family composition, the largest proportion of the sample has only one child (43.6%) and this condition prevails among women (53.6% versus 33.3% of men). About a quarter of entrepreneurs (25.2%) are parents of two or more children, while 31.2% of the sample has no children. Only 16% of parents have at least one child less than or equal to 10 years old, while 84% have one or more children over 10 years old. Results from the empirical survey are presented and discussed in the following sections.

4. Results

4.1. How the Economic Crisis Affected the Work-Family Balance

The crisis does not seem to have had a disruptive effect on the entrepreneurs' work–family balance (Table 1).

Table 1. With regard to the last 5 years, has the capacity to balance family and work domains changed?

	Whole Sample		Men		Women	
	N°	%	N°	%	N°	%
Yes, it has improved	23	10.6	7	6.5	16	14.5
Yes, it got worse	16	7.3	5	4.6	11	10.0
No, it has unchanged	179	82.1	96	88.9	83	75.5
Total	**218**	**100**	**108**	**100**	**110**	**100**

In fact, 82.1% of the interviewees stated that, despite the recession, their ability to balance work activities and family commitments has not changed. However, this does not mean that the respondents were not confronted with any work–family balance problems. Rather, it means that during the crisis, they did not experience substantial changes in their ability to manage their work–family balance. In some cases, the stability is due to the fact that, as we will see later, respondents fall into the categories that experienced less problems related to work–family balance (for example, singles and those who do not have children). In other cases, it is possible to hypothesise that no changes related to the entrepreneur's life cycle or the family ménage occurred, such as the modification of the work–family balance. Mostly men asserted that they did not notice significant changes in their work–family balance (88.9% versus 75.5% of women). Therefore, women perceived a (positive or negative) change in their ability to balance work and family obligations more than men, confirming their greater responsiveness to issues related to work–family balance. It was also found that 17.9% of the whole sample stated that the management of work–family balance changed in the period 2008–2013, and 10.6% claimed it improved, while the remaining 7.3% said it worsened.

Women claimed that their work–family balance improved more than men during the crisis (14.5% versus 6.5%). However, more women referred a worsening of their ability to achieve balance than men (10% versus 4.6% of men). These who noticed a change are quite few in number and thus percentages are highly sensitive even in very small differences in absolute value. Therefore, the analysis is limited to descriptive statistics and results cannot be considered statistically generalizable. However, data highlight some interesting trends, and it seems useful to analyse the three sub-samples (improved, worsened, and unchanged work–family balance) with regard to some variables that, emerging from the literature review, can influence the management of work–family balance: marital status, number of children and presence of children aged 10 years or younger.

An improvement in work–family balance was experienced by interviewees who have a less complex family situation. In fact, in the group of these who refer to an improvement in their work–family balance, the percentages of entrepreneurs with only one child (60.9%) or with children over the age of 10 (86.4%) (Table 2) are higher than in the other groups, and especially with respect to the "worsened work–life balance" group. Accordingly in this group, the percentages of those who have two or more children, with at least one under the age of 10, achieved relatively low rates (34.8% and 13.6%, respectively).

Table 2. Improved work–family balance: classification of the sub-sample by marital status, number and age of children.

	Whole Sample		Men		Women	
	N°	%	N°	%	N°	%
Marital status						
Married	20	87.0	6	85.7	14	87.5
Life partners	1	4.3	1	14.3	0	-
Single	0	-	0	-	0	-
Divorced/Separated	2	8.7	0	-	2	12.5
Widower/Widow	0	-	0	-	0	-
Total	**23**	**100**	**7**	**100**	**16**	**100**

Table 2. *Cont.*

	Whole Sample		Men		Women	
Number of children						
No one	1	4.3	0	-	1	6.3
1 child	14	60.9	4	57.1	10	62.5
2 or more children	8	34.8	3	42.9	5	31.3
Total	**23**	**100**	**7**	**100**	**16**	**100**
Age of children						
At least one child aged less than or equal to 10 years	3	13.6	1	14.3	2	13.3
Children aged more than 10 years	19	86.4	6	85.7	13	86.7
Total	**22**	**100**	**7**	**100**	**15**	**100**

Based on analysis of the motivations of these who refer to an improvement in their work–family balance, results show that for almost all women (81.3%), this change was determined by the age of their children. On the contrary, male entrepreneurs never mentioned this factor (Table 3). For them, in fact, the improvement was mainly due to the reduction of work due to the recession and the consequent increase in free time (85.7%). Therefore, the economic crisis seems to have had a positive impact on male entrepreneurs' work–family balance, while for female entrepreneurs, no influence emerged as the improvement of their work–family balance was mainly linked to the age of their children, an aspect that is obviously not conditioned by the recession.

Table 3. If your work–family balance has improved, can you tell us why?

	Whole Sample		Men		Women	
	N°	%	N°	%	N°	%
Children have grown up	13	56.5	0	-	13	81.3
Less work, more free time	7	30.4	6	85.7	1	6.3
Separation	1	4.3	0	-	1	6.3
Other reasons	1	4.3	1	14.3	0	-
No response	1	4.3	0	-	1	6.3
Total	23	100	7	100	16	100

Those who stated that their work–family balance worsened live with a partner and have one or more children (87.5%). Although they are not necessarily very young (42.9%), they have at least one child aged 10 years or younger, while the remaining 57.1% have children older than 10 (Table 4). By distinguishing the results according to gender, we observed that all men who expressed a deterioration in balancing work and family are married (100%), while women are divided into married (81.8%) and life partner (18.2%). Among women entrepreneurs, 18.2% (versus 0% of men) complained a deterioration despite having no children, while 66.7% (against 40% of men) of them have children over ten years old. On the one hand, therefore, children certainly increase the family obligations, but, on the other hand, it is not the only factor affecting women's work–family balance.

With regard to the factors indicated as the cause of the work–family balance worsening, the following prevail: (1) for women, the increase in commitment required by the entrepreneurial activity (82%) and the rise of family obligations and responsibilities (55%) (for instance, after getting married, beginning cohabitation, having sick parents, etc.); (2) for men, the same reasons emerging, but with a lower percentage (40%).

Table 4. Worsened work–family balance: classification of the sub-sample by marital status, number and age of children.

	Whole Sample		Men		Women	
	N°	%	N°	%	N°	%
Marital status						
Married	14	87.5	5	100	9	81.8
Life partners	2	12.5	0	-	2	18.2
Single	0	-	0	-	0	-
Divorced/Separated	0	-	0	-	0	-
Widower/Widow	0	-	0	-	0	-
Total	16	100	5	100	11	100
Number of children						
No one	2	12.50	0	-	2	18.2
1 child	9	56.25	3	60	6	54.5
2 or more children	5	31.25	2	40	3	27.3
Total	16	100	5	100	11	100
Age of children						
At least one child aged less than or equal to 10 years	6	42.9	3	60	3	33.3
Children aged more than 10 years	8	57.1	2	40	6	66.7
Total	14	100	5	100	9	100

The sub-sample of entrepreneurs who have not observed changes in their work–family balance is, as anticipated, the most numerous and articulated (Table 5). With regard to marital status, the percentage of married entrepreneurs is lower than that of the other groups (62%), as there is a fair percentage of single (16.8%). Limited is the presence of divorced/separated entrepreneurs (6.7%) or widows/widowers (5.6%, the percentage rising to 9.6% for women). Considering the number of children, the proportion of these with no child is higher than that of the other groups: 36.3% against 4.3% in the "improved work–family balance" sub-sample and 12.5% in the "worsened work–family balance" sub-sample. Compared to the latter group, the presence of interviewees with children over the age of 10 years also greatly increases: 86.8% of the parent-entrepreneurs belong to this sub-sample (the rate is similar to that of the "improved work–family balance", equal to 86.4%), compared to 57.1% for the "worsened work–family balance" sub-sample.

Table 5. Unchanged work–family balance: classification of the sub-sample by marital status, number and age of children.

	Whole Sample		Men		Women	
	N°	%	N°	%	N°	%
Marital status						
Married	111	62.0	63	65.6	48	57.8
Life partners	16	8.9	5	5.2	11	13.3
Single	30	16.8	18	18.8	12	14.5
Divorced/Separated	12	6.7	8	8.3	4	4.8
Widower/Widow	10	5.6	2	2.1	8	9.6
Total	179	100	96	100	83	100
Number of children						
No one	65	36.3	39	40.6	26	31.3
1 child	72	40.2	29	30.2	43	51.8
2 or more children	42	23.5	28	29.2	14	16.9
Total	179	100	96	100	83	100
Age of children						
At least one child aged less than or equal to 10 years	15	13.2	8	14.0	7	12.3
Children aged more than 10 years	99	86.8	49	86.0	50	87.7
Total	114	100	57	100	57	100

4.2. The Cost of Services to Support a Work–Family Balance during the Crisis

In regard to the costs of services used to support the family and household, most of sample (about 85% without gender differences) declared that, despite the crisis, the spending remained stable (Table 6). The cost did not greatly increase or decrease for anyone, and only a small percentage stated that it decreased (9.63%) or increased (5%).

Table 6. With regard to the last 5 years, how have the costs for your family changed for schools, domestic help, caregivers, nannies and other services in support of family?

	Whole Sample		Men		Women	
	N°	%	N°	%	N°	%
Much increased	0	-	0	-	0	-
Increased	11	5.05	7	6.5	4	3.6
Stable	186	85.32	92	85.2	94	85.5
Decreased	21	9.63	9	8.3	12	10.9
Much decreased	0	-	0	-	0	-
Total	**218**	**100**	**108**	**100**	**110**	**100**

An open-ended question also allowed us to gather the reasons that explain the trend of spending devoted to these kinds of services (Table 7). Half of the whole sample (68.35%) stated that the costs did not increase because they do not use these kinds of services. In particular, more men (75%) than women (61.8%) stated that they do not have such costs. In this case, those who are single were also included (97%) in the sample. Seventeen percentage of sample, on the other hand, supports these kinds of costs but declared that the spending as a whole remained unchanged. In this case, the percentage of women (23.6%) exceeds that of the men (10.2%). The reasons for the increase in incurred costs, on the other hand, are generally attributable to the increase in family care needs. They are determined by the need to enrol children in nursery school or hire babysitters, or by need to hire a caregiver for their parents who are no longer self-sufficient. Only two entrepreneurs (0.98%) stated that spending increased due to the increase in the cost of services. In parallel, the drop of spending is due, in large part, to the reduction of family needs and in primis to the growth of children. Only three women entrepreneurs (1.38%) stated that the reduction of income was determined by the crisis and forced them to renounce the external help. Finally, the reasons for those who said they do not support any kind of cost to access external services were investigated (Table 8).

Table 7. Reasons to explain the trend of costs for family support services.

	Whole Sample		Men		Women	
	N°	%	N°	%	N°	%
I haven't this kind of expense	149	68.35	81	75.0	68	61.8
Costs remained unchanged	37	16.97	11	10.2	26	23.6
Children have grown up	14	6.42	8	7.4	6	5.5
I eliminated the services because of decreased income	3	1.38	0	-	3	2.7
I have no longer nannies or maid because my partner no longer works	2	0.92	0	-	2	1.8
Needs have diminished because the family situation has changed	1	0.46	1	0.9	0	-
I fired the maid because I don't work anymore	1	0.46	0	-	1	0.9
I added the costs for the nursery school	4	1.83	2	1.9	2	1.8
I hired a caregiver	3	1.38	3	2.8	0	-
Costs for services have increased	2	0.92	0	-	2	1.8
I added a nannie because the partner has begun to work	1	0.46	1	0.9	0	-
No answer	1	0.46	1	0.9	0	-
Total	**218**	**100**	**108**	**100**	**110**	**100**

Table 8. Why do you not support this kind of cost?

	Whole Sample		Men		Women	
	N°	%	N°	%	N°	%
We don't need this services	120	80.54	70	86.4	50	73.5
My partner takes care of it	9	6.04	9	11.1	0	-
I'll take care of it	16	10.74	0	-	16	23.5
Parents and relatives help me	4	2.68	2	2.5	2	2.9
Total	**149**	**100**	**81**	**100**	**68**	**100**

It was found that 80.5% of the sample (more men, 86.4%, than women 73.5%) did not have this kind of cost because they stated that they did not need these services (they did not have little children or parents that are not self-sufficient). On the other hand, 19.5% of the sample specified that they did not need external services because there was already someone taking care of the house and family. Moreover, 6.4% stated that their partner takes care of the house and family, while 10.7% declared that they take care of the house and family themselves.

The interesting as well as predictable aspect is that only men answered: "My partner takes care of it", while only women said: "I take care of it". It is a little, but meaningful, sign, without statistical relevance, that there is a clear division of roles in force in our society between men and women in the family environment. The rest—2.7%—refers to parents or other relatives who supported them in managing the house and/or family.

5. Conclusions

Our research findings show that the work–family balance of women entrepreneurs does not seem to have been particularly affected by the crisis. However, some differences between men and women remain, regardless of the recession. For some men entrepreneurs, the crisis indicated an improvement in the work–family balance, due to a diminishing of work and an increase in available free time, while for women entrepreneurs, the improvement of work–family balance was confirmed mainly due to the age of the children. Only a few declared a deterioration, while most of the sample stated that work–family balance remained stable during the crisis, as well as the spending devoted to services that support the balance between family and work. Concerning balance, a difference between men and women entrepreneurs emerged. As expected, only women stated that they personally take care of the house and family.

Our findings allowed us to observe the psychological implications of work–family balance, confirming some data that have emerged in recent researches. Basically, they are:

- different perceptions of the crisis between men and women, which remain as a consequence of gender stereotypes: women have to bear the burden of household work and needs, while men think more about work commitments. Women experienced difficulties in coordinating different areas of their lives, and in particular, family influenced some conflicting demands (children and other responsibilities). On the contrary, men perceived a better balance between work and family (Emslie and Hunt 2009);
- different perceptions of the work–family balance during times of crisis, revealing greater female difficulty in having an internal psychological balance of the double role than men, who were more involved in the implementation of external balance and focused on corporate and social provisions (Girelli and Mapelli 2016). Women perceive recent or current problems as demanding sources. For men, their role as father was associated with attending key family events and was not a problem; this can explain why men perceive conflicts as an individual problem for their family to solve.

Difficulties in managing relations between firm and family are confirmed as more structural, that is, mostly related to the person's family condition and the disparity of roles between men and women in the family context, than conjunctural, that is, determined by the reduction in services due to the recession. However, this result should not be interpreted as something that does not require services to support the family. Rather, it seems to suggest, mainly to policy makers who deal with gender equality and supporting policies of work–family balance, the opportunity to manage the question considering two aspects: gender culture and services offered. The provision of services is a necessary but perhaps insufficient condition to support women entrepreneurs and female workers, especially if it is not accompanied by actions that can facilitate gender equality. On the one hand, indeed, it is true that some aspects cannot be separated from women, i.e., maternity; on the other hand, it is equally certain that a different work organization, a fair distribution of tasks in the family and the presence of services and means to support the family can relieve women from numerous tasks and considerably simplify her work–family balance. For such changes to occur, a cultural change is necessary, which modifies the common way of thinking about the division of roles between men and women within the family and, more generally, in society. In part, these changes are already taking place, but this process can be accelerated thanks to appropriate measures promoted by policy makers, such as the mandatory parental leave for fathers.

This study has the merit to thoroughly examine the issue of work–family balance of women entrepreneurs during economic recession. However, our research presents some important limitations. Among them, the composition of the sample seems to be the most relevant. Having defined a statistically representative sample of the population of the reference companies, on the one hand, and needing to exclude newly established companies, on the other hand, caused an underrepresentation of categories which may have experienced balance problems. Indeed, within the sample, the percentage of subjects under the age of 35 with at least one child under 10 years old is low. Therefore, our data referred to rather low numbers, permitted only a simple descriptive analysis and obtained results that are not statistically generalisable. Further quantitative analysis can be done on a wider and more targeted sample. In order to obtain more insight into changes in work–family balance caused by the crisis, further research should also consider questions about particular aspects of work–family balance (e.g., hours worked, times family events missed, etc.), in order to triangulate them against the overall question about work–family balance.

Author Contributions: All the Authors equally contributed to this article. They have been equally involved in the phases of conceptualization, data analysis, drafting, writing and critical revision of the manuscript. Finally, all authors approved the final content manuscript.

Funding: This research received no external funding.

Conflicts of Interest: The authors declare no conflicts of interest.

References

Ahl, Helene. 2006. Why research on women entrepreneurs needs new directions. *Entrepreneurship Theory and Practice* 30: 595–621. [CrossRef]

Alesina, Alberto F., Francesca Lotti, and Paolo Emilio Mistrulli. 2013. Do Women Pay More for Credit? Evidence from Italy. *Journal of the European Economic Association* 11: 45–66. [CrossRef]

Bates, Timothy. 2002. Restricted Access to Markets Characterizes Women-Owned Businesses. *Journal of Business Venturing* 17: 313–24. [CrossRef]

Boden, Richard J., Jr. 1999. Flexible Working Hours, Family Responsibilities, and Female Self-Employment. *American Journal of Economics and Sociology* 58: 71–83. [CrossRef]

Boden, Richard J., Jr., and Alfred R. Nucci. 2000. On the Survival Prospects of Men's and Women's New Business Ventures. *Journal of Business Venturing* 15: 347–62. [CrossRef]

Bornstein, Stephanie, Joan C. Williams, and Genevieve R. Painter. 2012. Discrimination against Mother Is the Strongest Form of Worker Gender Discrimination: Lessons from US Caregiver Discrimination Law. *The International Journal of Comparative Labour Law and Industrial Relations* 28: 45–62.

Cardon, Melissa S., and Pankaj C. Patel. 2015. Is stress worth it? Stress-related health and wealth trade-offs for entrepreneurs. *Applied Psychology* 64: 379–420. [CrossRef]

Carter, Sara, Samuel Mwaura, Monder Ram, Kiran Trehan, and Trevor Jones. 2015. Barriers to ethnic minority and women's. enterprise: Existing evidence, policy tensions and unsettled questions. *International Small Business Journal* 33: 49–69. [CrossRef]

Cesaroni, Francesca Maria, and Annalisa Sentuti. 2014. Women and family businesses. When women are left only minor roles. *The History of the Family* 19: 358–79. [CrossRef]

Cliff, Jennifer E. 1998. Does One Size Fit All? Exploring the Relationship Between Attitudes Towards Growth, Gender, and Business Size. *Journal of Business Venturing* 13: 523–42. [CrossRef]

Collins-Dodd, Colleen, Irene M. Gordon, and Carolyne Smart. 2004. Further evidence on the role of gender in financial performance. *Journal of Small Business Management* 42: 395–417. [CrossRef]

Cross, Christine, and Margaret Linehan. 2006. Barriers to Advancing Female Careers in the High-Tech Sector: Empirical Evidence from Ireland. *Women in Management Review* 21: 28–39. [CrossRef]

DeMartino, Richard, and Robert Barbato. 2003. Differences Between Women and Men MBA Entrepreneurs: Exploring Family Flexibility and Wealth Creation as Career Motivators. *Journal of Business Venturing* 18: 815–32. [CrossRef]

DeMartino, Richard, Robert Barbato, and Paul H. Jacques. 2006. Exploring the career /achievement and personal life orientation differences between entrepreneurs and non-entrepreneurs: The impact of sex and dependents. *Journal of Small Business Management* 44: 350–69. [CrossRef]

Eddleston, Kimberly A., and Gary N. Powell. 2012. Nurturing entrepreneurs' work-family balance: A gendered perspective. *Entrepreneurship Theory and Practice* 36: 513–41. [CrossRef]

Emslie, Carol, and Kate Hunt. 2009. Live to Work' or 'Work to Live'? A Qualitative Study of Gender and Work–life Balance among Men and Women in Mid-life. *Gender, Work and Organization* 16: 151–72. [CrossRef]

Fairlie, Robert W., and Alicia M. Robb. 2009. Gender differences in business performance: Evidence from the characteristics of business owners survey. *Small Business Economics* 33: 375–95. [CrossRef]

Farina, Fatima. 2012. *La Complessa Tessitura di Penelope*. Napoli: Liguori Editore.

Fischer, Eileen M., A. Rebecca Reuber, and Lorraine S. Dyke. 1993. A theoretical Overview and Extension of Research on Sex, Gender, and Entrepreneurship. *Journal of Business Venturing* 8: 151–68. [CrossRef]

Girelli, Laura, and Adele Mapelli. 2016. *Genitori al Lavoro. L'arte di Integrare Figli, Lavoro, Vita*. Milano: Guerini.

Greenhaus, Jeffrey H., and Nicholas J. Beutell. 1985. Sources of conflict between work and family roles. *Academy of Management Review* 10: 76–88. [CrossRef]

Greenhaus, Jeffrey H., and Gary N. Powell. 2006. When Work and Family are Allies: A Theory of Work-Family Enrichment. *Academy of Management Review* 31: 72–92. [CrossRef]

Greenhaus, Jeffrey H., Karen M. Collins, and Jason D. Shaw. 2003. The relation between work-family balance and quality of life. *Journal of Vocational Behavior* 63: 510–31. [CrossRef]

Heilman, Madeline E. 2001. Description and prescription: How Gender Stereotypes Prevent Women Ascent up the Organizzational Ladder. *Journal of Social Issues* 57: 657–74. [CrossRef]

Heilman, Madeline E., and Julie J. Chen. 2003. Entrepreneurship as a Solution: The Allure of Self-Employment for Women and Minorities. *Human Resource Management Review* 13: 347–64. [CrossRef]

Higgins, Christopher Alan, and Linda Elizabeth Duxbury. 1992. Work-Family Conflict in the Dual-Career Family. *Organizational Behavior and Human Decision Processes* 51: 51–75. [CrossRef]

Hisrich, Robert, and Candy Brush. 1984. The Woman Entrepreneur: Management Skills and Business Problems. *Journal of Small Business Management* 22: 30–37.

Hughes, Karen D. 2003. Pushed or Pulled? Women's Entry into Self-Employment and Small Business Ownership. *Gender, Work & Organization* 10: 433–54.

ILO. 2017. World Employment Social Outlook. Available online: www.ilo.org (accessed on 26 October 2018).

Istat. 2014a. Bes 2014. Il Benessere equo e Sostenibile in Italia. Available online: www.istat.it/it/files/2014/06/Rapporto_Bes_2014.pdf (accessed on 3 September 2018).

Istat. 2014b. Rapporto annuale 2014—La situazione del Paese. Available online: http://www.istat.it/it/archivio/120991 (accessed on 3 September 2018).

Jennings, Jennifer E., and Megan S. McDougald. 2007. Work-family Interface Experiences and Coping Strategies: Implications for Entrepreneurship Research and Practice. *Academy of Management Review* 32: 747–60. [CrossRef]

Johansson Sevä, Ingemar, and Ida Öun. 2015. Self-Employment as a Strategy for Dealing with the Competing Demands of Work and Family? The Importance of Family/Lifestyle Motives. *Gender, Work & Organization* 22: 256–72.

Kickul, Jill R., Lisa K. Gundry, and Susan D. Sampson. 2007. Women Entrepreneurs Preparing for Growth: The Influence of Social Capital and Training on Resource Acquisition. *Journal of Small Business & Entrepreneurship* 20: 169–81.

Kirkwood, Jodyanne, and Beth Tootell. 2008. Is entrepreneurship the answer to achieving work-family balance. *Journal of Management & Organization* 14: 285–302.

Kollmann, Tobias, Christoph Stöckmann, and Julia M. Kensbock. 2018. I can't get no sleep—the differential impact of entrepreneurial stressors on work-home interference and insomnia among experienced versus novice entrepreneurs. *Journal of Business Venturing*. in press. [CrossRef]

Kim, Jean, and Choo Seow Ling. 2001. Work-Family Conflict of Women Entrepreneurs in Singapore. *Women in Management Review* 16: 204–21.

Loscocco, Karyn A. 1997. Work-family Linkages among Self-employed Women and Men. *Journal of Vocational Behavior* 50: 2014–226. [CrossRef]

Loscocco, Karyn A., Joyce Robinson, Richard H. Hall, and John K. Allen. 1991. Gender and Small Business Success: An Inquiry into Women's Relative Disadvantage. *Social Forces* 70: 65–85. [CrossRef]

Macchioni, Elena. 2012. "Welfare aziendale. Buone pratiche di conciliazione Famiglia-Lavoro", Osservatorio nazionale sulla famiglia, ebook/3. Available online: www.osservatorionazionalefamiglie.it/ (accessed on 15 June 2018).

Marks, Stephen R., and Shelley M. MacDermid. 1996. Multiple roles and the self: A theory of role balance. *Journal of Marriage and the Family* 58: 417–32. [CrossRef]

Marlow, Susan. 1997. Self-employed Women—New Opportunities, Old Challenges? *Entrepreneurship & Regional Development* 9: 199–210.

Martins, Luis L., Kimberly A. Eddleston, and John F. Veiga. 2002. Moderators of the Relationship Between Work-Family Conflict and Career Satisfaction. *Academy of Management Journal* 45: 399–409.

McGowan, Pauric, Caroline Lewis Redeker, Sarah Y. Cooper, and Kate Greenan. 2012. Female entrepreneurship and the management of business and domestic roles: Motivations, expectations and realities. *Entrepreneurship & Regional Development* 24: 53–72.

Milkie, Melissa A., and Pia Peltola. 1999. Playing All the Roles: Gender and the Work-Family Balancing Act. *Journal of Marriage and the Family* 61: 476–90. [CrossRef]

Ocse. 2013. How's Life? 2013. Measuring Well-Being. Available online: http://www.oecd.org/statistics/how-s-life-23089679.htm (accessed on 3 September 2018).

Parasuraman, Saroj, Yasmin S. Purohit, Veronica M. Godshalk, and Nicholas J. Beutell. 1996. Work and Family Variables, Entrepreneurial Career Success, and Psychological Well-Being. *Journal of Vocational Behavior* 48: 275–300. [CrossRef]

Poggesi, Sara, Michela Mari, and Luisa De Vita. 2017. Women Entrepreneurs and Work-Family Conflict: Insights from Italy. *Academy of Management Proceedings* 17: 209–28. [CrossRef]

Posig, Margaret, and Jill Kickul. 2004. Work-role expectations and work family conflict: gender differences in emotional exhaustion. *Women in Management Review* 7: 373–386. [CrossRef]

Rehman, Sumaira, and Muhammad Azam Roomi. 2012. Gender and work-life balance: a phenomenological study of women entrepreneurs in Pakistan. *Journal of Small Business and Enterprise Development* 19: 209–28. [CrossRef]

Shelton, Beth A. 1992. *Women, Men, and Time: Gender Differences in Paid Work, Housework, and Leisure*. New York: Greenwood.

Shelton, Lois M. 2006. Female Entrepreneurs, Work–Family Conflict, and Venture Performance: New Insights into the Work–Family Interface. *Journal of Small Business Management* 44: 285–97. [CrossRef]

Unioncamere. 2016. Impresa in genere. Available online: http://www.imprenditoriafemminile.camcom.it/P42A2350C321S410/3--Rapporto-nazionale-sulla-imprenditoria-femminile--Impresa-in-genere---Unioncamere.htm (accessed on 15 June 2018).

Walker, Elizabeth, and Beverley Webster. 2006. Management competencies of women business owners. *International Entrepreneurship and Management Journal* 2: 429–529. [CrossRef]

Walker, Elizabeth, Calvin Wang, and Janice Redmond. 2008. Women and work-life balance: Is home-based business ownership the solution? *Equal Opportunities International* 27: 258–75. [CrossRef]

Watson, John, and Sherry Robinson. 2003. Adjusting for Risk in Comparing the Performances of Male-and Female-Controlled SMEs. *Journal of Business Venturing* 18: 773–88. [CrossRef]

WEF. 2015. Global Gender Gap Report 2015, World Economic Forum. Available online: http://www3.weforum.org/docs/GGGR2015/cover.pdf (accessed on 11 June 2018).

Williams, Donald R. 2004. Effects of Childcare Activities on the Duration of Self-Employment in Europe. *Entrepreneurship Theory and Practice* 28: 467–85. [CrossRef]

administrative
sciences

MDPI

Article

Women Career Paths in Accounting Organizations: Big4 Scenario

Adriana Tiron-Tudor *and Widad Atena Faragalla

Faculty of Economic Sciences and Business Administration, Babeş-Bolyai University, Cluj-Napoca 400084, Romania; atena.faragalla@econ.ubbcluj.ro
* Correspondence: adriana.tiron@econ.ubbcluj.ro; Tel.: +40-726-779-474

Received: 29 August 2018; Accepted: 15 October 2018; Published: 17 October 2018

Abstract: In this paper, we analyze the gender issues that are present in the accounting profession, and more precisely, on the career paths one could follow in the accounting profession and what the underlying reasons are for each option. Our conclusions show that some of the factors that influence women career paths are discrimination, motherhood, glass-ceiling, double standard and a lack of visibility.

Keywords: accounting profession; women; gender issues; career paths; gender stratification; glass ceiling

---

1. Introduction

Professions such as lawyers, engineers, architects, doctors (liberal professions) have at least one aspect in common—the common trait of conservatism. The accounting profession, also a liberal profession, is no exception. This is precisely why gender issues linked to the accounting profession are a subject of interest and their very existence in accounting organizations is no surprise. There have been studies and early contributions that attested to the gendered nature or accounting organizations (Kirkham and Loft 1993; Loft 1992; Lehman 1992; Fogarty et al. 1998; Grey 1998; Ud Din et al. 2017). Using these studies as a benchmark and a starting point, later on, other contributions to the literature emerged, mostly empirical studies of gender in accounting organizations (Anderson-Gough et al. 2005; Ciancanelli 1998; Dambrin and Lambert 2008, 2012; Lupu 2012; Kornberger et al. 2010; Mueller et al. 2011).

The aim of the study is to identify which are the main gender issues women face in the accounting profession and in the different career paths that one can choose to follow. For this, a qualitative approach was used, by conducting a literature review of articles on the topic of women in the accounting profession and also articles that mentioned the possible challenges one may face if they were to follow one certain career path. There are no similar studies conducted in the literature that would approach the aforementioned subject, which is precisely why the paper is a novelty. At the same time, it also addresses an existing research gap, which is the motivation behind approaching this area of research.

The type of literature review that was pursued in what follows was a structured one (Massaro et al. 2016) since it was based on carefully selected keywords from the approached area of research; a sample of relevant materials that would suit the purposes of the paper were chosen. In doing so, the paper provides answers to two major research questions:

- Which are the main career paths in accounting?
- What are the underlying reasons for the existence of glass ceiling and gender stratification inside accounting organizations?

Adm. Sci. **2018**, *8*, 62

In regards to the years taken into consideration when selecting articles, there was not a time span that was pre-considered, nor only a certain period in time. The keywords used were an important, and deciding factor regarding why some articles were considered and some were not. What is specific for this research is the fact that the analyzed articles come from a wide range of publishing years.

One of the first discoveries was that, from all the career paths one could follow in the accounting profession, the most disputed one, gender- and otherwise, was the auditing one. In the literature the most disputed career path is choosing to work in a Big Four (the four large accounting firms specialized in worldwide services such as audit and finance, business and financial advisory) thus the focus was mainly on studies that were approaching the Big Four. A second result of this paper was the realization that gender discrimination has as one of the major underlying reasons, motherhood, which is represented as a drawback in the case of career advancement and influences the extent of the heaviness of glass ceiling in those organizations.

The results of the paper are structured in three parts. The first part includes the used theories, such as gender stratification and the related notions such as double standard and glass ceiling. These theories are also explained and demonstrated using the Big Four case as an example. The second part includes the most common gender issues that can be associated with working in a large auditing firm based on the findings in the literature, and that influence the women to leave Big Four and start their own businesses, or to change employer even to continue in another audit and/or accounting firm or to change the environment by working in a company as a CFO, internal controller, internal auditor or other similar positions. The main contribution of the paper is the application of gender theories to carrier path issue by using sources from the literature. This usage of theories has led to the discovery of the underlying factors that are the cause of the impassibleness of breaking the ceiling.

The remainder of the paper is organized as follows. In the next section, the methodology will be presented, followed by presenting the main career paths in the accounting profession and by elaborating upon the main gender issues in the accounting profession. The last section concludes the paper.

2. Gender Stratification Theory

Gender stratification theory can be applied to a large range of situations (Brinton 1998; DuBose 2017; Blumberg 1984; Keister and Southgate 2012) and conditions including historical comparisons (Scott 1986; Wermuth and M 2002). Gender stratification can be used to explain the problems of building a theory that contains numerous factors which are directly linked.

The theory debates about a social ranking of some sort, where men typically inhabit a higher status than women. Gender stratification and gender inequality are the same facets of one idea. Gender stratification considers criteria as class, race, and sex (male/female). One of the things the theory suggests is that gender stratification exists to create in an efficient way, a division of labor or a social system in which a segment of the population oversees certain parts of labor, while the other segment is responsible for different parts that can be more important or not (Collins et al. 1993).

It analyzes all the aspects of the social life and cuts across social classes concerning the unequal access of men and women to power, prestige, and property all based on nature of their sex (Treas and Tai 2016; Collins et al. 1993).

Linked to the theory are concepts such as differential access, glass ceiling, and occupational distribution. The differential access refers to the fact that men have greater access to the labor market than women do, or that if they still do enter the labor market, they are doing it for lower paid jobs, or they have to periodically leave. The occupational distribution refers to the kind of work an individual does, work that can place him in a certain category or provide him with a certain label. The glass ceiling theory emphasizes upon the idea that it is harder for women to break through that ceiling which can lead them towards the upper level of organizations—a vertical promotion (Treas and Tai 2016; Collins et al. 1993).

From a sociological point of view, gender stratification is regarded as a theory proposing the existence of gender inequalities as a means to create a system, a social one, inside which one part of the population bears the responsibility of certain labor acts while the other part is responsible for other labor acts. Basically, the inequalities that have as a source gender, exist to create differences in the degree of responsibilities; the main issue is that there is a tendency, as in any other social group, for one group to become dominant and maybe suppress the other one (Treas and Tai 2016; Collins et al. 1993).

If conflict theory, which claims that society is in a state of continuous competition over resources (theory suggested by Karl Marx) (Collins 1990; Joas and Knöbl 2011) is introduced in relation to gender stratification theory, then it can be argued that gender can be understood as men overpowering women and trying to hold on to power and privilege, since society is defined by the on-going fight for dominance. In the case of gender, the dominant group are men and the subordinate group are women, which goes back to the two laborer categories. In time, the dominant group can change, but in most cases it does not, because the dominant group will always work and try to hold on to power. And this led in many cases, at least in the early days when women's rights were almost nonexistent, to social change and uprisings (Collins et al. 1993).

Gender stratification theory or social stratification and gender, how it is also called in the literature (Grusky and Szelényi 2011; Grusky and Weisshaar 2014) emphasizes creating layers inside society, and how always one layer will be powerful than the other; if we put together gender and the theory of stratification, from this equation we get that men are the more powerful layer, and women as a group, will always take a back seat to history and to the public scene or to positions of power; elements that are leading to this conjunction are glass ceiling (Cotter et al. 2001; Ragins et al. 1998; Davidson and Cooper 1992), sexism, prejudice, double standard, discrimination, and last and not least the point, the underlying element to all of the above: the assumption that men are superior to women (Treas and Tai 2016; Collins et al. 1993).

Inside an organization you may have some of the discriminating factors present as dominant ones, while the others might be less striking. In either case, to some extent they could all be noticed. Sexism for example is strongly linked to double standards; at first sight one might not recognize or understand what is referred to when discussing it, but sexism is most recognizable in situations where women avoid pursuing certain career paths because they are viewed to be more masculine and suitable to a man; the glass ceiling also applies, because if they do have the courage to enter into such a profession, they have trouble meeting the expectations (that are molded after a man's image) and thus in most cases they have trouble with being promoted (Treas and Tai 2016; Collins et al. 1993).

3. Methodology

3.1. Literature Search Approach

The paper is a literature review, and from a methodological point of view, a thorough analysis of the literature available was conducted. The selection of articles started by searching in the databases (ProQuest Central, Springer Link, Emerald, EBSCO) using keywords such as *accounting profession, gender issues, women in the accounting profession*. One of the first discoveries was that from all the career paths one could follow in the accounting profession, the most disputed one, gender and otherwise, was the auditing one. So, the perspective was shifted and the key words changed to *auditing, gender issues, Big Four, women, accounting profession* and any combination of the aforementioned words. In the literature, the most disputed career path is choosing to work in a Big Four, thus the focus was mainly on studies that were approaching the Big Four case.

The approached methodology explained above is a structured literature review since we used keywords that would suit our research topic, and based on the returns, we eliminated the articles that did not suit our purpose. As compared to a traditional literature review, which would provide a broad overview of the research topic, a structured literature review is providing a high-level overview of the primary research and answers to one or multiple research questions.

Through the structured literature review the paper is trying to respond to the below questions:

- Which are the main career paths in accounting?
- What are the underlying reasons for the existence of glass ceiling and gender stratification inside accounting organizations?

3.2. Selection of Articles for Review

The search returned several results, but many of the articles contained just one or two of the keywords, and the content of the article was not relevant for the purpose of this paper. Their titles and abstracts were reviewed by one author for the relevance of the study. After these articles were overlooked a number of 80 articles remained. From these articles those who were approaching the subject briefly and who did not elaborate on gender issues were eliminated as well as the ones who were duplicates. A total of 33 articles met the criteria. Papers were included if they approached the subject of gender in Big Accounting Firms or gender in accounting, in general (Table 1).

Table 1. Number of articles used.

Articles	Number
Initial Number of Articles	80
Articles eliminated	38
Duplicate articles	9
Articles about gender issues in accounting	33

Source: author's projection.

The articles that were used for the literature review are published in 19 different journals, including Critical Perspectives on Accounting (CPA), Accounting, Organizations and Society (AOS), Accounting, Auditing and Accountability Journal (AAAJ), so journals that are specialized on the accounting area but also in journals that do not have a connection to it such as European Sociological review (ESR), Gender, Work and Organization (GWO) or Gender in Management: An International Journal (GMIJ). The Journals that are more inclined to publish in the area are CPA, AOS and AAAJ if we take a closer look at the outcome represented in Table 2.

Table 2. Main articles used.

Reference	Title of the Article	Journal	Methodological Approach
Anderson-Gough et al. (2002, 2005)	Helping them to forget: the organizational embedding of gender relations in public audit firms; Accounting Professionals and the Accounting Profession: Linking Conduct and Context	Accounting organizations and society (AOS); Accounting and Business Research (ABR)	Study employed a qualitative methodology based principally upon a programmer of semi structured interviews
Barker and Monks 1998	Irish women accountants and career progression: a research note	Accounting organizations and society (AOS)	Qualitative research based on interviews and questionnaires
Carnegie and Walker 2007	Household accounting in Australia: Prescription and practice from the 1820s to the 1960s	Accounting, Auditing & Accountability Journal (AAAJ)	Literature review and a micro historical approach involving the detailed scrutiny of 18 sets of accounting records and relevant biographical and family data on the household accountants involved.
Charron and Lowe 2005	Factors that affect accountant's perceptions of alternative work arrangements	Accounting forum	Traditional literature review
Ciancanelli 1998	Survey research and the limited imagination	Critical Perspectives on Accounting (CPA)	Quantitative research
Crompton and Harris 1998	Explaining women's employment patterns: 'orientations to work' revisited	The British Journal of Sociology (BJS)	Traditional literature review

Table 2. *Cont.*

Reference	Title of the Article	Journal	Methodological Approach
Czarniawska 2008	Accounting and gender across times and places: an excursion into fiction	Accounting organizations and society (AOS)	Structured literature review
Dambrin and Lambert 2008	Mothering or auditing? The case of two Big Four in France	Accounting, Auditing & Accountability Journal (AAAJ)	Qualitative review; from 24 interviews with male and female auditors of various hierarchical levels, one seeks to reveal the specificity of the difficulties encountered by auditor mothers.
Duff 2011	Big Four accounting firms annual reviews: A photo analysis of gender and race portrayals	Critical Perspectives on Accounting (CPA)	Structured literature review
Carli and Eagly 2007	Women and the labyrinth of Leadership	Harvard business review	Traditional literature review
Fearfull and Kamenou 2006	How do you account for it? A critical exploration of career opportunities for and experiences of ethnic minority women	Critical Perspectives on Accounting (CPA)	Structured literature review
Gendron and Spira 2010	Identity narratives under threat: a study of former members of Arthur Andersen	Accounting organizations and society (AOS)	Quantitative research
Grey 1998	On being a professional in a 'Big Six' firm	Accounting organizations and society (AOS)	Qualitative case study
Hakim 1991	Grateful slaves and self-made women: fact and fantasy in women's work orientations	European Sociological Review (ESR)	Structured literature review
Hewlett 2007	Off-ramps and on-ramps. In: Keeping women on the road to success	Harvard business review	Traditional literature review
Jeny and Santacreu-Vasut 2017	New avenues of research to explain the rarity of females at the top of the accountancy profession	Palgrave communications	Systematic literature review
Johnson et al. 2008	Alternative work arrangements and perceived career success: current evidence from the Big Four firms in the US	Accounting organizations and society (AOS)	Structured literature review
Kornberger et al. 2010	Changing gender domination in a Big Four accounting firm: Flexibility, performance and client service in practice	Accounting organizations and society (AOS)	Qualitative case study
Lehman 1992	Herstory in accounting: the first eight years	Accounting organizations and society (AOS)	Traditional literature review
Loft 1992	Making sense of career in a Big Four accounting firm	International sociological association (ISA)	Empirical study approach
Lupu 2012	Approved routes and alternative paths: The construction of women's careers in large accounting firms. Evidence from the French Big Four	Critical Perspectives on Accounting (CPA)	Systematic literature review and qualitative research
Lyonette and Crompton 2008	The only way is up? An examination of women's "under-achievement" in the accountancy profession in the UK	Gender in management: an international journal	Systematic literature review and qualitative research
Macintosh and Scapens 1990	Structuration theory in management accounting	Accounting organizations and society (AOS)	Structured literature review
Martin 2000	Hidden gendered assumptions in mainstream organizational theory and research	Journal of management inquiry	Structured literature review
McKeen and Richardson 1998	Education, Employment and Certification: An Oral History of the Entry of Women into the Canadian Accounting Profession	Oxford University Press	Traditional literature review
Mueller et al. 2011	Making sense of career in a Big Four accounting firm	Current Sociology	Systematic literature review
Procter and Padfield 1999	Work orientations and women's work: a critique of Hakim's theory of the heterogeneity of women	Gender work and organization	Traditional literature review

Table 2. *Cont.*

Reference	Title of the Article	Journal	Methodological Approach
Reed et al. 1994	Job satisfaction, organizational commitment, and turnover intentions of United States accountants. The impact of the locus of control and gender	Accounting, Auditing and Accountability Journal	Qualitative review
Spruill and Wootton 1995	The struggle of Women in accounting: The case of Jennie Palen, Pioneer Accountant, Historian and Poet	Critical Perspectives on Accounting (CPA)	Traditional literature review and case study based on interviews
Windsor and Auyeung 2006	The effect of gender and dependent children on professional accountant's career progression	Critical Perspectives on Accounting (CPA)	Traditional literature review
Ud Din et al. 2017	Women's skills and career advancement: a review of gender (in)equality in an accounting workplace	Economic Research	Traditional literature review

Source: author's projection.

All the used articles were analyzed based on the year they were published, and the outcome is in the chart below where the trend can be noticed. The years 1998, 2008 and 2017 are seen as pique years (see Figure 1).

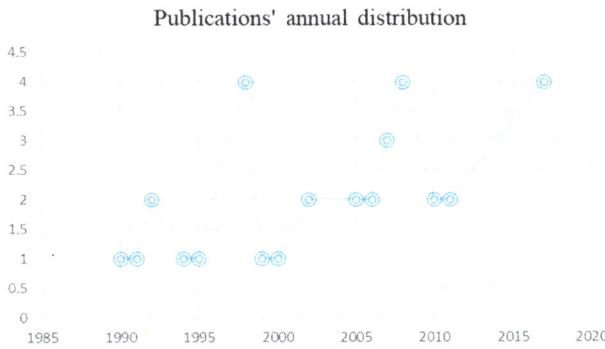

Figure 1. Publications' annual distribution, based based on selected articles. Source: author's projection.

3.3. Development of Topics

The 33 articles that remained were analyzed based on the gender issues that they were approaching, in order to better review them and in order to have a logic in the discourse that was approached.

4. Results and Discussion

The section is divided in three parts. The first part is analyzing the career paths one could follow inside the accounting profession, with emphasis on Big Four accounting environment. Even if an approach where all possible career paths to follow were scrutinized, the literature provided mostly information regarding the auditing environment; thus, the focus of the research shifted.

The second part is looking into the glass ceiling phenomenon in the context of the aforementioned organizations and also as a primary component of the gender stratification theory. Lastly, the ultimate part is investigating the primary reasons for the existence of the glass ceiling, with a key finding of motherhood as a main and underlying component and factor.

4.1. Career Paths in the Accounting Profession

There are three main categories of career paths in accounting that one can follow after graduating, and all three of them refer to the idea of being employed. One of them is working in a Big Four company, the other refers working in a multinational and the last one working in a small practice as a bookkeeper.

Each one of these career paths has its own upsides and downsides, its requirements, its challenges and set of skills that are demanded. These requirements and challenges could be underlying factors that could influence the decision to follow that career path or not, or if already followed to explain the decision of choosing a different career path than the one initially chosen.

Accounting firms, and the major auditing companies in particular, often lose a considerable number of their new workers, as they choose to follow a different career path altogether after they leave. There is also a particular concern in these companies, about retaining women at higher levels of the hierarchy; it seems that even though women represent 50% of all entry level positions, 10 or 12 years later, the pool of women candidates is depleted (Greenhaus et al. 1997; Emery et al. 2002; Grey 1998).

The ones that choose the option of working in a Big Four company after that period of three to five years have several options: they remain in Big Four and advance on management positions, they go to one of their former clients in high level management positions, or they go to a multinational in management positions, or as a last option, they open their own business, since the know-how acquired is sufficient to ensure the business will not collapse.

The name of Big Four is given to a number of 4 firms that are specialized worldwide in services such as audit and finance, business and financial advisory, cyber, tax, governance, risk and regulation, property/real estate strategy and operations.

The group is comprised of PwC (PricewaterhouseCoopers), Deloitte (Deloitte Touche Tohmatsu), EY (Ernst & Young) and KPMG (Klynveld Peat Marwick Mitchell Main Goerdeler). They are called Big Four because they have a global presence, both in terms of size and reputation (Brock and Powell 2005; Perera et al. 2003; Builders of a Better Working World n.d.; The Big 4 Accounting Firms n.d.; The Big Four Accounting Firms n.d.; Small and Medium Practices n.d.).

One thing that is known about Big Four firms, even before one joins them, is that it is not a 9 to 5 job and that employees work very hard, sometimes even 70–80 h a week during the peak season to finish projects. It is the general trait for all 4 of them since all of them perform the same kind of work and the profile of the candidates is the same (Brock and Powell 2005; Perera et al. 2003; KPMG n.d.; Builders of a Better Working World n.d.; Deloitte n.d.; PwC n.d.).

Currently, each one of them is highly present in the professional services market and offering a wide range of services. For example, PwC is the second largest professional services firm in the world for the value of revenue, and third for the number of employees. Its headquarters is in the UK and the president of the company is Bob Moritz. The company has branches in 157 countries, with some 700 locations. The main focus of PwC is auditing and assurance services. They have the biggest number of clients from Fortune 100 and the largest audit fees from all the Big 4s (Brock and Powell 2005; Perera et al. 2003; KPMG n.d.; Builders of a Better Working World n.d.; Deloitte n.d.; PwC n.d.).

The impact that Big Four companies have on the markets is significant, considering that they are the ones that decide if the financial statements of one company are compliant or not, or if they accurate or not (Kirsch et al. 2000; Berger et al. 2000).

The majority of the literature is focused on Big Accounting firms, mainly because they have a special organizational structure, and the career ladder is visible and well structured. Furthermore, these organizations are very often compared with an escalator, precisely due to the speediness with which things are happening in terms of promotion and structure changes.

A job candidate can actually plan his or her career ahead and know what to expect in the future, and at least for the first few hierarchical levels, promotion comes quickly. To become a partner, one will have to be with the firm for a continued association of at least 13 to 14 years. Between the associate position and the partner position, there are nearly 6 more designations. Many firms have a policy of working at a particular designation for at least 2 to 3 years before getting promoted. Two years staff, three years senior (two years if you get promoted early), three years manager (two years if you get promoted early) and 3 to 5 years senior manager (where coaching for partnership begins) (Burrowes et al. 2004).

Generally, in all four of them, the structure remains the same and there are 4 levels for the professional staff (divided vertically into seniority grades), up until one can make it to the top to the role of partner: junior auditor, senior auditor, manager and finally partner (they are also divided in small other positions). For the role of junior auditors (junior audit associates) they usually recruit directly from the faculty and start preparing the new joiners for future higher roles (Burrowes et al. 2004).

A junior auditor will be responsible for up to three people and at first will be assigned small and medium sized client assignments; after acquiring more experience, they will be involved in various clients' assignments and they are directly reporting to the senior audit associate. A senior audit associate is involved in major client's assignments and has a bigger staff responsibility and directly reports to the junior audit manager. A junior audit manager is responsible with a large team of staff and major clients' assignments, they report back to the senior manager, who is responsible for the entire department and with almost all the clients of that department (Baker and Hayes 2004).

The last hierarchical step is Partner, to which a senior manager reports. A partner is in charge of the development of clients, bringing more clients and satisfying their requirements. Partners, delegate decisions of routine management to the managing partners (senior audit managers). They are responsible for the service they are providing to the clients, even though the managing partner is the one in charge of the whole audit mission, including the staff (Burrowes et al. 2004).

Aside from the vertically division there is a lateral one, dividing the staff into departments: audit, taxation, legal, consultancy, liquidation. The professional staff together with the partners maintains accurate time records, meaning that they will track how much time a certain activity took, since the Big Four companies bill their clients at hourly rates. They have to be able to justify the bill and moreover, to accurately bill the clients (Baker and Hayes 2004).

Regarding women's presence in Big Four companies, a recent study by Catalyst (January, 2018 citing Financial Reporting Council) showed that, contrary to the reality of over 50% females in the accounting profession, in the Big Four companies, the number of women principals (partners) is below 20%, EY 19% (highest rate), PwC 17%, Deloitte-15% and KPMG-15%. The same study revealed that, as stated before, women were 50.2% of all auditors and accountants and that the proportion of women studying accounting worldwide has increased up to 49%. Moreover, the gender pay gap is still a problem and that women working as auditors and accountants are paid $1600 less per month than men with the same job and responsibilities.

Since an overwhelming number of studies about career paths in the accounting profession are focusing on the Big Four environment, it explains why the review is done on articles that are focusing on the topic. Even though we identified multinationals and small accounting practices as the other two career paths, they were not included, because the studies based on them were not sufficient.

4.2. Glass Ceiling as a Part of Gender Stratification Theory

In the literature, there are a number of studies focusing on Big Four accounting firms and gender stratification implications in their work culture. It only serves to prove that whatever happened in the past in terms of gendered issues for women, continues in the present. These issues never disappeared, nor did they surface only recently. They were there since the beginning of time, since women entered the profession, and they will continue to be present.

Glass ceiling represents the invisible barrier that prevents women and minorities from climbing up the hierarchical ladder. It is a metaphor used to represent an invisible barrier that keeps a certain demographic from rising beyond a certain level in a hierarchy. In the case of women breaking the barrier, this would imply their efforts are recognized by their superiors, who in most cases happen to be men (Smith and Caputi 2012; Helfat et al. 2006).

The work hours in a Big Four firm are modeled after the client's program and often, in order to complete audit missions and projects, employees work 70–80 h per week; which is considerable, and not very flexible. With a job that demanding, it is difficult to find balance between work life and personal life. One must suffer. And the question is who is willing to make sacrifices?

The studies focus on glass ceiling theory and gender inequality at work for women in particular. There are several studies in the literature that approach the subject of women inequality at the work place, but more precisely, the effects of the gender stratification theory in Big Four companies (Lupu 2012; Kornberger et al. 2010; Dambrin and Lambert 2008; Duff 2011; Anderson-Gough et al. 2005; Anderson-Gough et al. 2002).

These Big Four accounting firms were and are the subject of numerous studies because of the style of working, which is entirely and utterly different from any other workplace. Of course, every work environment is different and has its own particularities, but when it comes to Big Fours, it's an entirely different story. Why? First of all, due to the long hours that employees pull and second of all, due to strict requirements one must meet in order to be able to join such a company.

One of the papers that investigate the glass ceiling theory and the case of women in Big Fours is written by Lupu (2012). The article focuses on the accounting profession in France and depicts the work environment and the way women were treated in these firms.

Regarding the accounting profession in France, in the early beginnings of the profession the presence of women was rare, similar to many other countries (Dambrin and Lambert 2008; Lupu 2012). Female public accountants were hard to find and the situation remained like that up until 1980 when women started to be more present in the profession. The presence increased from 9% in 1980 to 19% in 2010, but compared to other French professions, the process of feminizing the accounting process is lagging (Lupu 2012).

The same phenomenon can be seen in the Big Four companies where at the moment the study was made, women partners in all the firms in the country, were between 10% and 18%. There are certain approved routes when it comes to career paths that are already in place and that are acknowledged. And these career paths are modeled after the image and skills of men, meaning they are more suitable for men (Duff 2011; Anderson-Gough et al. 2005; Lupu 2012).

It is also brought to discussion that if one were to propose some alternative paths, these routes would not have the same impact as the paths that were already approved because they would lack legitimacy and would derail women careers from early on. Basically, the approved routes of the career paths are gendered and biased (Duff 2011; Anderson-Gough et al. 2005).

There are two theories that explain the lack of women in the higher ranks of organizations. The first theory was developed by Catherine Hakim, and is called the preference theory, preference between market work and family work. Hakim argues that in order to find the reasons for the presence of women in inferior positions rather than in higher ranks, it is necessary to look for factors that are dispositional and not functional, meaning for example, the nature of their work (Hakim 1991; Procter and Padfield 1999).

Hakim (1991) argues that the choices one makes career wise (and other choices) are influenced by the lifestyle preferences one has. She creates three categories of people called home centered, work centered or the ones that show adaptive lifestyle preferences. Hakim argues that the latter who want to reconcile the work life with the family life will not give priority to work life. That is precisely what is required to get to the top levels of an organization, namely, giving priority to work. Thus, women who wish to balance they work life with their family life will never make it to the top. It was also reinforced by Procter and Padfield (1999).

Basically, the bottom line is that the rarity of women at top levels is explained by the choice women make to prioritize family over work, period. There are others that argue against the idea, suggesting that women are as focused on their careers as men are, and they want promotion as much as men do.

The second theory that could explain the rarity of women in top positions could be the influence of social and organizational context and the influence of stereotyping that makes it hard for people in general to take roles that are in different register from what it was prescribed to them (Lehman 1992; Duff 2011; Hakim 1991).

Earlier there was mentioned the reasons one would like to follow a career in a Big Four company and why the Big Four environment is so appealing to researchers. There are other similar arguments that these large firms, even though difficult to access information, have a professional culture which is based on processes and practices that are highly standardized, have a transparent hierarchical structure and the career model is based on "up or out" model. The career model basically means that those deserving of promotion, are given it. It is considered that accounting practices are shaped in these Big Four companies that they are regulated here (Lyonette and Crompton 2008; Kornberger et al. 2010).

Statistical data in a study published in 2011 shows that the highest percentage of women as partners in a Big Four company could be found at Deloitte and KPMG, 18.8%, in the United States, while PwC had the lowest rate, only 16.9%. By comparison in France, the ranges varied form 10% (KPMG) to 18% (PwC) (Lupu 2012).

4.3. Gender Issues that Influence the Women Carrier Paths in the Accounting Profession

4.3.1. Double Standard in Career Advancement and Recruiting

In terms of recruitment, what Lupu (2012) has discovered in her research is that first of all, that Big Four companies (in France) had a habit of recruiting amongst the candidates that graduated only from Grandes Ecoles, because they were considered to be elite places with prepared candidates who had un upper hand, in comparison the graduates from other schools: they could pick up on things faster, write better, progress better. They had other skills that the candidates from other places did not, skills that were more valuable than knowing accounting, which was considered something that could be easily learned. One additional factor that was considered, was that these graduates were coming from good families, and thus ten years later, they could bring clients in the firm by using their familial connections.

Recruiting from Grandes Ecoles ensured a homogeneity of the candidates because they would have the same behavior, same profile that would fit the firm's values and culture. The firm had little or no work to do when it came to "formatting" the recruits to the highly formalized culture. A different aspect when it came to recruiting discovered through the interviews was that even though the Big Fours wanted to seem gender balanced, in reality, the situation was not like that at all (Lupu 2012).

Women had a better academic situation than men, but this was not taken into consideration. The partners who recruited were told to be a little bit harder on women because otherwise there would have been more women in the organization than men, and that would not have been okay when they would go on maternity leaves. It would have affected an entire generation. One of the interviewees said that if they would have been fair to all candidates during the interviews, and they would have disregarded the gender. Currently, the situation would have been very different because women's records were far better than men's (Anderson-Gough et al. 2005; Grey 1998).

The career path and advancement in a Big Four is far more stringent than in any other companies; it can be compared to an escalator that it is always moving, and if you step out for just a bit then you will be surpassed by your colleagues and the entire work scene will seem different when you get back (for example maternity leave in the case of women) (Mueller et al. 2011).

In some studies, the Big Four environments are described as a workplace that is very demanding, where work never stops nor does the rhythm. However, employees do not seem to be bothered by it since they see it as a competition with their peers who were often their college mates. So inside these firms, there is a cohort effect created, that makes it okay for the staff to leave work at 11 because they have the feeling of belonging to a group, to a team with people that have the same age (Anderson-Gough et al. 2005; Lehman 1992).

What it seems conventional inside the Big Four firms (crazy rhythm of work, long hours, huge workload, becoming better, more efficient, working harder to be able to promote) it is tough to understand for people who have never worked in such a place. And here comes the differentiating factor for women, namely that they relate to time differently than men do, they have to fit in the same amount of time more activities and that is why they will allocate less time to networking activities than men will; just because they have to deal with personal matters, they do not have the luxury of spending their free time networking (Anderson-Gough et al. 2005; Duff 2011; Lehman 1992).

The consequence of the double responsibility is that the career of women often takes a different turn when they have children. They temporarily leave the work environment, the time during which their male colleagues are promoted and the whole dynamic at work changes, and the whole hierarchical structure. The idea of working hard in a Big Four firm is only bearable because at the end of the day one knows that eventually he/she will be promoted. But when you reach the end of the hierarchical ladder and you are not considered as partner material, it is hard to accept, and many leave (Lehman 1992).

4.3.2. Motherhood as a Primary Gender Issue

Motherhood came up several times during the interviews and it was one of the reasons why women were excluded from the path of reaching partner or excluded themselves since they were preoccupied with other matters and work was not their main focus anymore. Advancing with the interviews, the authors discovered three main reasons that led to the rarity of women in higher ranks of organizations. The first one is that the audit firms are the ones that, through their policies and practices, are pushing women away and do not give them the same opportunity.

The second one is the exact opposite; women start to separate themselves from "the crowd" in anticipation of the event and to try to reconcile both private and professional life. The third one is in direct link to the second one, a direct consequence, an aftermath, and it refers to the idea that struggling to make peace between personal and professional life women often choose a different professional path, that is different from what the rest of the colleagues are doing and which is not in accordance with the organizations practice. That path alienates them from the highest levels, thus the rarity of women in higher ranks (Mueller et al. 2011; Crompton and Sanderson 1990; Loft 1992).

What it means to work in an audit firm was detailed earlier, based on Lupu (2012) article, which described the job requirements in the context of French firms. Grey (1998) also explains the bottom line of what it means to be an auditor in a Big Four firm is that is it a career model is "up or out", a model that is for all employees and which has as an ultimate goal the partnership of the firm.

In auditing, the system is that employees work on teams on different clients and the competition between teams is very high. Each team has a junior, a senior and a manager. The fees for auditing are established with the client and highly negotiated before the audit mission started. The firm is on a budget, and the idea is to be productive and efficient. That is why managers tend to maximize the productivity of the teams by belittling the amount of work they perform. And they continually ask for more and more effort. The employees are also made accountable in front of the clients, creating a relationship with the client from the smallest member of the team. At the end of all of these lies the possibility that if you make partner, you can earn a percent of the profit, but also the risks of signing off on the audit opinion and bearing the responsibility.

It is precisely why motherhood will never be a good fit in an audit company, because it represents everything that and audit firm would want to avoid, since becoming a mother means that that person will be missing for a longer period from the firm and will be disconnected from everything (clients, networking, colleagues) (Carnegie and Walker 2007; Johnson et al. 2008; McKeen and Richardson 1998).

Pregnancy, according to the statements given by the interviewees, when it is announced, is not seen in favorable light, especially if it is in the busiest work season. One of the women interviewed stated that if you announce a pregnancy during the audit season and you do not plan it for the summer, it means that you have done it on purpose and that somehow you are announcing your resignation. A downside brought up by several women was that often, after announcing a pregnancy, they would get their bonuses cut even though many of them still work the same hours as before, and they are passed over for promotion that year (Dambrin and Lambert 2008; Spruill and Wootton 1995).

Furthermore, during the period she is missing, her client portfolio gets transferred to another member of the organization, and the clients that are big and represented the best assignments are the ones that go first (the clients that are the most prestigious and most comfortable to work with). A woman in that situation loses all her visibility in the firm and all the pre-acquired knowledge that made her visible in the organization (Charron and Lowe 2005; Johnson et al. 2008).

Nevertheless, there are still some barriers that could be considered as being glass ceiling barriers and taken into consideration, such as the fact that the director position is occupied by women in a proportion of 60% because it is the end point of their careers in a Big Four. The level is dedicated to those who were senior managers for a long time and who will never make partners (Ciancanelli 1998).

These spots are usually reserved for people who do not have the skills to search for clients, or negotiate fees. Described above are different forms of discrimination women are subjected to once they announce their pregnancy. But how do they cope with work and maternity? According to Dambrin and Lambert (2008), they start organizing themselves in time to be prepared for the future. They start delegating their assignments and make sure they choose the right persons to do that, to be able to recover their clients once they get back (Reed et al. 1994).

The second way women try to manage motherhood in their work life is by imposing different work habits on their team, such as starting work earlier, taking no breaks, including lunch break and finishing work earlier by a certain time. These work practices that are imposed are not necessarily received without backlash since basically, these women are imposing crazy deadlines with the same workload as before (Barker and Monks 1998; Lehman 1992).

One other option would be that they choose to specialize in certain areas such taxation, that will make developing expertise easier, and more importantly, will make juggling their personal life with work life easier, since they do not have to travel anymore and go on assignments. Nevertheless, the role of an expert is difficult to be left, and usually, when a woman becomes an expert she remains there and is automatically separated from the prospect of becoming a partner. Aside from the expert position, a different one is the one of the support function, meaning that women leave their branches as auditors and go, in most cases in the human resources department. For both of these positions, it is not impossible to become partner; there are cases, but it is harder and rare (Barker and Monks 1998; Kornberger et al. 2010; Lehman 1992).

The conclusion of the study is that if women choose to favor their pregnancy over the work life, they gain no recognition and are offered positions that mean that they will not advance to be partners. There are women who make it as a partner, but they are not viewed as a true partner, not like men are seen, precisely because they still have families to deal with (Dambrin and Lambert 2008).

The bottom line is that these accounting organizations are gendered through their policies and practices. At first sight, they may seem to be conventional and neutral because it is standard to have promotion procedures and performance indicators and reviews. But at a second glance, one may discover that they are indeed gendered since they are modeled after a man's profile or that it fits better to a man than it fits a woman (Kornberger et al. 2010; Anderson-Gough et al. 2002). When it comes to how things can be changed, nobody takes the initiative.

5. Conclusions

The article intended to discover the gendered issues one may have, in current times, when choosing a certain career path. The paper focused on gender issues women currently face in the accounting profession. The first intention of the paper was to analyze all possible career paths

Adm. Sci. **2018**, *8*, 62

in the accounting profession and to find what the reasons are behind choosing a certain career path or not, as well as the gender issues one may face when pursuing that particular career path.

Based on the findings of the article, we draw two conclusions: the first part is comprised of the actual career paths we were able to analyze and the second part the gender issues one may face with the underlying reasons and as well the solutions that were found.

The first part of the findings reveals that the most disputed career path in the literature is working in a large auditing firm. The other career paths such as small accounting firms or multinationals are not investigated to any extent. They did not pose interest to researchers neither from a gendered perspective nor from an organizational perspective. This is a gap in the literature and can constitute the agenda for future research. When more papers that would approach the subject of the other career paths in the accounting profession is available in the literature, then another possible agenda for future research would be a comparison between career paths and the gender issues they face.

The second part of the findings is comprised of the gender issues women face in large auditing firms and one of the most important discoveries is that gender discrimination is very much present through glass ceiling phenomena, double standard, motherhood and the aftermath that comes with it. The findings showed that motherhood is an important reason why women do not advance to partnership as easily or fast as men, or that it is okay for a man with a family to consider his job a priority, but it is not okay for women.

The main contribution of the paper is the application of gender theories to career path issues by using sources from the literature. This usage of theories led to the discovery of the underlying factors that are the cause of the impassibleness of breaking the ceiling.

The overall findings revealed that breaking through the ceiling and overcoming all of the obstacles in the way of reaching the top level, for women, is still difficult and this may be the cause for some of them to decide to try to be independent and become entrepreneurs.

Entrepreneurship is not the only possible solution to the glass ceiling phenomenon and gender discrimination in accounting organizations; a more proactive attitude in trying to accommodate solutions in order to prevent or diminish the impact of it, can be the answer as well and this is a limitation of the current research.

Author Contributions: The authors' individual contribution are the follows: A.T.-T., part 1, 2 and 5 and W.A.F., part 3 and 4.

Funding: This research received no external funding.

Conflicts of Interest: The authors declare no conflicts of interest.

References

Anderson-Gough, Fiona, Christopher Grey, and Keith Robson. 2002. Accounting Professionals and the Accounting Profession: Linking Conduct and Context. *Accounting and Business Research* 32: 41–56. [CrossRef]

Anderson-Gough, Fiona, Christopher Grey, and Keith Robson. 2005. "Helping them to forget": The organizational embedding of gender relations in public audit firms. *Accounting Organizations and Society* 30: 469–90. [CrossRef]

Baker, C. Richard, and Rick Hayes. 2004. Reflecting form over substance: The case of Enron Corp. *Critical Perspectives on Accounting* 15: 767–85. [CrossRef]

Barker, Patricia C., and Kathy Monks. 1998. Irish women accountants and career progression: A research note. *Accounting, Organizations and Society* 23: 813–23. [CrossRef]

Berger, Allen N., Robert DeYoung, Hesna Genay, and Gregory F. Udell. 2000. Globalization of Financial Institutions: Evidence from Cross-Border Banking performance. *Brookings-Wharton Papers on Financial Services* 1: 23–120. [CrossRef]

Blumberg, Rae Lesser. 1984. A general theory of gender stratification. *Sociological Theory* 2: 23–101. [CrossRef]

Brinton, Mary C. 1998. The Social-Institutional Bases of Gender Stratification: Japan as an Illustrative Case. *American Journal of Sociology* 94: 300–34. [CrossRef]

Brock, David M., and Michael J. Powell. 2005. Radical strategic change in the global professional network: The "Big Five" 1999–2001. *Journal of Organizational Change Management* 18: 451–68. [CrossRef]

Builders of a Better Working World. n.d. Available online: http://www.ey.com/gl/en/about-us (accessed on 20 January 2018).

Burrowes, Ashley W., Joseph Kastantin, and Milorad M. Novicevic. 2004. The Sarbanes-Oxley act as a hologram of post-Enron disclosure: A critical realist commentary. *Critical Perspectives on Accounting* 15: 797–811. [CrossRef]

Carli, Linda L., and Alice H. Eagly. 2007. Overcoming resistance to women leaders: The importance of leadership style. In *Women and Leadership: The State of Play and Strategies for Change*. Edited by Barbara Kellerman and Deborah L. Rhode. San Francisco: Jossey-Bass.

Carnegie, Garry D., and Stephen P. Walker. 2007. Household accounting in Australia: Prescription and practice from the 1820s to the 1960s. *Accounting, Auditing & Accountability Journal* 20: 41–73.

Charron, Kimberly Frank, and D. Jordan Lowe. 2005. Factors that affect accountant's perceptions of alternative work arrangements. *Accounting Forum* 29: 191–206. [CrossRef]

Ciancanelli, Penny. 1998. Survey research and the limited imagination. *Critical Perspectives on Accounting* 9: 387–9. [CrossRef]

Collins, Randall. 1990. Conflict theory and the advance of macro-historical sociology. In *Frontiers of Social Theory*. Edited by George Ritzer. New York: Columbia University Press, pp. 68–87.

Collins, Randall, Janet Saltzman Chafetz, Rae Lesser Blumberg, Scott Coltrane, and Jonathan H. Turner. 1993. Toward an integrated theory of gender stratification. *Sociological Perspectives* 36: 185–216. [CrossRef]

Cotter, David A., Joan M. Hermsen, Seth Ovadia, and Reeve Vanneman. 2001. The Glass Ceiling Effect. *Social Forces* 80: 655–81. [CrossRef]

Crompton, Rosemary, and Fiona Harris. 1998. Explaining women's employment patterns: 'Orientations to work' revisited. *The British Journal of Sociology* 49: 118–36. [CrossRef] [PubMed]

Crompton, Rosemary, and Kay Sanderson. 1990. *Gendered Jobs and Social Change*. London: Routledge.

Czarniawska, Barbara. 2008. Accounting and gender across times and places: An excursion into fiction. *Accounting, Organizations and Society* 33: 33–47. [CrossRef]

Dambrin, Claire, and Caroline Lambert. 2008. Mothering or auditing? The case of two Big four in France. *Accounting, Auditing & Accountability Journal* 21: 474–506.

Dambrin, Claire, and Caroline Lambert. 2012. Who is she and who are we? A reflexive journey in research into the rarity of women in the highest ranks of accountancy. *Critical Perspectives on Accounting* 23: 1–16. [CrossRef]

Davidson, Marilyn J., and Cary L. Cooper. 1992. *Shattering the Glass Ceiling: The Woman Manager*. London: Paul Chapman Publishing.

Deloitte. n.d. About Deloitte. Available online: https://www2.deloitte.com/global/en/pages/about-deloitte/articles/about-deloitte.html (accessed on 20 January 2018).

DuBose, Renalia. 2017. Compliance Requires Inspection: The Failure of Gender Equal Pay Efforts in the United States. *Mercer Law Review* 68: 445–60.

Duff, Angus. 2011. Big four accounting firms annual reviews: A photo analysis of gender and race portrayals. *Critical Perspectives on Accounting* 22: 20–38. [CrossRef]

Emery, Michelle, Jill Hooks, and Ross Stewart. 2002. Born at the Wrong Time? An Oral History of Women Professional Accountants in New Zealand. *Accounting History* 7: 7–34. [CrossRef]

Fearfull, Anne, and Nicolina Kamenou. 2006. How do you account for it? A critical exploration of career opportunities for and experiences of ethnic minority women. *Critical Perspectives on Accounting* 17: 883–901. [CrossRef]

Fogarty, Timothy J., Larry M. Parker, and Thomas Robinson. 1998. Where the rubber meets the road: Performance evaluation and gender in large public accounting organizations. *Women in Management Review* 13: 299–311. [CrossRef]

Gendron, Yves, and Laura F. Spira. 2010. Identity narratives under threat: A study of former members of Arthur Andersen. *Accounting, Organizations and Society* 35: 275–300. [CrossRef]

Greenhaus, Jeffrey H., Karen M. Collins, Romila Singh, and Saroj Parasuraman. 1997. Work and Family Influences on Departure from Public Accounting. *Journal of Vocational Behaviour* 50: 249–70. [CrossRef]

Grey, Christopher. 1998. On being a professional in a 'Big Six' firm. *Accounting, Organizations and Society* 23: 569–87. [CrossRef]

Grusky, David B., and Szonja Szelényi. 2011. *The Inequality Reader. Contemporary and Foundational Readings in Race, Class and Gender*. Abingdon: Routledge, Milton Park: Taylor and Francis.

Grusky, David B., and Katherine R. Weisshaar. 2014. *Social Stratification: Class, Race, and Gender in Sociological Perspective*. Abingdon: Routledge, Milton Park: Taylor and Francis.

Hakim, Catherine. 1991. Grateful slaves and self-made women: Fact and fantasy in women's work orientations. *European Sociological Review* 7: 101–21. [CrossRef]

Joas, Hans, and Wolfgang Knöbl. 2011. Conflict sociology and conflict theory. In *Social Theory: Twenty Introductory Lectures*. Edited by Hans Joas and Wolfgang Knöbl. Cambridge: Cambridge University Press, pp. 174–98.

Helfat, Constance E., Dawn Harris, and Paul J. Wolfson. 2006. The Pipeline to the Top: Women and Men in the Top Executive Ranks of U.S. Corporations. *Academy of Management Perspectives* 20: 42–64. [CrossRef]

Hewlett, Sylvia Ann. 2007. Off-ramps and on-ramps. In *Keeping Women on the Road to Success*. Brighton: Harvard Business School Press.

Jeny, Anne, and Estefania Santacreu-Vasut. 2017. New avenues of research to explain the rarity of females at the top of the accountancy profession. *Palgrave Communications* 3: 17011. [CrossRef]

Johnson, Eric N., D. Jordan Lowe, and Philip M. J. Reckers. 2008. Alternative work arrangements and perceived career success: Current evidence from the big four firms in the US. *Accounting, Organizations and Society* 33: 48–72. [CrossRef]

Keister, Lisa A., and Darby E. Southgate. 2012. *Inequality: A Contemporary Approach to Race, Class, and Gender*. Cambridge: Cambridge University Press.

Kirkham, Linda M., and Anne Loft. 1993. Gender and the construction of the professional accountant. *Accounting, Organizations and Society* 18: 507–58. [CrossRef]

Kirsch, R.J., K. Laird, and T Evans. 2000. The Entry of International CPA Firms into Emerging Markets: Motivational Factors and Growth Strategies. *The International Journal of Accounting* 35: 99–119. [CrossRef]

Kornberger, Martin, Chris Carter, and Anne Ross-Smith. 2010. Changing gender domination in a Big Four accounting firm: Flexibility, performance and client service in practice. *Accounting, Organizations and Society* 35: 775–91. [CrossRef]

KPMG. n.d. KPMG 2017 Citizenship Report. Available online: https://home.kpmg.com/us/en/home/about.html (accessed on 20 January 2018).

Lehman, Cheryl R. 1992. Herstory in accounting: The first eight years. *Accounting organization and Society* 17: 262–85. [CrossRef]

Loft, Anne. 1992. Accountancy and the gendered division of labour: A review essay. *Accounting, Organizations and Society* 17: 367–78. [CrossRef]

Lupu, Ioana. 2012. Approved routes and alternative paths: The construction of women's careers in large accounting firms. Evidence from the French Big Four. *Critical Perspectives on Accounting* 23: 351–69. [CrossRef]

Lyonette, Clare, and Rosemary Crompton. 2008. The only way is up? An examination of women's "under-achievement" in the accountancy profession in the UK. *Gender in Management: An International Journal* 23: 506–21. [CrossRef]

Macintosh, Norman B., and Robert W. Scapens. 1990. Structuration theory in management accounting. *Accounting, Organizations and Society* 15: 455–77. [CrossRef]

Martin, Joanne. 2000. Hidden gendered assumptions in mainstream organizational theory and research. *Journal of Management Inquiry* 9: 207–16. [CrossRef]

Massaro, Maurizio, John Dumay, and James Guthrie. 2016. On the shoulders of giants: Undertaking a: Structured Literature Review. *Accounting, Auditing & Accountability Journal* 29: 767–801.

McKeen, Carol A., and Alan J. Richardson. 1998. Education, Employment and Certification: An Oral History of the Entry of Women into the Canadian Accounting Profession. *Business and Economic History* 27: 500–21.

Mueller, Frank, Chris Carter, and Anne Ross-Smith. 2011. Making sense of career in a Big four accounting firm. *Current Sociology* 59: 551–67. [CrossRef]

Perera, Hector B., Asheq R. Rahman, and Steven F. Cahan. 2003. Globalisation and the major accounting firms. *Australian Accounting Review* 13: 27–37. [CrossRef]

Procter, Ian, and Maureen Padfield. 1999. Work orientations and women's work: A critique of Hakim's theory of the heterogenity of women. *Gender, Work and Organization* 6: 152–62. [CrossRef]

PwC. n.d. Our Purpose and Values. Available online: http://www.pwc.com/gx/en/about/purpose-and-values.html (accessed on 20 January 2018).

Ragins, Belle Rose, Bickley Townsend, and Mary Mattis. 1998. Gender gap in the executive suite: CEOs and female executives report on breaking the glass ceiling. *Academy of Management Perspectives* 12: 28–42. [CrossRef]

Reed, Sarah A., Stanley H. Kratchman, and Robert H. Strawser. 1994. Job satisfaction, organizational commitment, and turnover intentions of United States accountants. The impact of the locus of control and gender. *Accounting, Auditing and Accountability Journal* 7: 31–58. [CrossRef]

Scott, Joan Wallach. 1986. Gender: A Useful Category for Historical Analysis. *American Historical Review* 91: 1053–75. [CrossRef]

Small and Medium Practices. n.d. Available online: https://www.ifac.org/about-ifac/small-and-medium-practices (accessed on 20 January 2018).

Smith, Paul, and Peter Caputi. 2012. A Maze of Metaphors. *Faculty of Health and Behavioral Sciences* 27: 436–48. [CrossRef]

Spruill, Wanda G., and Charles W. Wootton. 1995. The struggle of Women in accounting: The case of Jennie Palen, Pioneer Accountant, Historian and Poet. *Critical Perspectives on Accounting* 6: 371–89. [CrossRef]

The Big 4 Accounting Firms. n.d. Available online: https://www.big4careerlab.com/big-4-accounting-firms/ (accessed on 20 January 2018).

The Big Four Accounting Firms. n.d. Available online: https://www.wikijob.co.uk/content/financial-terms/accounting/big-four-accounting-firms (accessed on 20 January 2018).

Treas, Judith, and Tsuio Tai. 2016. Gender inequality in housework across 20 European Nations: Lessons from Gender Stratification Theories. *Sex Roles* 74: 495–511. [CrossRef]

Ud Din, Nizam, Xinsheng Cheng, and Shama Nazneen. 2017. Women's skills and career advancement: A review of gender (in)equality in an accounting workplace. *Economic Research-Ekonomska Istraživanja*, 1–14. [CrossRef]

Wermuth, L., and Monges M. 2002. Gender Stratification: A Structural Model for Examining Case Examples of Women in Less-Developed Countries, Gender stratification. *Frontiers. A Journal of Women Studies* 23: 22. [CrossRef]

Windsor, Carolyn, and Pak Auyeung. 2006. The effect of gender and dependent children on professional accountant's career progression. *Critical Perspectives on Accounting* 17: 828–44. [CrossRef]

administrative sciences

MDPI

Article

Women's Role in the Accounting Profession: A Comparative Study between Italy and Romania

Mara Del Baldo [1],*, Adriana Tiron-Tudor [2] and Widad Atena Faragalla [2]

[1]   Department of Economics, Society and Politics, University of Urbino Carlo Bo, 61029 Urbino, Italy
[2]   Department of Accounting, Babes-Bolyai University, Cluj-Napoca 400084, Romania;
      adriana.tiron.tudor@gmail.com (A.T.-T.); faragallaatena@gmail.com (W.A.F.)
*   Correspondence: mara.delbaldo@uniurb.it; Tel.: +39-0722-305-529

Received: 16 October 2018; Accepted: 20 December 2018; Published: 24 December 2018

Abstract: Historically, in most countries, the accounting profession has always been male-dominated. Liberal professions such as lawyers, engineers, architects and doctors share the common trait of conservatism. The accounting profession, which is also a liberal profession, is no exception. Starting from this premise, this work aims to provide, using a historical and institutional perspective, a picture of the past and current "journey" in the accountancy profession of women-chartered accountants and auditors in Italy and Romania. Drawing from the theoretical framework of gendered construction of the accounting profession, the paper points out issues affecting the presence, the degree of representativeness and the role (concerning the presence among the higher level of professional activities and governance positions) of women within the National Chartered Association and their continued under-representation in Italy and Romania. Findings contribute to providing insights useful to develop a future agenda and fill in the research gaps in this field.

Keywords: accounting profession; chartered public accountants; gender; governance; women

---

1. Introduction

Accounting as a liberal profession (Cooper and Robson 2006; Rodrigues et al. 2003; Marlow and Carter 2003) such as the other liberal professions—lawyers, notaries, engineers, architects, doctors (Adler et al. 2008; Kirkpatrick and Muzio 2011) is characterized by a marked intellectual character and requires a high-level qualification and specialized training. A common trait shared by liberal professions is conservatism. In the context of this paper, conservatism refers to the commitment to the traditional structure of organisations, namely to values, principles and ideas, the unwillingness to adopt changes, the resistance to innovation (Muller 1997; Grigsby 2008) and the attitude towards gender aspects (Kyriakidou et al. 2013; Dambrin and Lambert 2012).

Gender issues can be common inside the structure of liberal professions, like the accounting one (Kyriakidou et al. 2013; Keiran 2017). According to the Milburn Report, which looked at fair access to professions, accountancy was the most socially exclusive amongst them all. Therefore, a multitude of recommendations required all professions to review their current practices on equitable access and develop ideas and strategies for improvement (Milburn Report 2009).

Dambrin and Lambert (2012) suggest that until stereotypes are challenged, gender issues and gender inequality will still be a common issue, thus posing the need to perform critical and reflective research on gender with an ongoing struggle to improve the position of women's representation in the accounting profession. Given the masculine history of the profession, stereotypes are difficult to shift and continue to affect the male organisational homo-sociality of the profession (Anderson-Gough et al. 2005; Kanter 1977).

However, international literature findings, as well as recent surveys (AFECA and FEE 2016), suggest that the under-representation of women in senior roles in the accounting profession continues to be a challenge (Kornberger et al. 2010) and points out that the accounting profession has traditionally been dominated by established male power structures that make it difficult for women to progress in their careers (Gammie and Gammie 1997; Gallhofer 1998; Adapa et al. 2015).

Gender inequality, giving voice to women and the empowerment of women, was represented in the third Millennium Development Goal (MDG) of UN (Kabeer 2005), and it is included in the Sustainable Development Goal (SDG) (EC 2014; EC 2015a, 2015b). Thus, in a profession characterised by a strong female presence as the accountancy profession, analysing how these women are represented is nonetheless, something worth investigating (Kirkham and Loft 1993).

Internationally, the presence of women in the accounting profession varies (Ciancanelli et al. 1990; Adapa et al. 2015; Kyriakidou et al. 2013) from region to region, primarily because of the cultural differences throughout history (Ried et al. 1987; Komori 1998, 2008, 2012; OhOgartaigh 2000; Paris 2016). However, some conventional aspects emerge, no matter the country, and point out issues, such as the glass ceiling, that is tied to the reasons behind the low percentage of women in higher ranks of organisations (Kyriakidou et al. 2013).

In the context of the aforementioned facts, gender stratification and institutional theory were used in order to better understand and explain the gender differences and issues between the two selected countries (Brinton 1998; Dubose 2017; Blumberg 1984; Keister and Southgate 2012). Historical comparisons were applied as well for the scope mentioned above (Scott 1986; Wermuth and Monges 2002). Namely, these frameworks help in understanding the context of women accountants in different regional settings and timeframes and interpret data relative to their presence and (under)representativeness within the chartered associations.

Starting from these premises, the paper's contribution is (1) to provide a picture of the past and current "journey" in the accountancy profession of women-chartered accountants in Italy and Romania by (2) grounding it on the theoretical framework of gender construction of the accounting profession and as well on historical facts from the literature. In doing so, the paper also (3) underlines the issues affecting the presence, the representativeness and the role (regarding their presence among the higher level of professional activities and governance positions) of women within the National Chartered Association and the under-representation in Italy and Romania. Inequality between women and men in Europe (EU 2017) still represents a critical key to contrast since gender segregation affects occupations in all economic sectors.

The paper contributes to the domain of cross-cultural studies in accounting by providing greater insight into the depth, richness and complexity of cultural similarities and differences between two European countries (Italy and Romania) by complementing the quantified dimensional based cultural measures with relevant historical and sociological insights. The underlying reasons for choosing Italy and Romania for the purposes of this paper are: (a) they can be considered extreme cases with a very different political and institutional setting; (b) their accounting history is very different as well; and (c) the linguistic similarities are very striking. Thus given the above, it is interesting to analyse the representation of women in higher ranks of accounting organisations.

The remainder of this paper is organised as follows. The next section introduces the theoretical framework, addressing attention on the gender stratification and gender inequality theory in general and applied to the specific case of the accounting profession. Section 3 presents the methodological aspects of the paper, while in Section 4 the results comprised of the comparative analysis are presented. Section 5 presents the discussion part. Following this, the paper finishes with concluding reflections.

2. Theoretical Framework

Based on the literature findings, the paper's theoretical framework pillars are constructed on gender stratification theory and institutional theory in the case of women in the accounting profession.

2.1. Gender Stratification Theory

Gender stratification theory or social stratification and gender (how it is also called in the literature) can be applied to an extensive range of situations (Brinton 1998; Dubose 2017; Blumberg 1984; Keister and Southgate 2012) and conditions including historical comparisons (Scott 1986; Wermuth and Monges 2002). Gender stratification or gender inequality refers to women not having the same chances or opportunities as men do, because of their gender.

Gender stratification debates about a social ranking of some sort, where men typically inhabit a higher status than women, taking into consideration criteria such as class, race, and sex (male/female). Gender stratification and gender inequality are the same facets of one idea. One of the things the theory suggests is that gender stratification exists to create in an efficient way a division of labour or a social system in which a segment of the population is in charge of certain parts of labour and while the other portion is responsible for different parts that can be more important or not (Collins et al. 1993; Brinton 1998). It analyses all the aspects of the social life and cuts across social classes mentioning about the unequal access of men and women to power, prestige, and property all based on nature of their sex (Treas and Tai 2016; Collins et al. 1993). Linked to the theory are concepts such as differential access, occupational distribution and glass ceiling. Namely, the glass ceiling theory emphasises upon the idea that it is harder for women to break through that ceiling which can lead them towards the upper level of organizations—a vertical promotion (Treas and Tai 2016; Collins et al. 1993; Anderson et al. 1994; Baxter and Wright 2000; Bell et al. 2002; Goodman et al. 2003; Broadbent and Kirkham 2008; Bryant 2010).

From a sociological point of view, gender stratification theory suggests the idea of the existence of gender inequalities as a means to create a system, a social one, inside which one part of the population bears the responsibility of certain labour acts while the other part is responsible for other labour acts. The inequalities that have as a source gender, exist to create differences in the degree of responsibilities; the main issue is that there is a tendency like in any other social group, for one group to become dominant and maybe suppress the other one (Treas and Tai 2016). If conflict theory which claims that society is in a state of continuous competition over resources (method suggested by Karl Marx) (Collins 1990; Hans and Knöbl 2011) is introduced as a component then it can be argued that gender can be understood as men overpowering women and trying to hold on to power and privilege, since the on-going fight for dominance defines society. In time the dominant group can change, but in most cases, the dominant group will always work and try to hold on to power. Moreover, this occurred in many cases, at least in the early days when women's rights were almost non-existent (Collins et al. 1993).

Gender stratification theory emphasises upon creating layers inside the society and about how always one layer will be more powerful than the other. Accordingly, from a gendered perspective, men are the more important layer, and women as a group will always take a back seat to history and the public scene or positions of power. Elements that are leading to this conjunction are glass-ceiling, sexism, prejudice, double standard, and discrimination. The point that is the underlying element to all of the above lies is the assumption that men are superior to women (Treas and Tai 2016; Collins et al. 1993; Keister and Southgate 2012). Consequently, if the latter do however have the courage to enter into a profession, they have trouble to meet the expectations (that are moulded in a man's image) and thus in most cases they have difficulty in performing a distinguishing career path (Treas and Tai 2016; Collins et al. 1993; Brinton 1998).

2.2. Institutional Theory

Insights from critical theories such as institutional theory (Boxenbaum 2006) could provide a platform for problematizing the discourses that are assumed to enhance women's role and legitimacy within governing bodies of accounting organisations (Tremblay et al. 2016). If identity in organisations is viewed as fluid rather than fixed, then greater attention should be paid to the study of the representation of identity in accounting organisations. "This would suggest more work focusing on the representation of identity in accounting organisations, specifying how representations create and sustain inequality in accounting" (Kyriakidou et al. 2013, p. 7). Kyriakidou et al. (2013) claim the need of scholars to focus their attention on what diversity addresses in accounting organisations, across different international contexts. The institutional approach refers to how multiple elements such as structures, schemes, rules, norms and routines work together to influence or affect social behaviours, thus societal behaviours and in the end how society is constructed and how it changes the mindset and mentality (Marquis and Tilcsik 2016; Scott 2004).

2.3. Gendered Nature of the Accounting Profession

While before the 1960s little attention was paid to the study of gender in accounting, after the introduction of equal employment and anti-discrimination legislation and with the impact of social movements in many countries, scholars' attention turned to the issues in accounting organisations (Kyriakidou et al. 2013, p. 3). As Hopwood (1987) underlined studies on gender started to question a vast array of practices and fields of knowledge, raising issues on how, where and by which instruments and through which players, knowledge is produced as well as identifying strategies through which male supremacy had been built and perpetuated in these contexts. Interaction of accounting and gender has been the subject of debate for many decades. Scholars have addressed, among other things, the gendered functioning of the profession in the labour market; the historical progress of women in the profession and their career trajectories; the gendered nature of accounting itself; and subjected the profession and accounting rationalities to feminist critique (Haynes 2017). The issue of accounting analysis and the accountancy profession considered from a feminist perspective was dealt with in the works of Burrell (1987) and Shearer and Arrington (1989).

Several studies and contributions attested to the gendered nature of accounting organisations (Hines 1992; Loft 1992; Lehman 1992; Kirkham and Loft 1993; Fogarty et al. 1998; Grey 1998; Napier 2001; Dambrin and Lambert 2006; Roberts 2013). Using these studies as a benchmark and starting point, other contributions began to emerge in the literature, mostly empirical studies of gender in accounting organisations and academia (Anderson-Gough et al. 2002; Dambrin and Lambert 2006, 2008, 2012; Lupu 2010; Kornberger et al. 2010; Broadbent 1998, 2016; Komori 2007; Virtanen 2009; Samkin and Schneider 2014; Baldarelli et al. 2016).

In most countries, the accounting profession has always been male-dominated. Starting from the 1970s, the gender composition of accounting began to change dramatically (Wootton and Kemmerer 2000; Walker 2008; Roberts 2013) and currently women represent a relevant percentage of the accounting workforce in the world (Ried et al. 1987; Carnegie and Napier 2010). However, though they started to be as numerous as men, their advancement on the hierarchical ladder was (and remains) difficult for them, since they suffered from discrimination and work inequality (Bryant 2010). By difficult it is meant that breaking through the glass ceiling is hard and not an easy task and women face many more obstacles as compared to men in the pursuit of career advancement and promotion.

Due to historical cultural and legal causes, as well as economic and educational forces, increases in the aggregate workforce were not (and are not currently) accompanied by subsequent proportional increases in participation at the upper-management levels of accounting firms (Lehman 1992; Haynes 2008a, 2008b; Laughlin 2011). A re-genderisation of the aggregate workforce, rather than an overall re-genderisation of the accounting profession occurred (Wootton and Kemmerer 2000). Among the theories used to explain such a phenomenon, the glass ceiling theory argues that vertical segregation operates mainly at the highest levels of organisations and professions (Collins et al. 1993; Anderson et al. 1994; Baxter and Wright 2000; Cotter et al. 2001; Bell et al. 2002; Goodman et al. 2003; Broadbent and Kirkham 2008; Dambrin and Lambert 2006). This theory refers to invisible barriers based on prejudices and stereotypes preventing qualified individuals advancing in the higher ranks of organisations (Bryant 2010).

It can be attributed to the fact that the 'accounting logic' which underpins the practice of accounting is gendered, because it represents the values and the profile of an accountant as 'universal masculine', namely the expectations are set on the profile of a man (Broadbent 1998).

As Anderson-Gough et al. (2005) point out research on gendering processes in the accounting profession necessarily combines consideration of both the formal mechanisms of organisational structuration—such as recruitment and training—and the informal processes concerning cultural norms, values and beliefs through how the legal methods are enacted and reproduced.

3. Methodology

3.1. Country Selection

The two countries (Italy and Romania) were selected for the following reasons. They can be considered extreme cases (Yin 2003) characterised by many differences relative to the political and institutional setting, being a Western and Eastern country, respectively; the level of sectoral segregation; and the diffusion of women accountants. Finally, they are marked by a different "history" of accounting, Italy having a "historical" tradition and Romania dating back to the previous century. But at the same time, one certain argument for our selection refers to the linguistic similarities between Italian and Romanian as well as Italy's close geographical proximity to Romania. Moreover, the two states have a rich history together, and the close link between them is visible even today, on various levels, thus helping the two countries to prosper together.

3.2. Method Selection

Comparative research method has been defined as a method of analysis that focuses on several objects of study to identify similarities and differences and can be made with structuralist and culturalist theory (Paisey and Paisey 2010). Structuralist approach asserts that similarities are to be expected across countries sharing similar structures (e.g., levels of industrialisation, industrial or occupational systems). Culturalist theory assumes that dissimilarities are to be expected as a result of intrinsic country-specific characteristics (Paisey and Paisey 2010), in other words assuming that culture modifies the effect of social structure on individuals (Gauthier 2000).

Comparative research has been criticised because each social system is unique and that, because of the volumes involved, it can be challenging to cover a sufficient number of cases to satisfy doubts about representation and validity (Goedegebuure and Vught 1996). However, there are also researchers that consider it like alternative research methodologies that can provide new ways of seeing, addressing the partial nature of accounting with its focus on what is happening to the exclusion of what might, or should, happen (Llewellyn 1996).

Cross-cultural research is nowadays increasingly recognised as an essential area in accounting. (Patel 2004) International comparative studies in the accounting profession point to the existence of similarities and/or distinct national differences, in relation with cultural profile, cross-cultural accounting research (Patel 2006) related to management accounting practices (Pistoni and Zoni 2000), standard setting (Bloom and Naciri 1989), accounting harmonization (Christensen et al. 2015), auditors' independence (Patel and Psaros 2000), ethics (Waldmann 2000) education (Rhoades 2001) and women in accounting profession (Whiting et al. 2015), to mention just some of the most well-known articles. These studies draw on a variety of methodological approaches, like questionnaires, surveys, or secondary resource analyses as in the case of this paper.

This study responds to the call for qualitative cross-cultural research in accounting (Patel 2004) that provides greater insight into the depth, richness and complexity of cultural and acculturational similarities and differences between and across nations by complementing the quantified dimensional based cultural measures with relevant historical, sociological and psychological literature.

3.3. Data Selection

Data for the comparative analysis were drawn from four sources:

- data from the literature and accountancy national bodies archives concerning the historiography of the accounting profession in both countries

- data on cultural factors, using Hofstede six dimensions (Hofstede et al. 2010)
- data on gender diversity useful to introduce the context of comparative gender analysis, have been extracted from the Report on equality between women and men in Europe (EU 2017), relative to the following features: gender segregation in occupations (all economic sectors), the proportion of women on boards of the largest publicly listed companies; the percentage of women in the single/lower houses of the national/federal parliaments and federal governments. The index "gender segregation" in occupations and economic sectors reflects the proportion of the employed population that would need to change occupation/sector to bring about an even distribution of men and women across occupations or sectors. The index varies between 0 (no segregation) and 50 (complete segregation).
- the AFECA's (Association des Formations Européennes a la Comptabilité et l'Audit) survey. AFECA represent a European benchmark on valorising women's capital in the accountancy profession. The study conducted by AFECA aimed to obtain an overview of progress within the 24 institutes from 22 countries concerning the valorisation of women capital and provoke exchanges and the sharing of best practices (AFECA and FEE 2016). This benchmark, useful for the assessment and comparison of the respective situations, was intended to generate dynamic movement (without stigmatisation and making value-based judgments) and allow each institute member (FEE or EFAA) to learn some lessons for their strategies in the field of the development and balance of human capital. Moreover, the key findings of the survey contribute to the reinforcement of collective action for parity and professional balance. Both countries were included in the international AFECA's survey, thus allowing a comparison based on a similar dataset.

3.4. Research Design

A historical approach was used in order to understand better the position of women in the accounting profession over time and to be able to compare and comprehend the social and economic context of Italy and Romania. The Italian and Romanian normative and socio-cultural context helped to interpret the statistical data presented in the following sections and provide insights useful to compare the Italian and Romanian contexts. Moreover, it is useful to acknowledge the reasons for gender inequality in Italy and Romania and, in more general terms, the way in which these factors are then manifested in the professional field of accounting in other countries (Broadbent 1998; Komori 2007; Virtanen 2009; Samkin and Schneider 2014; Baldarelli et al. 2016).

While the main focus of the paper is the accounting profession, and part of the study case is based on the accounting profession data, other areas were taken into consideration such as women on boards presence, gender segregation on occupations, sectors etc. in order to be able to provide a better context over the gender gap between and inside the two compared countries.

4. Results

4.1. Accounting Profession and Women Accountants in Italy and Romania: The Historical and Institutional Framework

4.1.1. Women in the Accounting Profession in Italy between Past and Present Times

The law that regulates the accounting profession in Italy dates back to the early 1900s. In 1906, a royal decree gave formal recognition to the accountancy profession. The introduction of the specific degree (*ragioniere*) was issued by the first Higher Schools of Commerce that were founded in Italy in the second half of the nineteenth century: The Venice School of Commerce, located in Cà Foscari, which was inaugurated in 1868; the Advanced School of Business Studies in Genoa, established in 1884 and the Bari School of Commerce, established in 1886.

Indeed, the profession of chartered accountants (*dottore commercialista*) was formally recognised later on, with the opening of a university that offered economics matters. Milan's Bocconi University graduates established private associations of accountants, and in 1910 they set up the first informal provincial professional bodies (Cantagalli 1996).

Ever since the beginning the Italian profession has always been characterised by its academic nature. The Order was established at the first National Congress of Italian Commercial Science graduates (*Dottori in Scienze Commerciali*), which was held in 1911, while the Public Chartered Accountants (*Dottore Commercialista*) professional qualification was coined in 1913.

In 1929 the profession was further regulated thanks to the adoption of two sets of professional rules, one for accountants and the other for chartered accountants. After the advent of Fascism—which entailed the dissolution of all professional associations (FNC 2015, p. 10; FNC 2017)—the profession of Chartered Accountancy was officially recognised in 1953 through the establishment of a special professional Order and a professional governing body with the enactment of the Presidential Decree 1067/1953. That same year, a further Decree (1068/1953) regulated the professions of accountancy and commercial experts. Only recently, namely in 2008, were the two professional bodies merged in a single public body, thus giving life to a unified profession. Over time, and with the evolution of the national regulatory models, the profession now is organised according to the Legislative Decree 139/2005 and the related regulations. At present, the national Order of Public Chartered Accountants and Accounting Experts—CNDCEC—has 117,916 registered members (January 2017), divided into 144 local branches (*Ordini territoriali*) based on a territorial jurisdiction principle following that of Italian courts. At a national level, the profession is exclusively represented by CNDCEC, which is based in Rome. The regional chapters are public entities, subject to the supervision of the Ministry of Justice and CNDCEC. Their widespread presence throughout the national territory allows the local orders to promote relations with local public authorities and, more generally, to become the local interlocutors of the public sector, academia and other professions.

At the beginning of the twentieth century, the profession of accountancy was a territory barred to women. By law, the professional accountant performed a public function and, therefore, could not be carried out by women who could not take on public offices. The presence of men was predominant or absolute in all professional orders (engineers, doctors, lawyers, accountants). The admission of women "equally with men to exercise every profession and to be able to hold every public position" was forbidden to them. Consequently, many professional careers (such as doctors, lawyers and accountants) remained far from the women's grasp for a long time, like the possibility to undertake university studies and an academic path (Ulivieri 1986). The turning point in the long and difficult fight for the inclusion of women in university studies (De Vivo and Genovesi 1986; Branciforte and Tazzioli 2001; De Rossi 2007; Frattini 2011) and professions occurred during the First World War, which opened up new areas of work for women, due to the male mortality reported in the post-war period. In 1919 the approval of a law (Law No 1176, the so-called "Sacchi Law") declared the abolition of the Institute of Marital Authorisation (*Istituto dell'autorizzazione maritale*) and allowed women's access to technical degrees (agriculture, economics, engineering and architecture), which prepared them for professions that dealt with the productive and economic aspects of society.

Namely, the history of the "female" accounting profession began in 1908 (Coronella 2014) when, for the first time, a woman applied for admission to the College of Accountants of Milan, which rejected her. This rejection marked the beginning of a fight that affected the institutions and opened the door for women's entry. Pierina Pavoni and Bianca Salvetti were the first to be admitted to the Register of Practitioners of the College of Accountants of Rome in 1911. Contextual factors favoured their entry. The first (P. Pavoni), after completing an apprenticeship at her father's office, passed the entrance examination for the profession with merit in 1913 and then applied to the Register of Accountants, which was accepted on 21 March 1914. At the same time, the Attorney General of the Court of Appeal requested the cancellation of the prior provision that sanctioned the male-dominated construct. Pavoni filed an appeal, and the Court (11 July 1914) definitively declared the right of women to enter the professional accounting world, provided they met the requirements (Bachelor's degree, professional training and passing the State examination). The enrolment of women in the Register of Accountants could not be prohibited because the Law 327 of 1906 was cancelled. This ruling marked an important step in the process of the emancipation of women, and not just for accountants because it formally marked the end of gender discrimination for the development of the accounting profession in Italy (Italian Ministry of Public Education 1878). However, it did not change the typically male system for several years (Coronella 2014). Many male accountants expressed negative judgments about women's entrance into the profession, highlighting that women should be considered legally incapacitated (Gambusera 1908, p. 93).

A fundamental step occurred in 1919 when the institution of marital authorisation was abolished, and the legal capacity of women was introduced—overcoming one of the main obstacles to females in the profession. However, after this, six years passed before another woman enrolled in the register of Accountants with Pavoni, and in the first twenty years, only six women were chartered (three in Rome, one in Bologna, one in Mantova and one in Vercelli). In 1941 they rose to 17 out of 1790 professionals, less than 1% (Liparini 2005; Cantagalli 2006), and in the following decades (1967) the percentage rose to 2% out of a total of about 10,000 professionals (Biographical Dictionary of Chartered Accountants 1967). Since then, the number of those registered has continued to increase, although more contained than their male counterparts.

Thus, three periods are distinguished in the female path of entry into the profession. The first, from the birth of the profession to the Fifties is characterised by the exclusion of women, while the second, from the Fifties to the Eighties, is characterised by the slow increase in female presence delayed by a hostile cultural heritage towards women that did not accept their presence in the profession. As a result, a process of self-exclusion was triggered, and women preferred to choose occupations more compatible with family life. The third period, which began in the Eighties and is still happening today, is marked by continued but still weak growth. In 2000, the percentage of chartered accountants was 22%, in 2004 it was 25%, increasing to 31.6% at the end of 2014 (FNC 2015, 2016). Currently, the percentage of women-chartered accountants is 33.8% (as per 1 January 2018; FNC 2018).

The numerical parity between women and men accountants is still far off, despite the positive trend. Although in 2015, among the new members, women enrolled in the National Training Register exceeded men (CNDCEC 2016), the picture gets worse if the gender reading is applied to the governance of the National Chartered Accounting association. Data shows predominant representativeness of the male component, both where the position is elective and where it is by appointment of the board. In other words, the National Council, that is the most important body of the association, is male-dominated: there are currently 21 members (including the President) of whom 19 are men (90.48%), and only two are women (9.52%).

The issue of gender imbalance in the liberal professions has been dealt with only in the last few years (CNDCEC 2016, Gender Report; European Economic and Social Committee 2014), urged by the global problem of the representation of genders (EC 2016—She Figures) in which the phenomenon of the glass ceiling (Bell et al. 2002; Goodman et al. 2003; Broadbent and Kirkham 2008; Bryant 2010) emerges. The same problem affects the governance of local accounting orders. In total, the composition of the Boards Councils of territorial Accountancy Orders in the period 2008–2012 was 88.69% of men and 11.31% of women and in the period 2013–2016, 79.07% of men and 20.93% of women (CNDCEC 2016, Gender Report, p. 23). It should be emphasised that in recent years over 50% of local orders have created equal opportunity organisms and committees: the latest survey (31 July 2015) detected 77 bodies (commissions) in 144 provincial laws.

However the paucity of the presence of women persists considering that in the bodies created within the CNDCEC Council, which in 2015 consisted of 58 between the commissions and study groups (i.e., commissions for relations with international institutions, for the professional order reform, etc.) for a total of 925 people of whom 737 are men (79.68%), and 188 are women (20.32%). These are mixed groups, except the Gender Equality Commission, made up exclusively of women. Overall, these commissions reflect a predominantly male composition.

4.1.2. The Accounting Profession from Romania—Key Highlights

The evolution of the accounting profession in Romania is very closely related to the development of trade education. As a consequence to the development of the industry and business, more and more knowledge about accounting was needed. Elementary accounting knowledge was taught in the schools of commerce. (Farcas and Tiron-Tudor 2016) Alexandru Ioan Cuza is the one that as early as 1859 states that the whole education system should be adapted to the needs Romania had at that time (Bunget et al. 2009; Hlaciuc and Deac 2014; Farcas and Tiron-Tudor 2016). Thus, the first Romanian Commercial School was opened in the year of 1864 at Galati and following this side of the country; the capital city is next, Bucharest and then Ploiesti, Iasi and Craiova. In Transylvania (belonging to the Austro Hungarian Empire since its unification with Romania in 1918) a school of commerce appeared in 1868 in Brasov and was the only one in the Romanian language belonging to this Romanian territory. (Farcas and Tiron-Tudor 2016).

The evolving economy from that time made it necessary in the minds of bank office-workers, companies' administrations and of course trade school graduates to form the basis of a professional body which happened in 1888 and it was called "The Body of Trade Accounting Schools Graduates".

In 1893 another organisation of this type took birth, and it was called The Association of National and International Trade School Graduates. The primary goals of the association were to defend their objectives and rights and to make a name for the accounting profession by "imposing the prestige of accountants, accounting and balance sheet".

The first major decision and movement that the new professional body made was to make sure that all accounts and commercial trades were handled by the graduates of business schools, people that were professionally prepared to handle such situations. At the first congress that happened in 1906 the work agenda was long, but the primary purpose, in the end, was to make sure that the accounting profession was very well represented either by establishing a proper remuneration, or by setting up a magazine (Bunget et al. 2009; Hlaciuc and Deac 2014; Farcas and Tiron-Tudor 2016). The key highlight of the Congress was the idea of setting up a Body of accounting experts. In 1907 another organisation related to accounting was being formed, The Union of Higher School of Commerce founded in 1907, which drafted the project for setting up the Body of Accounting. After several other procedures, the plan was finally submitted and was brought up to the Minister of Labour and Social Protection who was an accountant. This was a fortunate event since he is the one who expedited the process and made it possible for the project to be adopted by the Chamber of Deputies and the Senate in 1921 and then to be signed by King Ferdinand (Bunget et al. 2009; Hlaciuc and Deac 2014; Farcas and Tiron-Tudor 2016).

The professional accounting body from Romania (CEECAR) was established in September 1921, and it is more than ninety years old. The law of setting the professional body was published in Romania's official Monitor on 21st of October 1921. At the beginning of November, a formal meeting was organised, and the primary purpose of that meeting was to elect the Board of the professional body for two years, 1921–1923. By the end of the year 1921, there were 42 organisations across the country with over 3000 members.

At the meeting there were representatives from all regions of the country, the profession was represented by the best in the field at that time but one aspect was noticeable: they were all men, covering top positions and roles within private and public institutions (i.e., banks, chamber of commerce, national and regional public administrations, ministries), no exceptions (Bunget et al. 2009; Hlaciuc and Deac 2014; Farcas and Tiron-Tudor 2016).

On CEECAR's website, there is listed the professional's body's council members up until 1941. None of the members was a woman, and furthermore, there is no mention of women whatsoever during that period. The body had specific requirements for its members such as superior studies, a particular experience in the field which was impossible for the women to acquire at that time.

After the grounds of the profession were established between 1948–1994 came a period of regulation of the activity of chartered accountants, starting with the requirements to enter the business and ending with guidelines as to how accounting expertise should look. During this period the profession was limited and mostly restricted to legal auditing (Bunget et al. 2009; Hlaciuc and Deac 2014; Farcas and Tiron-Tudor 2016). After 1989 the profession had to adapt itself to the new economic reality and as well to the political events that happened during and after that year. Several restructurations occurred, and the profession started to grow and grow.

The change that happened during that year meant a crossing from a centralised economy to a market-based economy and a broader opening towards freedom of choice. Suddenly the options were more numerous, and all organisations started to change their structure for the better and to adopt a more democratic structure. After the revolution from 1989, the accounting profession from Romania became strongly reconnected with the European one and in 1990–1993 there was an attempt to rekindle the old accounting system (Jianu and Jianu 2012).

The 1990–1993 period was a transition one from a Soviet-style accounting system to a French one. The accounting law was adopted in 1991, and in 1992 the Body of Expert and Licensed Accountants of Romania (CECCAR) was reignited. Starting from 1994 a new accounting system, the French one was implemented (Jianu and Jianu 2012).

Even if in the historical documents there is no mention of women accountants' overtime (such as in the early days' meetings of the council) after 1990 the number of women in the profession started to grow from year to year as a consequence perhaps of the communist influence which encouraged women and minorities to overcome specific barriers. It is probably one of the reasons why as of now the number of women in the profession is almost 80% (AFECA and FEE 2016; Istrate 2012).

4.2. Comparative Results Concerning Cultural Factors in Italy and Romania

To understand the cultural context of both countries, we employed Hofstede's six dimensions (power distance, individualism, masculinity, uncertainty avoidance, long-term orientation and indulgence). The results obtained for Italy and Romania and the distance between the countries are in the following graph (Figure 1).

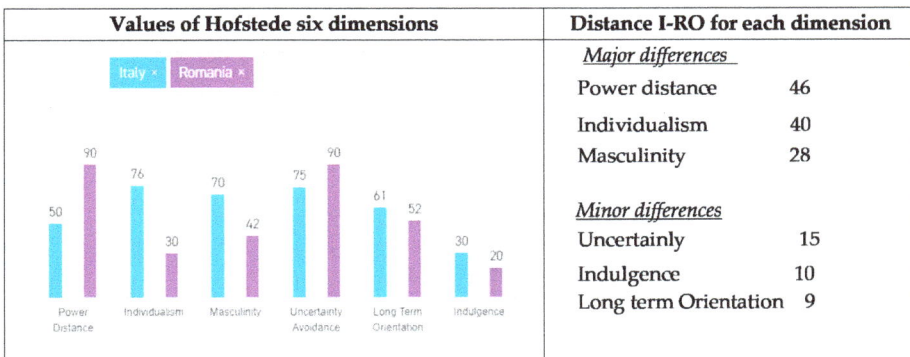

Values of Hofstede six dimensions	Distance I-RO for each dimension	
	Major differences	
	Power distance	46
	Individualism	40
	Masculinity	28
	Minor differences	
	Uncertainly	15
	Indulgence	10
	Long term Orientation	9

Figure 1. Cultural factors values of Italy and Romania. Source: Hofstede insights (https://www.hofstede-insights.com/country-comparison/italy,romania/).

There are significant differences concerning power distance, individualism and masculinity dimensions between Italy and Romania.

Power distance deals with the fact that all individuals in societies are not equal—it expresses the attitude of the culture towards these inequalities amongst us. Power Distance is defined as the extent to which the less powerful members of institutions and organisations within a country expect and accept that power is distributed unequally. Italy tends to prefer equality and a decentralisation of power and decision-making. Conversely, in Romanian organisations, centralised management with an autocrat manager which imposes a strict hierarchy is seen as being inherent (Hofstede insights).

Individualism dimension is the degree of interdependence a society maintains among its members. It has to do with whether people's self-image is defined regarding "I" or "We". In individualist societies like the Italy case, people are supposed to look after themselves and their direct family only. In collectivist societies, like the Romania case, people belong to 'in groups' that take care of them in exchange for loyalty (Hofstede insights).

The fundamental issue of the third indicator refers to what motivates people. A high score of masculinity (i.e., Italy) indicates that the society will be driven by competition, achievement and success, with success being defined by the winner/best in the field—a value system that starts in school and continues throughout organisational behaviour. However, a low score on the dimension means that the dominant values in society are caring for others and quality of life (i.e., Romania)

For the next three dimensions: uncertainty avoidance, long-term orientation and indulgence the differences are considered minor being under 15 (Hofstede insights).

The dimension's uncertainty avoidance, indulgence and long-term orientation have to do with the way that a society deals with the fact that the future can never be known. This ambiguity brings with it anxiety and different cultures have learnt to deal with this anxiety in different ways and is the case for both countries (Hofstede insights).

The long-term orientation dimension describes how every society must maintain some links with its past while dealing with the challenges of the present and future, and societies prioritise these two existential goals differently. Both countries count a culture which scores high, take a more pragmatic approach: they encourage thrift and efforts in modern education to prepare for the future.

Indulgence dimension is defined as the extent to which people try to control their desires and impulses, based on the way they were raised. There is a relatively weak control in both countries meaning an indulgent culture (Hofstede insights).

4.3. General Context of the Gender Comparative Study

Below we compare the Italy and Romania status with the EU average concerning gender segregation in occupations and economic sectors for 2005, 2010, 2015 and gender diversity measures used to monitor the gender gap in top positions in private and public organisations. The index "gender segregation" in occupations and economic sectors reflects the proportion of the employed population that would need to change occupation/sector in order to bring about an even distribution of men and women across occupations or sectors. The index varies between 0 (no segregation) and 50 (complete segregation).

For the EU, the figures are still high: 24.3% for occupational segregation and 18.9% for sectoral segregation. Table 1 summarizes Italy and Romania's situation and highlights the phenomenal growth in the case of Romania.

The purpose of presenting the gender segregation in occupations is to provide a better context of gender implications in the economy with a starting point for the context of the accounting profession and as well as a comparison between Romania and Italy. Using the gender segregation indicator has been in many cases used as a measure of gender inequality, or at least a reliable indicator of it (Blackburn et al. 2002). Table 2 presents the situation in the light of the European average as well, and the conclusion is that Romania is behind Italy and the European average, while Italy is always one step behind the EU for all three years analysed. There are some exceptions (1st category—2010; last category—2016) but overall Italy is much more advanced.

Table 1. Gender segregation in occupations and economic sectors (2005, 2010 and 2015).

	Gender Segregation in Occupations			Gender Segregation in Sectors		
	2005	2010	2015	2005	2010	2015
EU 27	24.8	24.9	24.3	17.8	19.1	18.9
EU 28		24.9	24.3		19.1	18.9
Italy	23.6	24.7	24.8	17.8	19.7	19.5
Romania	19.3	22	23	14.9	16.7	18.1

Source: Eurostat, Labour Force Survey (EU 2017, p. 57).

Table 2. Gender diversity measures.

	Proportion of Women in Boards of the Largest Publicly Listed Companies (%)			Proportion of Women in the Single/Lower Houses of the National/Federal Parliaments (%)			Proportion of Women among Senior Ministers in National/FEDERAL Governments (%)		
	2010	2013	2016	2010	2013	2016	2010	2013	2016
EU28	11.9%	17.8%	23.9%	24.4%	27.4%	28.7%	26.2%	26.6%	27.9%
Italy	4.5%	15.0%	32.3%	21.1%	31.3%	31.0%	21.7%	28.6%	29.4%
Romania	21.3%	7.8%	10.1%	11.4%	13.5%	14.2%	11.8%	21.4%	36.4%

Source: European Commission, Database on women and men in decision-making (EU 2017, p. 61).

The focus of the paper is on the accounting profession from Italy and Romania as a comparison, to see which, one is ahead, and which one is making more progress in the area of gender issues. Much like the prior data regarding gender segregation statistics on women on boards, parliaments and governments come to offer a macro context regarding the advancement of women in higher ranks of important organisations as a measure of comparison and starting point. The purpose is to provide a benchmark for the presence of women in the accounting profession of the two analysed countries (including Tables 3 and 4 which have the same purpose).

Italy is far ahead of Romania on all three chapters, and the representation of women is even higher than the EU average. On the opposite pole, Romania has a good representation only in the senior ministers and national federal governments if we look at the 2016 data. The outcome linked with the gender segregation results seems to offer a reasonable basis for a healthy presence of women in professions (in the accounting one for example) as well as a good representation in higher ranks of organisations.

In addition, further states' measures in key areas of gender analysis (Table 3) are represented by the women and men's employment rate, as well as the gender equality in decision-making, whose measures are monitored at the European level through the following indexes/proxies: proportion of women among members of the highest decision-making bodies of the largest nationally registered companies listed on the national stock exchange; percentage of women among presidents and CEOs of the largest nationally registered companies listed on the national stock exchange; and proportion of women among executive and non-executive members of the two highest decision-making bodies of the largest nationally registered companies listed on the national stock exchange.

Table 3. Women and men's employment rate and full-time equivalent (20–64 years old) in %.

Key Areas	Italy	Romania
Equal economic independence (2016) Source: Eurostat, LFS	Men 72.2% Women 51.7%	Men 76.8 Women 58.5
Women and men's employment rate in full-time equivalent (20–64 years old, 2015) Source: Eurostat, LFS	Italy Women 43.7 Men 68.3 Gender gap (men-women) 24.6	Romania Women 55.4 Men 73 Gender gap (men-women) 17.6

The following table depicts a brief European overview of the index mentioned above (Table 4).

Table 4. Measures of gender equality in decision-making.

	2015	2016
Presidents	7.1%	7.0%
CEOs	3.6%	5.1%
Non-executive directors:	22.5%	26.1%
Senior executives:	13.7%	14.9%

Source: our elaboration from EU (2017).

Going back to the gender stratification theory with its components (glass ceiling, double standard, inequality) which is used as a theoretical framework for the purpose of this paper and placing it in the context of the statistical data presented earlier and below as well, it can be asserted that there is still a lack of representation of women in organisations at a macro level and that the two countries present a significant difference in figures at all chapters.

4.4. Romania–Italy Country Level Comparison Based on AFECA Study

As aforementioned, in 2016 AFECA conducted a study over 24 professional bodies from different European countries. Professional bodies were willing to provide information on matters that concern mainly gender and gender diversity in their respective organisations. The analysis was performed following 12 main categories, related to gender, such as the law on gender equality, quotas on boards, the percentage of women on boards, women in accountancy, and the possibility of adopting a more flexible schedule to better balance work life with family life (Table 5).

Table 5. Romania–Italy comparisons on gender diversity in accounting professional bodies.

Gender Diversity Dimensions/Countries	Italy (CNDCEC—Consiglio Nazionale dei Dottori Commercialisti e degli Esperti Contabili)	Romania (CECCAR—Body of Expert and Licensed Accountants of Romania)
Law on gender equality	Establishes a gender quota for companies listed in the Stock Exchange—noncompliance results in a warning followed by financial sanctions and in the case of noncompliance the exclusion from the board YES	Law No 202/2002 on equal opportunities and treatment for women and men in labour market, education and the elimination of gender roles and stereotypes YES
Quotas on Boards	Mandatory 33.3%	NO
% Women on Boards	31%	12%
% Women in accountancy	31.60%	77.90%
Actions	working committees dedicated for gender equality; databases collecting resumes of women that are interested in being appointed to boards; collection of signs of discrimination in order to implement actions that promote gender equality YES	NO
Good Practices	NO	NO
Work from home	NO	NO
Flexible work hours	NO	NO
Part-time work	NO	NO
Internal quotas	NO	NO
Promotion rules	NO	NO
Services allowing workers to achieve a better balance between work and family life	NO	NO

Source: Author's projection after the data published in the AFECA and FEE study (2016).

When comparing the two countries, it emerges that Romania is far behind Italy in the case of all chapters except for the level of women in the professional body and the existence of the law on gender equality which is a "yes" in the case of both countries. Romania has a percentage of almost 80% of women in the profession while Italy has only 31.60% situating itself below average with 7% women accountants (the average was obtained by using all the percentages from all 24 countries present in the AFECA study).

The national legal framework for gender equality is different: the quotas of women on board are mandatory in the case of Italy, which enacted the so-called Law "Golfo-Mosca" (Law No 120 of 12 August 2011) to establish a gender quota (33.3%) in the boards of directors for the least represented gender. The law on gender equality in the case of Italy is directed towards companies listed on the Stock exchange, and it establishes a series of sanctions which are applied in the case of non-compliance. Non-compliance results in a warning, followed by financial penalties and, in the case of continued non-compliance, the potential dissolution of the board. On the other hand, Romania has a law since 2002 which is generally applicable to equal opportunities and treatment for women and men in the labour market, education and the elimination of gender roles and stereotypes. In the case of Romania, the quotas are not mandatory, and despite this, there is still 12% of women active on boards.

Regarding the good practices section that are basically actions that would improve women's work-life-balance (Windsor and Auyeung 2006), the ones that were identified based on the professional body answers were the possibility to work from home, introducing flexible hours approach, part-time work etc, neither of the countries has made any steps in this direction. However, Italy has taken actions to reduce discrimination and find possible solutions. Namely, efforts to develop attractiveness, support and value woman human capital include: the creation of working committees in charge of gender equality issues established in all the territorial chapters in order to create a network to exchange ideas; national database collecting résumés of registered women members of CNDCEC that are interested in being appointed to boards; collection at the national level of signs of discrimination to assess actions to promote gender equality; and promotion of legal reforms to enhance gender equality.

5. Discussion

A possible explanation of the reduced percentage of women in top positions and the high percentage of women in the Romanian accounting profession can be connected with some cultural factors. Romania scores high on the power distance cultural dimension (score of 90) which means that people accept a hierarchical order in which everybody has a place and which requires no further justification. The acceptance of hierarchical order determines inherent inequalities because subordinates expect to be told what to do by a benevolent autocratic boss. Also, the collectivist society culture can be taken into consideration; women would prefer to be loyal to the workgroup that values their skills. Employer/employee relationships are perceived in moral terms (like a family link), hiring and promotion decisions take into account the employee's in-group, interpersonal relations within the company (boss, peers) and are considered as extremely important (Mustata et al. 2010). At the extreme pole there is the Italian society, based on an individual mentality and moreover oriented towards success and driven, based on competition among colleagues for succeeding in their career. Concerning Romanian society, the focus is on "working in order to live", the focus on well-being and status is not shown, and promotion is not seen as a strong motivational factor (Mustata et al. 2010).

In Italy, the combination of high Masculinity and high Uncertainty Avoidance makes life very difficult and stressful. The highest score in Romania concerning Uncertainty Avoidance is related to maintaining rigid codes of belief and behaviour and is intolerant of unusual behaviour and ideas. In these cultures, there is an emotional need for rules (even if the rules never seem to work), time is money, people have an inner urge to be busy and work hard, precision and punctuality are the norms, innovation may be resisted, security is an essential element in individual motivation

Some countries are more diverse than others when it comes to women being part of the accountancy profession (AFECA and FEE 2016). Accordingly, the result shows that the presence of women in the profession varies strongly: women in accountancy in Italy are 31.6% and 77.9% in Romania. The comparative analysis between Italy and Romania first underlines that the existence of hard law aimed at enhancing professional equality does not necessarily guarantee a higher level of women in the profession (whereas soft laws seem to be working in several European countries).

One plausible reason for the high number of women in the accounting profession from Romania could be the numerous years in which Romania was under the communist ruling which was determined that minorities, poor classes and women had access to more and better opportunities than before. Women were placed on a pedestal and encouraged to get out from their households, get a degree and find a job. Another explanation could be the fact that the accounting field is inherently viewed as a feminine one which would explain the high number of female graduates in the field which transpires in the profession as well (Albu et al. 2011; Tudor and Mutiu 2007; Barbu et al. 2010).

Second, a geographical approach by zone (Western/Eastern countries) does not help to explain the different level or feminisation of the accountancy profession. In the same way, no correlation could be established between the number of women accountants and their inclusion in the boards of the National Orders. The legislative environments in Italy and Romania are diverse. Although both countries recognise the principle of gender equality in their law and constitution concerning rights, pay and opportunities, differences emerge regarding measures issued to fight against gender-based inequality, in particular, if one considers the more specific subject concerning the presence of women on boards of directors. There is, in fact, diversity in approaching the subject: while no provision is made in Romania, Italy has established mandatory quotas. In particular, the Italian Law introduced the obligation of the presence of both genders on the boards of listed companies and public subsidiaries that, starting from the second and third renewal of human organs, must be equal to at least one third, up to 2022. In this way, a process of cultural renewal to support greater meritocracy and growth opportunities has been triggered, to enhance women's opportunity to affirm their skills and competencies and contribute to the creation of economic and social value. Thus, in Italy, women, are 31% on boards while in Romania they are only 12%. The inclusion of women is increasing overall but at different rhythms: +3.29% in Italy and 3–6% in Romania.

Third, the professional contexts, despite the different features of the respective accounting traditions, point out a similar male-dominated construct (Loft 1992; Komori 2008; Dambrin and Lambert 2012; Bryant 2010; Kyriakidou et al. 2013). Both countries have not established specific policies for women accountants (such as, events for networking that consider gender in recruitment policies, the establishment of charters for best practices). Good practices (such as working from home, flexible work hours, part-time work, internal quota, promotion rules, services allowing workers to achieve a better balance between work and family life) are entirely absent both in Romania and Italy. In the former case, this can be attributed to the fact that women are already well represented in the profession (AFECA and FEE 2016). However, in the last few years in Italy, the CNDCEC has started to trigger the creation of dedicated associations or commissions, and the establishment of directories and studies. In particular, the first national gender report was released in 2016, following the recommendations of the European Parliament that, in 2003, through the Commission for Women's Rights and Equal Opportunities, presented a "Gender budgeting to encourage the implementation of public budgets according to the gender perspective". In February 2016, the Italian National Council of Accountants and Accounting Experts approved the guidelines for the presentation of disaggregated information by gender and gender-sensitive indicators in order to allow the Association to sensitize the Council, the employees of the body and the members to gender issues and the diversified impact of policies; to reduce gender inequalities through a more equitable distribution of resources; to improve the effectiveness, efficiency and transparency of the Association's action; to promote a reading and analysis of the population and the different needs present in the professional community and to respond coherently to them; and to develop "gender sensitive" data and statistics. We can read: "Besides covering all areas linked to all fields of professional activity, CNDCEC places a special focus on equal opportunities and the presence of women in the Profession" (FNC 2015, p. 40). Accordingly, in January 2011, the National Equal Opportunities Committee of the Order presented the ethical charter as a manifesto for all professional colleagues to disengage in any form of gender discrimination and value diversity within their professional structure. Also, in recent years, a series of training events at the national and local level dedicated to gender aspects has been organised by the national Order including psychological training, techniques for reconciling work and family time, self-knowledge, listening persuasion, the management of human resources within the firm and female leadership. We can read: "Besides covering all areas linked to all fields of professional activity, CNDCEC places a special focus on equal opportunities and the presence of women in the Profession" (FNC 2015, p. 40).

However, we cannot speak of the feminization of the category and the picture gets worse if the gender reading is applied to the governance of National Chartered Accounting Associations since the boards remain male-dominated in both countries and affected by the glass ceiling phenomenon (Bell et al. 2002; Broadbent and Kirkham 2008; Bryant 2010).

Fourth, the work has also managerial and political implications. From the managerial perspective, findings claim the need to pursue several challenges. First, achieving a balanced representation of men and women within the profession, among accountants, partners in the highest positions, governance, in accountancy governing bodies, private companies and national institutions is fundamental to increase the presence of female role models and help women aspire to leadership positions. In this regard, within extant literature, it has been widely demonstrated that mentored women are more likely to achieve the highest position in career. Mentoring—conceived as "a process by which an experienced individual provides career guidance and personal support to a less experienced individual" (Bailey et al. 2016, p. 160)—play a positive effect in favour of the mentee (Dreher and Ash 1990; Whitten 2016) because it enhances the self-confidence of the mentee, provides a role modeling, friendship and emotional support that are very important to support the psycho-social dimension of women (Merriam 1983; Burke and McKeen 1990). In other words, mentoring can be considered a possible tool to reinforce the women accountants' role within the National and Territorial Orders. Second, in a profession with high demands and time constraints, it is important to create a work environment that promotes gender equality by allowing workers to reconcile their work and private life (i.e., flexible working hours must be promoted and information technology opportunities used). There is a huge need for a comprehensive strategy capable of including a broad range of actions (i.e., measures to reconcile family and work life for both women and men; changing the political culture; overcoming gender stereotypes regarding leadership skills; ensuring women's equal access to financial resources; programs to support training/mentoring for women candidates and to build a pipeline of women politicians).

We therefore claim that there is a need to better understand complex and multiple motivations that can be attributed, like in other professional settings, to a higher difficulty of entering the profession compared to male colleagues, less opportunities to earn (as data relative to the gender pay-gap confirm in both countries) and less inclination toward the risk that an independent activity involves (EC 2016—She Figures; EC 2014; Broadbent 2016). In this regard, in both countries, a weakness in best practices emerges, with reference to work-life balance policies. All professions, especially accountancy, can support the economic independence and well-being of both men and women, if well designed and capable of allowing for the equal sharing of care responsibilities between women and men. In 2016, a country-specific recommendation related to the female labour market participation was addressed to 10 Member States, including Italy and Romania, notably encouraging them to improve the provision of quality, affordable full-time childcare, access to long-term care, remove obstacles and disincentives and promote economic independence (EU 2017, p. 13).

Neither Italy nor Romania is included among the few European Member States that are catching up, and where progress has been significant (i.e., Bulgaria, Latvia, Lithuania, Malta and Portugal), retrenchment is quite substantial in Romania (EU 2017, p. 14).

6. Conclusions

When the social orders of the Chartered Accountants and the local colleges of the Accountants and Commercial Experts were established both in Italy and Romania women's declination was common to all professional orders, as in many other countries. It was a matter of form and substance, the presence of men, as in all other professional orders (engineers, doctors, lawyers, accountants) was predominant or absolute. Currently, women in the accounting profession represent a fundamental resource for the evolution of the profession itself, although their presence has not yet been adequately valued and there is a lack of deep reflection on their role within the accountancy profession. In particular, we are not aware of previous studies aimed at comparing the women accountants' situation among different countries. Therefore, these works can contribute to trigger scientific debate and stimulate useful comparisons. The gap identified in literature and practice leads us to propose a research agenda on the following themes: the evolution of women's presence in the accounting profession over the years, aimed at focusing the obstacles encountered and the "strategies" adopted to overcome them; the analysis of the specific value that women can provide in the accounting profession, to point out how different male and female sensibilities can be integrated to enhance differences and improve the ethical foundation of the profession; the importance of role models in the accounting profession, capable of positively influencing new generations. The gaps mentioned above can be applied to practical study cases, a comparison between multiple countries placed in the professional accounting bodies from those respective countries. Thus, the suggestion is to take a more practical approach rather than a theoretical one (Wright and Wright 1987; Irvine et al. 2010).

Under the political implications, this study contributes to pointing out the need for a strong political will for further action and engagement of political parties to put gender balance on the political agenda and overcome the barriers to equal access of the boards of the National and Local Orders. While formal quotas are an effective way to encourage political parties to seek the participation of women, these nevertheless need to be well designed and effectively implemented within the professions, such as in the accountancy field, to achieve good results. Moreover, within the Chartered Accounting Associations, it would be necessary to intensify the opportunities for discussion and sharing, particularly involving the scientific institutions, because since its birth the profession has always been linked to the university and the development of accounting is related to both the practice and the research gained in the academic field. Finally, the availability of data to monitor the progress made, both quantitative and qualitative, is crucial.

In summary, despite the limitations of the study, due to the focus on the comparison on solely Romania and Italy and the incomplete availability and comparability of data, we can affirm that moving towards increasing openness and inclusive culture in the accountancy profession represents a consistent way to promote a vibrant and non-dominated culture.

Author Contributions: This paper represents the work of a common research project. However, M.D.B. wrote Sections 1, 4.1 and 4.4, A.T.-T. wrote Sections 3 and 4.3 and W.A.F. wrote Sections 2, 4.2 and 4.4. All three authors wrote together Section 5—discussion and Section 6—conclusions.

Funding: This research received no external funding.

Conflicts of Interest: The authors declare no conflict of interest. The funders had no role in the design of the study; in the collection, analyses, or interpretation of data; in the writing of the manuscript, and in the decision to publish the results.

References

Adapa, Sujana, Alison Sheridan, and Jennifer Rindfleish. 2015. Career enablers for women in regional and metropolitan accounting SMEs. *Australasian Journal of Regional Studies* 21: 178–201. Available online: http://www.anzrsai.org/publications/ajrs/ (accessed on 20 December 2018).

Adler, Paul S., Seok-Woo Kwon, and Charles Heckscher. 2008. Professional Work: The Emergence of Collaborative Community. *Organization Science* 19: 359–76. [CrossRef]

Association des Femmes diplômées d'Expertise Comptable Administrateurs Gender (AAECA), and Fédération des Experts Comptables Européens (FEE). 2016. *Diversity in the European Accountancy Profession. An AFECA Study with the Support of FEE.* Paris: AFECA.

Albu, Nadia, Catalin Albu, Maria Gîrbină, and Maria Sandu. 2011. The Implications of Corporate Social Responsibility on the Accounting Profession: The Case of Romania. *Amfiteatru Economic Journal, The Bucharest University of Economic Studies, Bucharest* 13: 221–34.

Anderson, John C., Eric N. Johnson, and Philip MJ Reckers. 1994. Perceived effects of gender, family structure and physical appearence on carreer progression in public accounting: A research note. *Accounting, Organization and Society* 19: 483–91. [CrossRef]

Anderson-Gough, Fiona, Christopher Grey, and Keith Robson. 2002. Accounting Professionals and the Accounting Profession: Linking Conduct and Context. *Accounting and Business Research* 32: 41–56. [CrossRef]

Anderson-Gough, Fiona, Christopher Grey, and Keith Robson. 2005. "Helping them to forget": The organizational embedding of gender relations in public audit firms. *Accounting Organizations and Society* 30: 469–90. [CrossRef]

Bailey, Sarah Frances, Elora C. Voyles, Lisa Finkelstein, and Kristina Matarazzo. 2016. Who is your ideal mentor? An exploratory study of mentor prototypes. *Career Development International* 21: 160–75. [CrossRef]

Baldarelli, Maria Gabriella, Mara Del Baldo, and Stefania Vignini. 2016. Pink accounting in Italy: Cultural perspectives over discrimination and/or lack of interest. *Meditari Accountancy Research* 24: 269–92. [CrossRef]

Barbu, Elena, Nicoleta Farcane, and Adina Popa. 2010. Looking for an Accounting Identity: The Case of Romania during the 20th Century. Available online: http://hal.archives-ouvertes.fr/docs/00/53/47/41/PDF/cr_2010_03_E2.pdf (accessed on 6 November 2018).

Baxter, Janeen, and Erik Olin Wright. 2000. The glass Ceiling Hypothesis: A Comparative Study of the United States, Sweden, and Australia. *Gender and Society* 14: 275–94. [CrossRef]

Bell, Myrtle P., Mary E. McLaughlin, and Jennifer M. Sequeira. 2002. Discrimination, harassment, and the glass ceiling: Women executives as change agents. *Journal of Business Ethics* 37: 65–76. [CrossRef]

Biographical Dictionary of Chartered Accountants. 1967. *Dizionario Biografico dei dottori commercialisti.* Roma: CNDCEC.

Blackburn, Robert M., Jude Browne, Bradley Brooks, and Jennifer Jarman. 2002. Explaining gender segregation. *British Journal of Sociology* 53: 513–36. [CrossRef] [PubMed]

Bloom, Robert, and M. Ahmed Naciri. 1989. Accounting standard setting and culture: A comparative analysis of the United States, Canada, England, West Germany, Australia, New Zealand, Sweden, Japan, and Switzerland. *The International Journal of Accounting* 24: 70–97.

Blumberg, Rae Lesser. 1984. A general theory of gender stratification. *Sociological Theory* 2: 23–101. [CrossRef]

Boxenbaum, Eva. 2006. Lost in translation? The making of Danish diversity management. *American Behavioral Scientist* 49: 939–48. [CrossRef]

Branciforte, Laura, and Rossana Tazzioli. 2001. *La presenza delle donne nella matematica e nel suo insegnamento.* Catania: Società di storia patria per la Sicilia Orientale.

Brinton, Mary C. 1998. The Social-Institutional Bases of Gender Stratification: Japan as an Illustrative Case. *American Journal of Sociology* 94: 300–34. [CrossRef]

Broadbent, Jane. 1998. The gendered nature of 'accounting logic': Pointers to an accounting that encompasses multiple values. *Critical Perspectives on Accounting* 9: 267–97. [CrossRef]

Broadbent, Jane. 2016. A gender agenda. *Meditari Accountancy Research* 24: 169–81. [CrossRef]

Broadbent, Jane, and Linda Kirkham. 2008. Glass ceilings, glass cliffs or new worlds?: Revisiting gender and accounting. *Accounting and Accountability Journal* 21: 465–73. [CrossRef]

Bryant, Lydia L. 2010. What role does the 'Glass ceiling' play for women in the accounting? *The York Scholar* 1: 2–13.

Bunget, Ovidiu-Constantin, Nicoleta Farcane, Alin-Constantin Dumitrescu, and Adina Popa. 2009. The Accounting Profession and Professions in Romania. Available online: https://mpra.ub.uni-muenchen.de/id/eprint/18408 (accessed on 25 January 2018).

Burke, Ronald J., and Carol A. McKeen. 1990. Mentoring in organizations: Implications for women. *Journal of Business Ethics* 9: 317–32. [CrossRef]

Burrell, Gibson. 1987. No Accounting for Sexuality. *Accounting, Organizations and Society* 12: 89–101. [CrossRef]

Cantagalli, Alessandra. 1996. La professione del dottore commercialista. In *Storia d'Italia. Annali, 10: I professionisti*. Edited by Maria Malatesta. Torino: Einaudi, pp. 225–58.

Cantagalli, A. 2006. Il Ragioniere Commercialista: Una storia lunga un secolo (1906–2006). *I ragionieri commercialisti in Italia. 100 anni della nostra storia.Summa* 23: 223.

Carnegie, Garry D., and Christopher J. Napier. 2010. Traditional accountants and business professionals: Portraying the accounting profession after Enron. *Accounting, Organization and Society* 35: 360–76. [CrossRef]

Christensen, Hans B., Edward Lee, Martin Walker, and Cheng Zeng. 2015. Incentives or Standards: What Determines Accounting Quality Changes around IFRS Adoption? *European Accounting Review* 24: 31–61. [CrossRef]

Ciancanelli, Penelope, Sonja Gallhofer, Christopher Humphrey, and Linda M. Kirkham. 1990. Gender and Accountancy: Some Evidence from the UK. *Critical Perspectives on Accounting* 1: 117–44. [CrossRef]

Consiglio Nazionale dei Dottori Commercialisti e degli Esperti Contabili (CNDCEC). 2016. *Gender Report, CNDCEC Bilancio di genere del Consiglio Nazionale dei Dottori Commercialisti e degli Esperti Contabili, Marzo 2016. A cura della Commissione Parità di Genere—Area Parità di Genere*. Rome: CNDCEC.

Collins, Randall. 1990. Conflict theory and the advance of macro-historical sociology. In *Frontiers of Social Theory*. Edited by George Ritzer. New York: Columbia University Press, pp. 68–87.

Collins, Randall, Janet Saltzman Chafetz, Rae Lesser Blumberg, Scott Coltrane, and Jonathan H. Turner. 1993. Toward an integrated theory of gender stratification. *Sociological Perspectives* 36: 185–216. [CrossRef]

Cooper, David J., and Keith Robson. 2006. Accounting, professions and regulation: Locating the site of professionalization. *Accounting, Organizations and Society* 31: 415–44. [CrossRef]

Coronella, Stefano, ed. 2014. L'ingresso delle donne nel mondo professionale. In *Storia della Ragioneria Italiana. Epoche, uomini e idee*. Milano: F. Angeli, pp. 349–51.

Cotter, David A., Joan M. Hermsen, Seth Ovadia, and Reeve Vanneman. 2001. The glass ceiling effect. *Social Forces* 80: 655–81. [CrossRef]

Dambrin, Claire, and Caroline Lambert. 2006. *La Question du Genre en Compatibilité. Analyses Theoriques et Metodologiques. Les Cahiers de Recherche 862*. Paris: HEC, pp. 1–26.

Dambrin, Claire, and Caroline Lambert. 2008. Mothering or auditing? The case of two Big four in France. *Accounting, Auditing & Accountability Journal* 21: 474–506.

Dambrin, Claire, and Caroline Lambert. 2012. Who is she and who are we? A reflexive journey in research into the rarity of women in the highest ranks of accountancy. *Critical Perspectives on Accounting* 23: 1–16. [CrossRef]

De Rossi, Roberta. 2007. *Le donne di Cà Foscari, Percorsi di emancipazione, Materiali di studi*. Venezia: Università Cà Foscari.

De Vivo, Francesco, and Giovanni Genovesi, eds. 1986. *Cento anni di Università l'istruzione superiore in Italia dall'Unità ai nostri giorni*. Napoli: Esi, Collana CIRSE, Frontiere dell'Educazione.

Dreher, George F., and Ronald A. Ash. 1990. A comparative study of mentoring among men and women in managerial, professional, and technical positions. *Journal of Applied Psychology* 75: 539–46. [CrossRef]

Dubose, Renalia. 2017. Compliance Requires Inspection: The Failure of Gender Equal Pay Efforts in the United States. *Mercer Law Review* 68: 445–60.

European Commission (EC). 2014. Gender Equality in Horizon 2020, 2014, Luxembourg. Available online: https://ec.europa.eu/research/swafs/pdf/pub_gender_equality/she_figures_2015-final.pdf (accessed on 8 November 2018).

European Commission (EC). 2015a. European Commission and the European External Action Service (EEAS) Joint Staff Working Document on "Gender Equality and Women's Empowerment: Transforming the lives of Girls and Women through EU External Relations 2016–2020 Brussels, 21.9.2015 SWD (2015) 182 Final. Available online: https://ec.europa.eu/europeaid/joint-staff-working-document-gender-equality-andwomens-empowerment-transforming-lives-girls-and_en (accessed on 2 February 2018).

European Commission (EC). 2015b. European Commission: Fact Sheet—Sustainable Development Goals and the Agenda 2030, Brussels, 25 September 2015. Available online: http://europa.eu/rapid/press-release_MEMO-15-5709_en.htm (accessed on 2 February 2018).

European Commission (EC). 2016. *She Figures 2015, Publication Office of the European Union*. Luxembourg: European Union.

Grigsby, Ellen. 2008. *Analyzing Politics*. Belmont: Cengage Learning, pp. 108–9, 112, 347. ISBN 978-0-495-50112-1.

European Union. 2017. *European Commission Report on Equality between Women and Men in the EU Justice and Consumers*. Belgium: European Union, p. 68. ISSN 2443-5228. [CrossRef]

European Economic and Social Committee. 2014. The State of Liberal Professions Concerning Their Functions and Relevance to European Civil Society. Available online: https://publications.europa.eu/fr/publication-detail/-/publication/f106f20b-36f7-4425-8e07-33db339da6e6 (accessed on 10 November 2018).

Farcas, Teodora Viorica, and Adriana Tiron-Tudor. 2016. An overlook into the Accounting History Evolution from a Romanian point of view. A Literature Review. *Economia Aziendale Online* 7: 71–84.

FNC (Fondazione Nazionale dei Commercialisti). 2015. *The Profession of Commercialista in Italy*, July 2015 ed. Rome: FNC.

FNC (Fondazione Nazionale dei Commercialisti). 2016. *Report on the Register of Chartered Accountants and Accounting Experts from the National Accountants Foundation*. Rome: FNC.

FNC (Fondazione Nazionale dei Commercialisti), ed. 2017. *Consiglio Nazionale dei Dottori Commercialisti e degli Esperti Contabili, Rapporto 2017 sull'Albo dei Dottori Commercialisti e degli Esperti Contabili, a cura di Di Nardo, T., Giugno 2017*. Roma: FNC.

Fondazione Nazionale dei Commercialisti (FNC), ed. 2018. *Rapporto 2018 Sull'albo dei DottoriCommercialisti e degli Esperti Contabili. Sintesi dei dati, a cura di Di Nardo, T., Giugno 2018*. Roma: FNC.

Fogarty, Timothy J., Larry M. Parker, and Thomas Robinson. 1998. Where the rubber meets the road: Performance evaluation and gender in large public accounting organizations. *Women in Management Review* 13: 299–311. [CrossRef]

Frattini, Romana. 2011. Le donne all'Università di Cà Foscari un percorso tormentato: Dati e problemi. In *Nominare per esistere: Nomi e cognomi*. Edited by Giuliana Glusti. Venezia: Libreria Editrice Cafoscarina, pp. 171–82.

Gallhofer, Sonja. 1998. The silence of mainstream feminist accounting research. *Critical Perspectives on Accounting* 9: 355–75. [CrossRef]

Gambusera, E. 1908. Le donne possono essere iscritti nei Collegi legali della Ragioneria? *Rivista dei Ragionieri* 1: 93.

Gammie, Bob, and Elizabeth Gammie. 1997. Career progression in accountancy. The role of personal and situational factors. *Women in Management Review* 12: 167–73. [CrossRef]

Gauthier, Lane Roy. 2000. The role of questioning: Beyond comprehension's front door. *Reading Horizons: A Journal of Literacy and Language Arts* 40: 239–52.

Goedegebuure, Leo, and Frans van Vught. 1996. Comparative higher education studies: The perspective from the policy sciences. *Higher Education* 32: 371–94. [CrossRef]

Goodman, Jodi S., Dail L. Fields, and Terry C. Blum. 2003. Cracks in the Glass Ceiling. In What Kinds of Organizations do Women Make it to the Top? *Group and Organization Management* 28: 475–501. [CrossRef]

Grey, Christopher. 1998. On being a professional in a 'Big Six' firm. *Accounting, Organizations and Society* 23: 569–87. [CrossRef]

Hlaciuc, Elena, and Veronica Deac. 2014. An Overview of Past and Present Romanian Accounting. *Procedia Economics and Finance* 15: 909–15. [CrossRef]

Hans, Joas, and Wolfgang Knöbl, eds. 2011. Conflict sociology and conflict theory. In *Social Theory: Twenty Introductory Lectures*. Cambridge: Cambridge University Press, pp. 174–98.

Haynes, Kathryn. 2008a. (Re)figuring accounting and maternal bodies: The gendered embodiment of accounting professionals. *Accounting, Organizations and Society* 33: 328–48. [CrossRef]

Haynes, Kathryn. 2008b. Moving the gender agenda or stirring chicken's entrails? Where next for feminist methodologies in accounting? *Accounting, Auditing and Accountability Journal* 21: 539–55. [CrossRef]

Haynes, Kathryn. 2017. Accounting as gendering and gendered: A review of 25 years of critical accounting research on gender. *Critical Perspectives on Accounting* 43: 110–24. [CrossRef]

Hines, Ruth D. 1992. Accounting: Filling the negative space. *Accounting Organizations and Society* 18: 313–41. [CrossRef]

Hofstede, Geert, G. J. Hofstede, and M. Minkov. 2010. *Cultures and Organizations: Software of the Mind: Intercultural Cooperation and Its Importance for Survival*, 3rd ed. New York and London: McGraw-Hill.

Hopwood, Anthony G. 1987. Accounting and Gender: An Introduction. *Accounting Organization and Society* 12: 65–69. [CrossRef]

Irvine, Helen, Lee Moerman, and Kathy Rudkin. 2010. A green drought: The challenge of mentoring for Australian accounting academics. *Accounting Research Journal* 23: 146–71. [CrossRef]

Istrate, Costel. 2012. Gender issues in romanian accounting profession. *Review of Economics Business Studies* 5: 21–45.

Italian Ministry of Public Education—Ministero della Pubblica Istruzione. 1878. *Programmi, osservazioni e memorie sullo insegnamento della Ragioneria e Computisteria negli Istituti tecnici del Regno con l'aggiunta di un elenco bibliografico di Computisteria e Ragioneria.* Roma: Tipografia Eredi Botta.

Jianu, Iulia, and Ionel Jianu. 2012. The told and retold story of Romanian accounting. *Accounting and Management Information Systems* 11: 391–423.

Kabeer, Naila. 2005. Gender equality and women's empowerment: A critical analysis of the third Millennium Development Goal. *Gender and Development* 13: 13–24. [CrossRef]

Kanter, Rosabeth Moss. 1977. *Men and Women of the Corporation.* New York: Basic Books.

Keiran, Sarah Elizabeth. 2017. Gender Roles in Public Accounting and the Absence of Women in Upper Level Management. Honors Theses and Capstones, University of New Hampshire Scholars' Repository, Durham, NH, USA. Available online: https://scholars.unh.edu/honors/358 (accessed on 2 September 2018).

Keister, Lisa A., and Darby E. Southgate. 2012. *Inequality: A Contemporary Approach to Race, Class, and Gender.* Cambridge: Cambridge University Press.

Kirkham, Linda M., and Anne Loft. 1993. Gender and the construction of the professional accountant. *Accounting, Organizations and Society* 18: 507–58. [CrossRef]

Kirkpatrick, Ian, and Daniel Muzio. 2011. Introduction: Professions and organizations—A conceptual framework. *Current Sociology* 59: 389–405. [CrossRef]

Komori, Naoko. 1998. In Search of Feminine Accounting Practice: The Experience of Women Accountants in Japan. The Second Asia Pacific Interdisciplinary Research in Accounting Conference. Available online: http://www.apira2013.org/past/apira1998/archives/pdfs/50.pdf (accessed on 7 July 2017).

Komori, Naoko. 2007. The "hidden" history of accounting in Japan: A historical examination of the relationship between Japanese women and Accounting. *Accounting History* 12: 329–58. [CrossRef]

Komori, Naoko. 2008. Towards the feminization of accounting practice: Lessons from the experiences of Japanese women in the accounting profession. *Accounting, Auditing and Accountability Journal* 21: 507–38. [CrossRef]

Komori, Naoko. 2012. Visualizing the Negative Space: Making Feminine Accounting Practices Visible by Reference to Japanese Women's Household Accounting Practices. *Critical Perspectives on Accounting* 26: 451–67. Available online: https://elsevier.conference-services.net/resources/247/2182/pdf/CPAC2011_0039_paper.pdf (accessed on 7 July 2017). [CrossRef]

Kornberger, Martin, Chris Carter, and Anne Ross-Smith. 2010. Changing gender domination in a Big Four accounting firm: Flexibility, performance and client service in practice. *Accounting, Organizations and Society* 35: 775–91. [CrossRef]

Kyriakidou, Olivia, Orthodoxia Kyriacou, Mustafa Özbilgin, and Emmanouil Dedoulis. 2013. Equality, diversity and inclusion in accounting. *Critical Perspective on Accounting, Special Issue* 35: 1–12.

Laughlin, Richard. 2011. Accounting research policy and practice: Worlds together or worlds apart? In *Bridging the Gap between Academic Research and Professional Practice.* Edited by Elaine Evans, Roger Burritt and James Guthrie. Sidney: Centre for Accounting, Governance and Sustainability, University of South Australia and Institute of Chartered Accountants of Australian, pp. 22–30.

Lehman, Cheryl R. 1992. Herstory in accounting: The first eighty years. *Accounting Organizations and Accounting* 17: 261–85. [CrossRef]

Liparini, Francesca. 2005. *Genere e professioni contabili. Fondazione dei Dottori Commercialisti di Bologna.* Zola Predosa: Tipolitografia Labor.

Llewellyn, Sue. 1996. Theories for theorists or theories for practice? Liberating academic accounting research? *Accounting, Auditing & Accountability Journal* 9: 112–18.

Loft, Anne. 1992. Accountancy and the gendered division of labour: A review essay. *Accounting, Organisation and Society* 17: 367–78. [CrossRef]

Lupu, Ioana. 2010. Women in the French Accountancy Profession: The Test of Labyrinth, GREG-CRC, Conservatoire National des Artes et Métieres (Paris), Académie d'Etudes Economiques, Bucares Working Paper. pp. 1–26. Available online: https://docplayer.net/38197254-Women-in-the-french-accountancy-profession-the-test-of-the-labyrinth.html (accessed on 3 June 2017).

Marlow, Susan, and Sara Carter. 2003. Accounting for change: Professional status, gender disadvantage and self-employment. *Women in Management Review* 19: 5–17. [CrossRef]

Marquis, Christopher, and András Tilcsik. 2016. Institutional Equivalence: How Industry and Community Peers Influence Corporate Philanthropy. *Organization Science* 27: 1325–41. [CrossRef]

Merriam, Sharan. 1983. Mentors and protégés: A critical review of the literature. *Adult Education Quarterly* 33: 161–73. [CrossRef]

Milburn Report. 2009. Unleashing Aspiration; The Final Report of the Panel on Fair Access to the Professions. Available online: http://www.cabinetoffice.gov.uk/accessprofessions (accessed on 10 November 2018).

Muller, Jerry Z. 1997. *Conservatism: An Anthology of Social and Political Thought from David Hume to the Present.* Princeton: Princeton University Press, p. 26. ISBN 0691037116.

Mustata, Razvan V., Szilveszter Fekete, and Dumitru Matis. 2010. Motivating accounting professionals in Romania. Analysis after five decades of communist ideology and two decades of accounting harmonization. *Accounting and Management Information Systems* 10: 169–201.

Napier, Christopher J. 2001. Accounting history and accounting progress. *Accounting History* 6: 7–31. [CrossRef]

OhOgartaigh, Ciaran O. 2000. Accounting for feminisation and the feminisation of accounting in Ireland: Gender and self-evaluation in the context of uncertain accounting information. *IBAR, Irish Business and Administrative Research* 21: 10–29.

Paisey, Catriona, and Nicholas J. Paisey. 2010. Comparative research: An opportunity for accounting researchers to learn from other professions. *Journal of Accounting & Organizational Change* 6: 180–99.

Paris, Dubravka. 2016. History of accounting and accountancy profession in Great Britain. *Journal of Accounting and Management* 6: 33–44.

Patel, Chris. 2004. Some theoretical and methodological suggestions for cross-cultural accounting studies. *International Journal of Accounting, Auditing and Performance Evaluation* 1: 61–84. [CrossRef]

Patel, Christopher. 2006. *A Comparative Study of Professional Accountants' Judgments—Studies in Managerial and Financial Accounting.* Amsterdam and Oxford: Elsevier.

Patel, Chris, and Jim Psaros. 2000. Perceptions of external auditors' independence: Some cross-cultural evidence. *The British Accounting Review* 32: 311–38. [CrossRef]

Pistoni, Anna, and Laura Zoni. 2000. Comparative management accounting education in Europe: An undergraduate education perspective. *The European Accounting Review* 9: 285–319. [CrossRef]

Ried, Glenda E., Brenda T. Acken, and Elise G. Jancura. 1987. A Historical perspective on women in Accounting. *Journal of Accountancy* 163: 338–55.

Rhoades, Gary. 2001. Introduction to special section: Perspectives on comparative higher education. *Higher Education* 41: 345–52. [CrossRef]

Roberts, Diane H. 2013. Women in accounting occupations in the 1880 US Census. *Accounting History Review* 23: 141–60. [CrossRef]

Rodrigues, Lúcia Lima, Delfina Gomes, and Russell Craig. 2003. Corporatism, Liberalism and the Accounting Profession in Portugal Since. *Accounting Historians Journal* 30: 95–128. [CrossRef]

Samkin, Grant, and Annika Schneider. 2014. The Accounting Academic. *Meditari Accountancy Research* 22: 2–19. [CrossRef]

Scott, Joan Wallach. 1986. Gender: A Useful Category for Historical Analysis. *The American Historical Review* 5: 1053–75. [CrossRef]

Scott, W. Richard. 2004. Institutional theory. In *Encyclopedia of Social Theory.* Edited by George Ritzer. Thousand Oaks: Sage, pp. 408–14.

Shearer, Teri L., and C. Edward Arrington. 1989. Accounting in other worlds: A feminism without reserve. *Accounting, Organizations and Society* 18: 253–72. [CrossRef]

Treas, Judith, and Tsuio Tai. 2016. Gender inequality in housework across 20 European Nations: Lessons from Gender Stratification Theories. *Sex Roles* 74: 495–511. [CrossRef]

Tremblay, Marie-Soleil, Bertrand Malsch, and Yves Gendron. 2016. Gender on board: Deconstructing the legitimate female director. *Accounting, Auditing & Accountability Journal* 29: 165–90.

Tudor, Adriana Tiron, and Alexandra Mutiu. 2007. Important stages in the development of Romanian accounting profession (from 1800 up to now). *Spanish Journal of Accounting History* 6: 183–99.

Ulivieri, Simonetta. 1986. La donna e gli studi universitari nell'Italia postunitaria. In *Cento anni di università—L'istruzione superiore in Italia dall'unità ai nostri giorni.* Edited by Francesco De Vivo and Giovanni Genovesi. Napoli: Edizioni Scientifiche Italiane, pp. 219–28.

Virtanen, Aila. 2009. Accounting, gender and history: The life of Minna Canth. *Accounting History* 14: 79–100. [CrossRef]

Waldmann, Erwin. 2000. Teaching ethics in accounting: A discussion of cross-cultural factors with a focus on Confucian and Western philosophy. *Accounting Education: An International Journal* 9: 23–35. [CrossRef]

Walker, Stephen P. 2008. Accounting histories of women: Beyond recovery? *Accounting, Auditing & Accountability Journal* 21: 580–610.

Wermuth, Laurie, and Miriam Ma'at-Ka-Re Monges. 2002. Gender stratification. A Structural Model for Examining Case Examples of Women in Less-Developed Countries. *Frontiers: A Journal of Women Studies* 23: 1–22. [CrossRef]

Whiting, Rosalind H., Elizabeth Gammie, and Kathleen Herbohn. 2015. Women and the prospects for partnership in professional accountancy firms. *Accounting and Finance* 55: 575–605. [CrossRef]

Whitten, Donna L. 2016. Mentoring and Work Engagement for Female Accounting, Faculty Members in Higher Education. *Mentoring & Tutorship: Partnership in Learning* 24: 365–82.

Windsor, Carolyn, and Pak Auyeung. 2006. The Effect of Gender and Dependent Children on Professional Accountants' Career Progression. *Critical Perspectives on Accounting* 17: 828–44. [CrossRef]

Wootton, Charles W., and Barbara E. Kemmerer. 2000. The changing genderization of the accounting workforce in the US, 1930–1990. *Accounting, Business & Financial History* 10: 169–90.

Wright, Cheryl A., and Scott D. Wright. 1987. The role of mentors in the career development of young professionals. *Family Relations* 36: 204–8. [CrossRef]

Yin, Robert K. 2003. *Case Study Research. Design and Methods*, 3rd ed. London: Sage Publications.

administrative
sciences

MDPI

Article

Opening the "Black Box". Factors Affecting Women's Journey to Top Management Positions: A Framework Applied to Chile

Katherina Kuschel [1,*,†] and Erica Salvaj [2,†]

1   Dirección de Investigación y Desarrollo Académico, Universidad Tecnológica Metropolitana,
    Santiago 8330378, Chile
2   School of Economics and Business, Universidad del Desarrollo, Santiago 7550000, Chile; esalvaj@udd.cl
*   Correspondence: kkuschel@utem.cl; Tel.: +56-952-580-035
†   These authors contributed equally to this work.

Received: 14 September 2018; Accepted: 19 October 2018; Published: 20 October 2018

Abstract: The issue of women's participation in top management and boardroom positions has received increasing attention in the academic literature and the press. However, the pace of advancement for women managers and directors continues to be slow and uneven. The novel framework of this study organizes the factors at the individual, organizational and public policy level that affect both career persistence and the advancement of women in top management positions; namely, factors affecting (1) career persistence (staying at the organization) and (2) career advancement or mobility (getting promoted within the organization). In the study location, Chile, only 32 percent of women "persist", or have a career without interruptions, mainly due to issues with work–family integration and organizational environments with opaque and challenging working conditions. Women who "advanced" in their professional careers represent 30 percent of high management positions in the public sector and 18 percent in the private sector. Only 3 percent of general managers in Chile are women. Women in Chile have limited access and are still not integrated into business power networks. Our findings will enlighten business leaders and public policy-makers interested in designing organizations that retain and promote talented women in top positions.

Keywords: gender; leadership; women in top management; career management; Chile

1. Introduction

In the last decade, talent management of women has become a priority in the agendas of countries, companies and social organizations. Many women are among the half of the active workforce with a college degree. However, this level of representation is not replicated in top management or director-level positions around the globe, as well as in Latin America (Abramo 2004; Zehnder 2016; PwC 2016). As a consequence, the growth potential of companies and countries that do not take advantage of the talents and education of their whole population is reduced.

With the purpose of preventing this loss of female talent and its collaboration to social and economic development, some governments have implemented practices and policies to increase women's participation in senior management. One of these decisions was especially disruptive: In 2008, Norway introduced a quota of 40 percent female participation in the boards of directors of publicly traded, cooperative societies and municipal enterprises.

Even though this norm met great opposition, the results obtained by the law have been quite positive so far. In his book, Dhir (2012) explains that democratization of board of directors in Norway improved decision making and governing board management culture. More precisely, he discovered that the incorporation of 40 percent women generated improvements in the process of decision-making, in prevention of the effects of groupthink, decrease of risk, an increment in the collective intelligence of government boards; it also forces the search and exploitation of women with talent to contribute to the business world in different networks, beyond the traditional corporate power network or the "old boys" (McDonald 2011).

Because of these results, many European countries have imitated or adapted this measure to their national reality. Norway's case was a trigger for new research and a reinterpretation of the role of women in corporate senior management, and of the causes that hindered their ascent to senior management positions.

It is precisely this new context that encouraged the realization of a study exploring all the academic and professional literature on women in senior management generated since 2009. Salvaj and Kuschel's work (Salvaj and Kuschel forthcoming) is based on a comprehensive study of the latest literature on the subject of women in top management. The first objective of their review was to open the "black box" that encloses all the factors that block the road to top management positions for women and visualize each one. From this starting point, their second objective was to map or organize these factors so women and organizations interested in the development of female talent can evaluate their weaknesses and strengths regarding each factor and focus on the design and implementation of concrete actions for the professional development and promotion of women in senior management. We will briefly describe the framework in the next section and then apply it to the Chilean context to reveal practical ways to increase women's participation at the top levels of management (see also the executive report in Supplementary Materials).

2. Framework for Women's Career Success

According to the recent literature review on empirical articles (published from 2009 to 2016) that supported this model, the reasons for the lack of participation of women in senior management are associated with complex and deeply-rooted aspects (Salvaj and Kuschel forthcoming).

2.1. Professional Success as Both Career Persistence and Career Advancement

Academic evidence regarding women in senior management indicate that professional success is associated with two actions: persistence and advancement. Women who are successful in their professional lives are those who persist, i.e., do not interrupt their career and/or advance, i.e., are promoted (Figure 1).

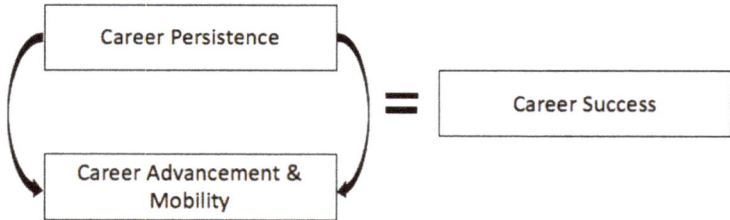

Figure 1. Components of women's professional success. Source: Salvaj and Kuschel (forthcoming).

2.2. Challenge 1: Persistence

A vast group of researchers has focused on understanding the factors that allow women to persist, or avoid interrupting their professional development. Persistence[1] is especially relevant for the case of women who aspire to occupy positions in senior management, since they (in contrast with men) tend

---

[1] When assessing the obstacles to persistence that women face in their professional lives, we find that only 32 percent of women manage to continue, uninterrupted, in the work market, according to data from Casen Survey 2013, Chile.

to face more challenges from hostile male organizational environments (Stamarski and Son Hing 2015; White and Massiha 2016); extended and rigid office schedules (Goldin 2014; Griffiths and Moore 2010); difficulties in integrating family and work life, which frequently drive them to prematurely interrupt or abandon their professional careers (Kossek et al. 2016), even when they are very talented and have great potential for promotion or advancement towards senior management positions (Hewlett and Rashid 2010). Academic papers show that those women in management positions that interrupt their professional activities experience great difficulty returning to the workforce in similar positions to those they held before the interruption, and that many never manage to achieve the same level in terms of position and remuneration (Kulich et al. 2011).

From an individual perspective, women need to set career as a primary—not secondary—domain (Sandberg 2013). Seth (2014) suggested that being career-driven is not a crime and encouraged women to ask for support from their partners and extended family, hire help, delegate both at work and at home, and either reframe the old job or find a part-time job. These strategies allow women to better manage their time and focus on strategic tasks.

From an organizational point of view, the solution might be to redefine job structures and remuneration so they do not punish flexibility (Goldin 2014) to avoid providing an organizationally hostile environment (White and Massiha 2016); to provide performance evaluation systems that are perceived as gender-inclusive (Festing et al. 2015); to avoid a gender pay gap (Blau and Kahn 2000; Hejase and Dah 2014); and to create a clear path for women to advance (Grant Thornton 2015). Finally, organizations can remove barriers and provide a more flexible and inclusive culture by providing intrapreneurial opportunities (i.e., corporate entrepreneurial ventures) for women (Mattis 2000, 2004). These are the organizational factors that need to be considered if organizations seek to retain talent. The individual and organizational factors affecting persistence are synthesized in Figure 2.

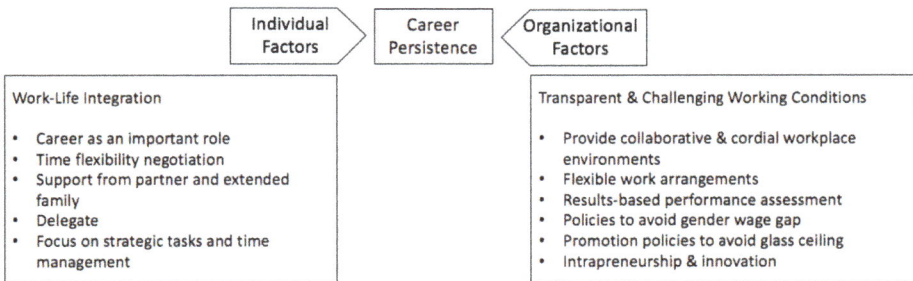

Figure 2. Factors that impact persistence and retention of women in senior management. Source: Salvaj and Kuschel (forthcoming).

2.3. Challenge 2: Advancement and Promotion

A second, larger group of studies have explored the factors that impact the professional advancement of women, i.e., their promotion towards managing positions of greater responsibility. According to the framework, there are factors or causes common to the persistence and advancement and other that are inherent to each of these components of women's professional success. Researchers working in this second group have been more prolific, not only in the number of studies, but also in the listing of factors: individual, organizational, and public policy (Figure 3).

At an individual level, performance and skills are of course critical to advance in organizations. While the literature highlights the technical/business ability to strategize and develop a vision (Appelbaum et al. 2013), most of the skills typically required from those at the top are "soft skills", such as adaptability and acquisition of novel knowledge, skills and capabilities (Ellemers et al. 2012); communication of performance (Grant and Taylor 2014; Ibarra and Obodaru 2009; Ibarra and

Sackley 2011); leadership (Sheaffer et al. 2011); negotiation (Hawley 2014); and networking skills (Brands and Kilduff 2014).

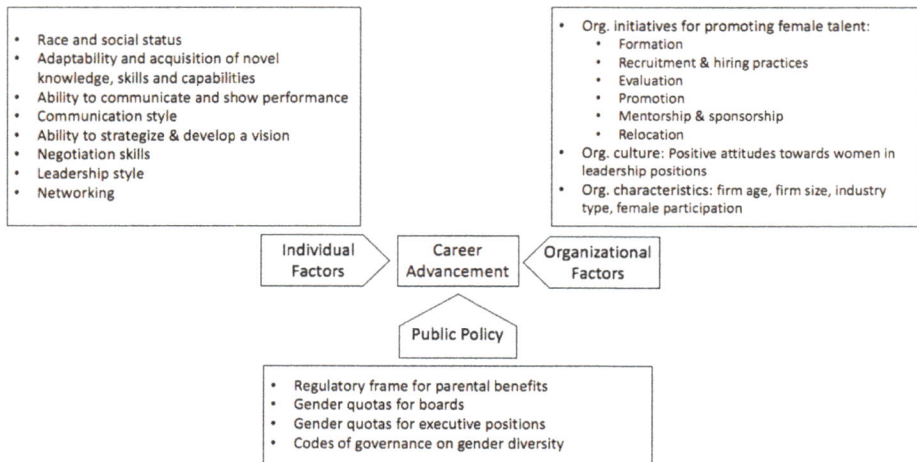

Figure 3. Factors that facilitate the advancement and promotion of female talent toward senior management. Source: Salvaj and Kuschel (forthcoming).

At an organizational level, the culture (generally reinforced by the supervisor), size and industry of the firm all matter, because the presence of a woman on a top management team reduces the likelihood that another woman occupies a position on that team (Dezső et al. 2016). Firms can advance women's careers by implementing diverse formal and informal organizational initiatives, from inclusive hiring practices to providing mentorship. Governments can provide the regulatory framework that can accelerate the cultural change in the attitudes towards women in senior positions.

In these two challenges, the same notions apply: (1) the factors affecting women's success in senior management interact with each other (e.g., as stated by Ibarra (1993), culture and context affects network structure, as well as networking skills or individuals' network development approaches or strategies for managing constraints); (2) each individual must understand how they perform or are assessed in their particular case; and (3) the importance of each of these factors and their relationships with each other are dynamic, i.e., they change constantly, so analyses of the ways in which these factors influence professional advancement must be reviewed periodically.

Persistence and advancement in professional life are related to and feed from each other. Women who persist in their careers have better chances of achieving advancements, but once these are achieved, the challenges and demands of an executive position with greater responsibility increase the difficulty of remaining in the professional career. Thus, persistence is a necessary condition to advance, and while women progress in their profession, persistence become harder. This is demonstrated by the decreasing percentage of women—in all industries—as they climb the organizational pyramid.

3. Results: The Framework Applied to the Chilean Case

3.1. Female Participation in Higher Education and Job Market

Currently in Chile, more than half of graduates from Chilean universities are women (52%), which demonstrates a high education level comparable to that of men (GET Report 2016). However, women tend to access careers with lower social rating, which could affect their legitimacy and status in their professional advancement. Eighty-seven percent of women who have a master's degree work, very close to the 89 percent of men. Additionally, it is estimated that 48.5 percent of women participate in the Chilean workforce (GET Report 2016).

Alarmingly, however, only 32 percent of women have a continuous career (CASEN 2013). This speaks of a low level of persistence in their professional careers because of temporary or permanent leaves. This, in part, explains why female talent only sit on and hold (approximately) 5 percent of boards[2] and 10 percent of senior management positions, according to Tokman (2011).[3] A recent report from the Chilean Civil Service in 2016 indicates that the percentage of positions occupied by women in public senior management reached 30 percent, while the corresponding rate in the private sector was only 18 percent.[4]

These values indicate that in Chile, the incorporation of women in positions of senior management is still low compared to other countries of the OECD, and even other countries in Latin America. It is worth mentioning, though, that the indicators have improved in the last few years, and that there is an important dynamism due to government commitment and the activism of organizations of women in senior management positions.

3.2. Individual Factors and Women in Senior Management Positions

Academic or professional research on the individual factors that facilitate persistence and advancement of women in senior management in Chile is exceedingly scarce. Table 1 presents a summary of the relevant existing research on the factors that affect women's success in senior management. This paper seeks to provide impetus for further research by showing the lack and inviting researchers to investigate each of the factors identified here.

In Chile, accessing positions in organizational leadership depends (greatly) on trust relationships with stakeholders. Salvaj and Lluch (2016) described that, up until the 90s, female chairwomen were associated with the family or controlling group of the company, and that in the last 10 years, this tendency has changed; even though "family chairwomen" are still an important percentage, "professional chairwomen" make up more than 50 percent of women on the boards of the 125 biggest companies in the country. They also analyzed the contact networks of women in managing positions; the results showed that, in addition to being a minority, multiple chairwomen (or those who sit on more than one board) tend to be less common than their male counterparts. Only 30 percent of chairwomen participated in two or more boards, while 40 percent of chairmen were members of at least 2 boards. Additionally, in 2010 and 2013, no chairwoman appeared in the top ten of better-connected chairpeople linked to the board network. In essence, Salvaj and Lluch's results suggest that, first, chairwomen represent a minority at the top levels of company management; and second, chairwomen have smaller networks or lower social capital than chairmen. Another interesting datum from that study is that the three women on the greatest number of boards in Chile in 2010 and 2013 were foreigners. The most popular chairwomen were from English-speaking countries or Colombia, and they were associated with regulated concessions and public services companies with foreign participation. They attained the chair position through their international networks, which allows us to state that none of the local or foreign women serving as chairpeople were completely integrated into the male networks, where the power is Chile is concentrated.

---

[2]   This value varies according to the sample size analyzed by the different studies. The most pessimistic are around 3 percent, while optimistic values are closer to 8 percent.
[3]   http://www.latercera.com/noticia/nacional/2016/03/680-671438-9-mujeres-ocupan-el-30-de-los-cargos-de-alta-direccion-del-sector-publico.shtml.
[4]   https://www.serviciocivil.cl/noticias/sin-categoria/servicio-civil-informa-que-las-mujeres-ocupan-el-30-de-los-cargos-de-alta-direcci-n-p-blica/.

Table 1. Summary of research on the factors that affect women's success in senior management.

	Factors Affecting Women's Success in Top Management	Research in Chile	Examples
Persistence	**Individual factors**		
	Career orientation	Non-existent	
	Negotiation of flexible hours	Non-existent	
	Support from the partner and extended family network	Non-existent	
	Delegation	Non-existent	
	Focus on strategic tasks and time management	Non-existent	
	Organizational factors		
	Intra-entrepreneurship	Non-existent	
	Innovation	Non-existent	
	Flexible work schedules	Limited	Chinchilla et al. (2017)
	Performance evaluation based on results	Non-existent	
	Wage policies that avoid gender pay gap	Non-existent	
	Promotion policies that avoid the glass-ceiling	Limited	Undurraga and Barozet (2015)
	Collaborative and cordial work environments	Non-existent	
	Individual factors		
	Social status	Non-existent	
	Ability to embrace and apply new knowledge and technologies	Non-existent	
	Ability to communicate and make her performance visible	Non-existent	
	Communication styles	Non-existent	
	Ability to articulate a strategic vision for the business	Non-existent	
	Negotiation skills	Non-existent	
	Leadership styles	Non-existent	
	Individual corporate networks	Limited	Salvaj and Lluch (2016)
Advancement and Mobility	**Organizational factors**		
	Organizational initiatives oriented to foster women's talent	Growing	Zehnder (2016)
	– Work and Family		Kelly et al. (2018)
	– Family-supportive supervisor behaviors		Las Heras et al. (2015)
	– Recruitment and hiring practices		Pezoa et al. (2011)
			Taser Erdogan et al. (2018)
			Undurraga and Barozet (2015)
	Organizational culture	Non-existent	
	Organizational characteristics	Limited	Tokman (2011)
	Public initiatives		
	Regulatory frameworks	Limited	Gabaldon (2015)Bosch et al. (2018)
	Quotas and women's participation on boards	Limited	Salvaj and Lluch (2016)
	Quotas and women's participation in executive positions	Non-existent	
	Gender diversity and corporate governance codes	Limited	Gabaldon (2015)

Source: Prepared by the authors.

As described in a report made by the Inter-American Development Bank (IDB) on female leadership in Chile (Gabaldón 2015), another relevant aspect is the quantity and dynamism of executive women's networks which seek to make visible the problem of female participation in senior management positions and to support women in executive positions. These studies have yet to analyze the effectiveness of said gender associations in reference to their capacity to ease access to senior management positions.

3.3. Organizational Factors and Women in Senior Management Positions

Similar to the subject of individual aspects, there is a dearth of research papers that explore the organizational factors that affect the management of female talent in senior management in Chile (see Table 1). We only identified reports from government agencies, consultancy firms and international organisms that describe the current situation of gender inequality.

Most of the previous studies have concentrated around the topic of corporate social responsibility (CSR), human resources best practices, and time flexibility at work (Chinchilla et al. 2017). Arguments have been made for flexibility as a route to more sustainable human development in Chilean society, but it carries the risk of becoming a burden for women if it is defined as a benefit just for them. Although flexible organizational policy (telework, part-time work, etc.) does not make firms sustainable, we acknowledge that it is a good way to start to change; it definitely moves the agenda forward to improve women's participation in the workforce. The gender equality and work-life balance certification for companies (NCh3262), Great Place to Work, and PROhumana foundation have been pushing this agenda forward.

New research is emerging to fill gaps. The ESE Business School is studying the profile of women in leadership positions in Chile (Bosch 2017; Bosch and Riumalló 2017a) and the impact of quotas (Bosch and Riumalló 2017b). Even in light of an "equal pay for equal work" law enacted in Chile (Law 20.348 of 2009[5]), the pay gap between men and women with the same responsibilities is still a reality in all the levels of organizations and in all job categories. It was still on the order of about 30 percent in the higher salary ranks as of 2015, according to estimates by the Dirección de Trabajo del Gobierno de Chile (Directorate of Labor of the Chilean Government) (Dirección del Trabajo 2015). According to the OECD (2018) the gender pay gap between individuals with higher education is 35 percent (OECD average is 26 percent), leaving Chile in 37th place, i.e., last among the OECD countries. In the Chilean public administration, the gender pay gap is 10.4 percent (ILO 2017). Law 20.348 of 2009 for equal remuneration for work of equal value has had little effect, and the rate of official complaints of differences in salary to the Directorate of Labor of the Chilean Government has been low.

In addition to the existence of an important wage gap, Chile also presents low indicators of female participation in senior management. Women in senior management make up only around 6 percent of working women (cf. the OECD average, 20 percent). Women occupy 6 percent of CEO positions, and approximately 12 percent in service management sector. In total, around 22 percent of management positions are held by women. Nevertheless, 36.6 percent of corporate governments still have no female participation (GET Report 2016).

The proportion of women on the boards of the most important companies (IPSA or Top 100 by size) is also very low. The ratio of female representation is never reported as higher than 8 percent (in 2018 it was 6.4 percent: 21 women in the 327 IPSA board of director positions). The report by Zehnder (2016) based on a sample of publicly held companies revealed that approximately half the boards of companies of the IPSA have at least one woman on their board; this could be perceived as progress, but it is far from a perfect situation: These companies may be adopting the strategy of "tokenism". The concept of tokenism refers to the policy and practice of making a superficial

---

[5] Equal remuneration for work of equal value (Law 20.348 of 2009) available at: https://www.leychile.cl/Navegar?idNorma=1003601.

gesture towards the inclusion of members of underprivileged or minority groups (King et al. 2010; Oakley 2000). In this context, an effort to include women on the board usually has the intention of creating the appearance of gender diversity, thereby deflecting accusations of discrimination.

Despite these low indicators, currently, there are no publicly held companies in Chile that have implemented programs or special policies to promote women to management positions (Zehnder 2016). This is in contrast with the cases of Argentina or Colombia, where 43 and 38 percent of companies (respectively) indicate they implement practices to develop female talent for promotion to senior management (Zehnder 2016). The lack of policies in the private sector[6] to ease or support the arrival of women to senior management is in line with Gabaldón (2015) report on the opinion of Chilean businessmen who were inclined toward the voluntary and progressive option of women in senior management, but did not define how they would exploit this process.

3.4. Public Policy Initiatives

There is also a dearth of research papers that explore the effectiveness of and ways in which public policy initiatives affect the management of female talent in senior management in Chile (Table 1). We only identify reports that describe the actions undertaken by the government and the prevailing situation of gender inequality.

The government of Chile has an explicit commitment to the advancement of women in senior management. Demonstrating this commitment, they set up the creation of a Ministerio de la Mujer y Equidad de Género (Ministry of Women and Gender Equality) as well as the Primer Plan de Acción de Responsabilidad Social 2015–2018 (First Action Plan of Social Responsibility 2015–2018) which incorporated concrete measures for the incorporation of gender dimension in companies according to the guidelines of the OECD.

In this framework, and with the objective of leading by example, an initiative that establishes a quota or goal for participation of women in the boards of Empresas del Sistema de Empresas Públicas (SEP) (Companies in the System of Public Companies) of 40 percent—as was done in several European countries (as described by Heemskerk and Fennema 2014) and as proposed by the norms of the EU—is being pushed. In 2015, the percentage reached 29.3 percent in SEP, while in non-SEP public companies, women's participation reached 25 percent (Pulso 2016).

Additionally, the Superintendency of Securities and Insurance (Superintendencia de Valores y Seguros—SVS) adopted measures (norm 386) that demand transparency regarding the number of women sitting on private companies' boards (SVS 2015). Among the changes to corporate government norms are the incorporation of data on the following aspects: diversity on the board (gender, nationality, age and seniority); diversity in general management and other managements that report to this management or to the board; diversity in the organization (gender, nationality, age, seniority); and pay gap by gender. Norm 385 also calls for firms to publicly report the adoption of the aforementioned policies to the diversity of the composition of the board and in the designation of the main executives of the society.

Finally, there is a developed regulatory framework related to gender in Chile. Exceptionally, and leading among American countries, Chile contemplated the "Law of Parental leave of 6 months", in force since 2011. Law 20.545 of 2011[7] modifies the norms on maternity protection and incorporates parent post-birth leave and allows Chilean mothers (and later fathers) to increase the time to be spent with newborn children. During this extension of 12 weeks (for a total of 24), mothers receive

---

[6] This observation is based in the non-existence of research that provide precise data on practices and policies in the private sector. However, it is worth mentioning that, from our experience, we know that there are some companies implementing CSR practices, family-friendly organizational culture, networking programs and non-discriminatory HR practices. Some examples are Movistar, BCI and Grupo Security. There are also programs to equalize female representation in senior management positions in multinational companies with branches in Chile, e.g., Adidas Chile.

[7] Modifies the norms on maternity protection and incorporates parental leave (Law 20.545 of 2011) available at: https://www.leychile.cl/Navegar?idNorma=1030936.

a maternity subsidy, financed by the State, which covers their remuneration during this time, for a maximum of 66 UF[8] monthly. Some companies cover the difference so leave pay matches the salary of women in executive positions with a greater salary. Normally, medium-sized organizations have explicit organization policy regarding how the rest should be covered. In smaller companies, this is open to negotiation between the employee and the employer.

4. Conclusions

This article highlights and integrates the most important factors that affect (allow or hinder) the persistence and advancement of women in top management positions. We map such factors with the intention of providing a practical guide for people interested in managing women's managerial talent within organizations; the factors are presented at the individual, organizational and institutional or government level.

The literature has shown that poor performance is *not* the reason women do not persist or advance in their professional careers, since companies with female executives in senior management positions present, in general, better financial results (Hoobler et al. 2018; Terjesen et al. 2016).

The real factors that would explain the success (or lack thereof) of women on their road to senior management are associated with aspects intrinsic to culture. Culture can change to take advantage of the value provided by female talent. However, all cultural changes require leaders who inspire and allow the advancement of women and can modify the application of policies and practices that aim to close gender gap as well as affirmative actions from both organizations and the government.

4.1. The Model as a Guide of Self-Assesment

This map of factors that impact women's professional development aims to help in self-evaluation (both on the personal and organizational level), identify aspects that could be obstructing female talent development, and aid in the development of design strategies for improvement. It is important to point out that the factors identified here are not all equally relevant in a specific moment, and that for each situation, the combination of factors that explain the difficulty to persist or move forward in professional development is different.

Organizations interested in managing their female talent can self-evaluate and identify the reasons why women leave their jobs prematurely or do not advance professionally. There are diverse organizational factors that affect the retention and promotion of female talent in each company. Therefore, it falls to women individually, as well as to individual organizations, to identify what factors have the greatest impact in each case, and to design practices or policies from the results of this analysis.

4.2. Future Research Opportunities

The existing research gaps in the literature on women's careers in Chile are highlighted in Table 1. Most of the relevant literature regarding Chile addresses the organizational level; there is a huge opportunity to explore the individual factors affecting women's ability to persist and advance in Chilean organizations, and make women's voice visible with more qualitative studies (Undurraga 2013).

Future academic research should close the gap of our understanding on the disadvantages women face at the entry level—especially with the introduction of (a) the gender equality and work-life balance certificate (NCh3262); (b) gender quotas for boards of directors; (c) the future law for universal access to early childhood education, and (d) retirement—with the future modification of retirement age.

---

[8] UF stands for *Unidad de Fomento*, a unit of account used in Chile. The exchange rate between the UF and the Chilean peso is constantly adjusted for inflation (http://www.hacienda.cl/glosario/uf.html) so that the value of the *Unidad de Fomento* remains constant on a daily basis during low inflation. 1 UF = 39.92 USD (18 October 2018).

It would be useful to address how specific contexts might affect women's development within organizations. For example, how women design their careers in STEM, and homosocial, i.e., male-dominated industries (Amon 2017; Holgersson 2013); what barriers women face when leading their own high-growth ventures (Kuschel and Labra 2018); how certain leadership perceptions have evolved over time (Appelbaum et al. 2013); and awareness of how situational factors such as tokenism (King et al. 2010) or the "glass cliff" phenomenon (Bruckmüller and Branscombe 2010) can artificially increase women's participation in senior positions.

4.3. Recommendations for the Chilean Actors

For the case of Chile, it is important to point out that the government is not the only actor that can help reduce gender gap in company leadership. Companies, through concrete actions and practices, play a fundamental role in addressing the current situation. This study shows dynamism in the public sector as well as organizations for women executives. Such efforts are not perceived to be made by companies, perhaps because of a lack of documentation. The lack of management of female talent is depicted in the lack of policies in large companies that ease the arrival of women in senior management would indicate a passive and uninterested position in generating change.

To achieve a greater ratio of women who persist, changes must be made in two directions: (1) facilitation of women's work–life integration; and (2) generation of challenging and interesting environments for them. Without women who persist in an organization, especially in mid-level and high-level positions, women will not be able to reach senior management positions or serve on boards.

Female talent management, necessary to increase economic and social development, must be understood as a process that starts the moment a woman enters a company and continues throughout her work life. Due to factors that affect the development of female talent at the individual, organizational and government levels, multiple actors must coordinate and contribute to this process.

Supplementary Materials: Executive Report (in Spanish: Abriendo la "caja negra": Factores que impactan en la travesía de las mujeres hacia la alta dirección) available online at http://www.redmad.cl/images/estudios/estudio13.pdf.

Author Contributions: K.K. and E.S. contributed to the design and implementation of the research, acquisition of data, analysis and interpretation of the results and to the writing of the manuscript.

Funding: This research was funded by *Red Mujeres para la Alta Dirección* (Women Top Executives Network) in Chile. http://www.redmad.cl/.

Conflicts of Interest: The authors declare no conflict of interest.

References

Abramo, Laís. 2004. ¿Inserción laboral de las mujeres en América Latina: Una fuerza de trabajo secundaria? *Revista Estudos Feministas* 12: 224–35. [CrossRef]

Amon, Mary J. 2017. Looking through the glass ceiling: A qualitative study of STEM women's career narratives. *Frontiers in Psychology* 8: 236. [CrossRef] [PubMed]

Appelbaum, Steven H., Barbara T. Shapiro, Katherine Didus, Tanya Luongo, and Bethsabeth Paz. 2013. Upward mobility for women managers: Styles and perceptions: Part two. *Industrial & Commercial Training* 45: 110–18.

Blau, Francine D., and Lawrence M. Kahn. 2000. Gender Differences in Pay. *Journal of Economic Perspectives* 14: 75–99. [CrossRef]

Bosch, María Jose. 2017. Women in management in Chile. In *Women in Management Worldwide: Signs of Progress*. Edited by Ronald J. Burke and Astrid M. Richardsen. New York: Routledge, pp. 249–67.

Bosch, María-José, and María-Paz Riumalló. 2017a. *Liderazgo Femenino*. Santiago: Cuaderno ESE.

Bosch, María-José, and María-Paz Riumalló. 2017b. *Ley de Cuota*. Santiago: Cuaderno ESE.

Bosch, María José, Carlos J. García Toledo, Marta Manríquez, and Gabriel Valenzuela. 2018. Macroeconomía y conciliación familiar: El impacto económico de los jardines infantiles. *El Trimestre Económico* 85: 543. [CrossRef]

Brands, Raina A., and Martin Kilduff. 2014. Just like a woman? Effects of gender-biased perceptions of friendship network brokerage on attributions and performance. *Organization Science* 25: 1530–48. [CrossRef]

Bruckmüller, Susanne, and Nyla R. Branscombe. 2010. The glass cliff: When and why women are selected as leaders in crisis contexts. *Social Pscychology* 49: 433–51. [CrossRef] [PubMed]

CASEN. 2013. *Encuesta de Caracterización Socioeconómica Nacional*. Santiago: Ministerio de Desarrollo Social.

Chinchilla, Nuria, Mireia Las Heras, María-José Bosch, and María-Paz Riumalló. 2017. *Responsabilidad Familiar Corporativa. Estudio IFREI Chile*. Santiago: ESE.

Dezső, Cristian L., David Gaddis Ross, and José Uribe. 2016. Is there an implicit quota on women in top management? A large-sample statistical analysis. *Strategic Management Journal* 37: 98–115. [CrossRef]

Dhir, Aaron. 2012. *Challenging Boardroom Homogeneity. Corporate Law, Governance, and Diversity*. Cambridge: Cambridge University Press.

Dirección del Trabajo. 2015. La desigualdad salarial entre hombres y mujeres. Alcances y limitaciones de la Ley Nº 20.328 para avanzar en justicia de género. Available online: http://www.dt.gob.cl/portal/1629/articles-105461_recurso_1.pdf (accessed on 20 October 2018).

Ellemers, Naomi, Floor Rink, Belle Derks, and Michelle K. Ryan. 2012. Women in high places: When and why promoting women into top positions can harm them individually or as a group (and how to prevent this). *Research in Organizational Behavior* 32: 163–87. [CrossRef]

Festing, Marion, Lena Knappert, and Angela Kornau. 2015. Gender-Specific Preferences in Global Performance Management: An Empirical Study of Male and Female Managers in a Multinational Context. *Human Resource Management* 54: 55–79. [CrossRef]

Gabaldón, Patricia. 2015. *Chile. Liderazgo Femenino en el Sector Privado*. Washington, DC: Banco Interamericano de Desarrollo.

GET Report. 2016. *Gender, Education and Labor. A Persistent Gap*. Santiago: Comunidad Mujer.

Goldin, Claudia. 2014. A Grand Gender Convergence: Its Last Chapter. *American Economic Review* 104: 1091–119. [CrossRef]

Grant, Anett D., and Amanda Taylor. 2014. Communication essentials for female executives to develop leadership presence: Getting beyond the barriers of understating accomplishment. *Business Horizons* 57: 73–83. [CrossRef]

Grant Thornton. 2015. *Mujeres directivas: En el camino hacia la alta dirección*. London: Grant Thornton International Ltd.

Griffiths, Marie, and Karenza Moore. 2010. Disappearing Women: A Study on Women Who Walked Away from their ICT Careers. *Journal of Technology Management and Innovation* 5: 95–107. [CrossRef]

Hawley, Stacey. 2014. *Rise to the Top: How Woman Leverage Their Professional Persona to Earn More and Rise to the Top*. Pompton Plains: Career Press.

Heemskerk, Eelke M., and Meindert Fennema. 2014. Women on bard: Female board membership as a form of elite democratization. *Enterprise and Society* 15: 252–84. [CrossRef]

Hejase, Ale, and Abdallah Dah. 2014. An Assessment of the Impact of Sticky Floors and Glass Ceilings in Lebanon. *Procedia—Social and Behavioral Sciences* 109: 954–64. [CrossRef]

Hewlett, Sylvia Ann, and Ripa Rashid. 2010. The Battle for Female Talent in Emerging Markets. *Harvard Business Review* 88: 101–8.

Holgersson, Charlotte. 2013. Recruiting Managing Directors: Doing Homosociality. *Gender, Work & Organization* 20: 454–66.

Hoobler, Jenny M., Courtney R. Masterson, Stella M. Nkomo, and Eric J. Michel. 2018. The business case for women leaders: Meta-analysis, research critique, and path forward. *Journal of Management* 44: 2473–99. [CrossRef]

Ibarra, Herminia. 1993. Personal Networks of Women and Minorities in Management: A Conceptual Framework. *The Academy of Management Review* 18: 56–87. [CrossRef]

Ibarra, Herminia, and Otilia Obodaru. 2009. Women and the vision thing. *Harvard Business Review* 87: 62–70, 117. [PubMed]

Ibarra, Herminia, and Nicole Sackley. 2011. *Charlotte Beers at Ogilvy & Mather Worldwide (A)*. Case Study. Boston: Harvard Business School Publishing.

ILO. 2017. Chile: Acortando las brechas de la desigualdad salarial en el sector público. Available online: http://www.ilo.org/santiago/sala-de-prensa/WCMS_555061/lang--es/index.htm (accessed on 20 October 2018).

Kelly, Ciara, Chidiebere Ogbonnaya, and María-José Bosch. 2018. Integrating FSSB with flexibility I-deals: The role of context and domain-related outcomes. *Academy of Management Proceedings* 2018: 11722. [CrossRef]

King, Eden B., Michelle R. Hebl, Jennifer M. George, and Sharon F. Matusik. 2010. Understanding tokenism: Antecedents and consequences of a psychological climate of gender inequity. *Journal of Management* 36: 482–510. [CrossRef]

Kossek, Ellen Ernst, Rong Su, and Lusi Wu. 2016. "Opting Out" or "Pushed Out"? Integrating Perspectives on Women's Career Equality for Gender Inclusion and Interventions. *Journal of Management* 20: 1–27. [CrossRef]

Kulich, Clara, Grzegorz Trojanowski, Michelle K. Ryan, S. Alexander Haslam, and Luc Renneboog. 2011. Who gets the carrot and who gets the stick? Evidence of gender disparities in executive remuneration. *Strategic Management Journal* 32: 301–21. [CrossRef]

Kuschel, Katherina, and Juan-Pablo Labra. 2018. Developing Entrepreneurial Identity among Start-ups' Female Founders in High-Tech: Policy Implications from the Chilean Case. In *A Research Agenda for Women and Entrepreneurship: Identity through Aspirations, Behaviors, and Confidence*. Edited by P. G. Greene and C. G. Brush. Boston: Edward Elgar, pp. 27–44.

Las Heras, Mireia, María-José Bosch, and Anneloes M. L. Raes. 2015. Sequential mediation among family friendly culture and outcomes. *Journal of Business Research* 68: 2366–73. [CrossRef]

Mattis, Mary C. 2000. Women entrepreneurs in the United States. In *Women in Management: Current Research Issues*. Edited by M. J. Davidson and R. J. Burke. Thousand Oaks: Sage, vol. II, pp. 53–68.

Mattis, Mary C. 2004. Women entrepreneurs: Out from under the glass ceiling. *Women in Management Review* 19: 154–63. [CrossRef]

McDonald, Steve. 2011. What's in the "old boys" network? Accessing social capital in gendered and racialized networks. *Social Networks* 33: 317–30. [CrossRef]

Oakley, Judith G. 2000. Gender-based barriers to senior management positions: Understanding the scarcity of female CEOs. *Journal of Business Ethics* 27: 321–34. [CrossRef]

OECD. 2018. *Education at a Glance 2018*. OECD. Available online: http://www.oecd.org/education/education-at-a-glance/ (accessed on 20 October 2018).

Pezoa, Alvaro, María-Paz Riumalló, and Karin Becker. 2011. *Conciliación Familia-Trabajo en Chile*. Santiago: ESE Business School y Grupo Security.

Pulso. 2016. Presencia femenina en directorios de empresas públicas bordeó el 30% en 2015. Date 2016-02-11. Available online: http://www.pulso.cl/economia-dinero/presencia-femenina-en-directorios-de-empresas-publicas-bordeo-el-30-en-2015/ (accessed on 20 October 2018).

PwC. 2016. *International Women's Day: PwC Women in Work Index*. London: PricewaterhouseCoopers LLP.

Salvaj, Erica, and Katherina Kuschel. Forthcoming. Opening the 'black box'. Factors affecting women's journey to senior management positions. A literature review. In *The New Ideal Worker: Organizations between Work-Life Balance, Women and Leadership*. Edited by Mireia Las Heras, Nuria Chinchilla and Marc Grau. Barcelona: IESE Publishing.

Salvaj, Erica, and Andrea Lluch. 2016. Women and corporate power: A historical and comparative study in Argentina and Chile (1901–2010). Paper presented at LAEMOS 2016, Viña del Mar, Chile, April 6–9.

Sandberg, Sheryl. 2013. *Lean in: Women, Work, and the Will to Lead*. New York: Random House.

Seth, Reva. 2014. *The Momshift: Women Share Their Stories of Career Success after Having Children*. Toronto: Random House Canada.

Sheaffer, Zachary, Ronit Bogler, and Samuel Sarfaty. 2011. Leadership attributes, masculinity and risk taking as predictors of crisis proneness. *Gender in Management: An International Journal* 26: 163–87. [CrossRef]

Stamarski, Cailin Susan, and Leanne S. Son Hing. 2015. Gender inequalities in the workplace: The effects of organizational structures, processes, practices, and decision makers' sexism. *Frontiers in Psychology* 6: 1400. [CrossRef] [PubMed]

SVS. 2015. Norma de carácter general N° 386. Available online: http://www.cmfchile.cl/normativa/ncg_386_2015.pdf (accessed on 20 October 2018).

Taser Erdogan, Didem, Maria Jose Bosch, Jakob Stollberger, Yasin Rofcanin, and Mireya Las Heras. 2018. Family motivation of supervisors: Exploring the impact on subordinate work performance. *Academy of Management Proceedings* 2018: 10750. [CrossRef]

Terjesen, Siri, Eduardo Barbosa Couto, and Paulo Morais Francisco. 2016. Does the presence of independent and female directors impact firm performance? A multi-country study of board diversity. *Journal of Management & Governance* 20: 447–83.

Tokman, Andrea. 2011. *Mujeres en puestos de responsabilidad empresarial.* Gobierno: Servicio Nacional de la Mujer.

Undurraga, Rosario. 2013. Mujer y trabajo en Chile: ¿qué dicen las mujeres sobre su participación en el mercado laboral? In *Desigualdad en Chile: La continua relevancia del género.* Edited by C. Mora. Santiago: Ediciones Universidad Alberto Hurtado, pp. 113–41.

Undurraga, Rosario, and Emmanuelle Barozet. 2015. Pratiques de recrutement et formes de discrimination des femmes diplômées—le cas du Chili. *L'Ordinaire des Amériques* 219. Available online: http://journals.openedition.org/orda/2357 (accessed on 20 October 2018).

White, Jeffry L., and G. H. Massiha. 2016. The retention of Women in Science, Technology, Engineering and Mathematics: A framework for persistence. *International Journal of Evaluation and Research in Education* 5: 1–8. [CrossRef]

Zehnder, Egon. 2016. *2016 Egon Zehnder Latin American Board Diversity Analysis.* Zurich: Egon Zehnder International, Inc.

administrative
sciences

MDPI

Article

Adoption of Gender-Responsive Budgeting (GRB) by an Italian Municipality

Giovanna Galizzi *, Gaia Viviana Bassani and Cristiana Cattaneo

Department of Management, Economics and Quantitative Method, University of Bergamo, Bergamo 24127, Italy; gaia.bassani@unibg.it (G.V.B.); cristiana.cattaneo@unibg.it (C.C.)
* Correspondence: giovanna.galizzi@unibg.it

Received: 30 September 2018; Accepted: 31 October 2018; Published: 3 November 2018

Abstract: Over the past few decades, many governments throughout the world have promoted gender-responsive budgeting (GRB). With its focus on equality, accountability, transparency and participation in the policy-making process, GRB shares some relevant principles with public governance that call governments at national and subnational levels to rethink their roles in the whole economic system. This worldwide political and managerial interest does not find sufficient space in academic discussion, mainly in terms of public administration and management studies. Adopting an interpretative approach, the present study aims to investigate how an Italian municipality has involved stakeholders in the GRB process. The case study shows that, when GRB is fully developed, the stakeholders involved are both internal and external, and these multiple actors, in pursuing gender equality, cooperate to achieve a common, public aim. In this way, GRB gives effectiveness to the public decision-making process, contributing to greater incisiveness in the local government's management and creation of a gender-sensitive governance process.

Keywords: gender-responsive budget; public governance; gender equality; stakeholder engagement

1. Introduction

Over the past few decades, many governments throughout the world have promoted initiatives to advance gender equality (Budlender 2002). More recently, European institutions have included gender topics among the European strategies for sustainable development, together with the fight against poverty and social exclusion (Council of the European Union 2006).

Owing to the predominance of economic criteria in policy design, one of the goals of gender initiatives is to criticise the neutrality of public budgets (i.e., the gender blindness of budgets, Elson (1998)), which ignore the differing impacts of revenues and expenditures on men and women because of their divergent gender roles in society (Elson 1999).

Thus, the expression "women's budget" (Budlender 2000) and, in recent times, gender-responsive budgeting (GRB), denote a national or local government budget that integrates the gender perspective into all phases of the budget cycle. The GRB aims to foster greater gender equality, efficiency and effectiveness, as well as transparency, accountability and the participation of civil society in the budget decision-making process.

Accordingly, in the gender framework, citizens are both beneficiaries and agents of the process whereby governments, at all levels, redesign their policy-making mechanisms and their accountability systems. As the GRB involves stakeholders and ensures that policy design and the allocation of resources meet the wide variety of citizens' needs, it must be considered as an important tool of public governance (Brody 2009).

Nevertheless, GRB is under-investigated in the public administration and management streams of literature. As Rubin and Bartle (2005, p. 260) have pointed out, "almost all of the research related to gender-responsive budgeting has taken a normative approach, promoting its use as a way to advance gender equality". While the authors examined "the potential of GRB for budget reform, following a long line of efforts to effectuate changes in the budget decision-making process" (Rubin and Bartle 2005, p. 260), the present study aims to investigate how the adoption of the GRB affects public governance and management through stakeholder engagement, in the awareness that "critical to the success of gender-responsive budgeting is the buy-in of stakeholders inside and outside government" (Rubin and Bartle 2005, p. 269).

The empirical focus of the paper is the municipality of Bologna, which introduced a GRB in 2008, incorporating the gender perspective into the planning stage of the budget cycle. The study sheds light on the enhancement of stakeholder engagement throughout the entire GRB process.

This paper contributes to the extant literature in three ways. First, it emphasises the GRB as a public governance tool with an in-depth case study. Second, it employs the stakeholder engagement strategy as a framework to investigate how GRB may enhance the participation of various stakeholders for the equal allocation of resources dedicated to men and women. Third, it highlights the way in which stakeholder participation in the GRB practices promotes the accountability of decision-making mechanisms in public domains. The study contributes to the present Special Issue by supporting the idea that the adoption of a stakeholder engagement strategy in forwarding GRB could enhance gender equality policy promoted by both public and private organisations, and addressing the challenges of diversity and gender inequalities.

The article is structured as follows: The second section illustrates the review of literature and the third one presents the conceptual framework used for the case study analysis; the fourth section regards methodology; the fifth section examines empirics from the case study; the sixth section is dedicated to the discussion of the results; and the seventh section proposes some concluding remarks.

2. Literature Review: Gender Equality, Gender-Responsive Budgeting, and Stakeholder Involvement

Gender equality is a long-established priority for the entire world. Since 1957, when The Treaty of Rome incorporated the right of men and women to equal pay for equal work, and since 1979, when the UN General Assembly adopted the Convention on the Elimination of All the Forms of Discrimination against Women, international agencies and national governments have committed themselves to advancing gender equality.

In 1995, the Fourth World Conference on Women, held in Beijing (Beijing Platform for Action 1995), called for governments to incorporate the perspective of gender equality at all stages and all levels of public policy-making, including the budgetary processes. Thus, GRB requires that the gender perspective be considered in every phase of budgetary decisions and in the drawing up of budgets. Before this awareness, different concepts ("women's budgets", "women's budget statements", "gender-sensitive budgets", "gender-responsive budgets" and "gender budget analysis") were used to describe the process of integration between gender and public budgets. Aiming to integrate gender into the decision-making process regarding expenditures and revenues, GRB indicates a government budget (at both national and local levels) (Council of Europe 2005) that incorporates a gender perspective in any or all parts of its process, in order to improve gender equality among its community (Budlender et al. 2002; Budlender and Hewitt 2002, 2003; Sharp 2002, 2003).

Therefore, GRB denotes a process that moves through two stages: (i) gender analysis or auditing; and (ii) gender budgeting. The former is related to the conceptual and analytical work done in order to assess the impact of budgets on different groups of women, men, girls, and boys. The latter refers to the ultimate goal of gender initiatives, namely a gender-aware formulation of the budget (Hofbauer Balmori 2003; Sharp 2002). The first stage of the process has raised awareness of gender issues and the government's accountability in terms of its commitment to gender equality (Sharp 2002, p. 90) by devising frameworks (Elson 2002; Sharp 2003) and tools for analysis (Budlender and Hewitt 2003; Sharp 2002), guidelines to support governments in their initiatives (Budlender et al. 1998; Budlender and Hewitt 2003; Hofbauer Balmori 2003), and gender-sensitive indicators (Beck 1999; Rubery et al. 2002). Although most GRB initiatives are still at this stage of the GRB process (Budlender et al. 2002; Budlender and Hewitt 2002; Rubin and Bartle 2005), there are some instances in which gender has been introduced into planning activities as a cross-cutting criterion (Budlender 2007; Sharp and Dev 2004) in an attempt "to bridge the gap between gender-sensitive budget analysis and the formulation of gender-sensitive budgets" (Hofbauer Balmori 2003, p. 45).

Gender budget exercises have been undertaken at international, national, and subnational levels of government in developed and developing countries (e.g., France, Sweden, Norway, Italy, the Netherlands, Uganda, and Tanzania), being coordinated and led by both governments (e.g., Australia and France) and civil society groups (e.g., UK, South Africa, and Tanzania) (Budlender et al. 1998, 2002). Unlike the majority of experiences worldwide, in Italy GRB is adopted by local governments, which perform a central role in regard to gender issues by designing policies, actions, and services to enhance gender equality in their communities.

Despite the governmental commitment to gender equality, there is a lack of substantial progress in reducing gender inequalities, particularly due to the predominance of economic criteria in policy design (Hofbauer Balmori 2003). In fact, macroeconomic frameworks do not consider the differences between men and women, as well as between different groups of men and women. As a result, the economic and statistical models are gender-blind, and the budget is considered to be a gender-neutral policy tool, thus ignoring the fact that a budget has a differentiated impact on men and women, because of their diverse gender roles in society (Elson 1999). Meanwhile, public budgets could be the main tools in transforming and redressing existing gender inequalities. Hence, GRB forms a specific process for advancing toward equality through the allocation of public resources.

Therefore, the main aim of the GRB process is to contest the alleged neutrality of government budgets (Elson 1998) by introducing and pursuing the goals of equality, efficiency, transparency, participation, and awareness in public economic policies. Not taking into account the differences between men and women means that the policies adopted are not neutral toward citizens.

The GRB aims to allocate resources deemed appropriate for the needs and priorities of men and women—needs and priorities that differ in nature—to allow men and women to achieve equality of outcomes from economic policies. While greater equality between men and women has been indubitably the most evident objective—and the one most frequently cited (at least initially) to justify GRB—other goals have arisen (Himmelweit 2002). The first of them is efficiency, to which governments and local authorities have grown sensitive in recent years. Because gender analysis requires knowledge of the gender differences among the population, it seeks: (i) to obtain a better use of resources, especially those, like unpaid work, not measured by economic and statistical indicators, so that there is a match between the demand expressed by the population and the supply of services by the government agency; and (ii) to show how apparently gender-neutral policy decisions have differing economic and social consequences for the male and female components of the population.

The adoption of GRB makes it possible to assess the effectiveness of economic policy measures on women and men, evaluating the consistency between outcomes achieved and pre-established objectives. In particular, adopting the gender perspective, the evaluation of effectiveness aims to verify whether the outcomes achieved by public policies meet the needs of both men and women.

The GRB highlights the link between governmental commitment toward gender equality and their responsibility to define a gender-sensitive form of collection and use of public resources (accountability). On the one hand, by pointing out the links between gender equality and efficiency and effectiveness, GRB makes institutions more aware of the consequences of their decisions on civil society, thus giving citizens a new tool to evaluate the use of public resources. On the other hand, GRB requires the involvement of civil society in the process of public policy analysis (Osborne et al. 2008).

The experience of GRB has seen an increase in the involvement of several actors (women's associations, non-governmental organisations, and civil society in general) who have exerted pressure to see gender equality substantially recognised.

Despite its improvement, to date there is still no reference standard for GRB models and a variety of analytical tools can be used (Budlender et al. 1998; Elson 1998). In the same way, there is still no reference for which actors to involve in the process. As mentioned by Osborne et al. (2008), there is a dichotomy between "expert-bureaucratic" and "participative-democratic" models of gender mainstreaming initiatives according to the extent to which the models incorporate strategies for community participation.

Evidence from gender initiatives worldwide (Budlender et al. 2002) demonstrates that the active involvement of many actors (experts on gender issues as well as civil society) enables GRB to be more effective (Krafchik 2002; Zuckerman 2005), i.e., to improve gender equality within society. The involvement of stakeholders also improves the transparency and accountability of the budgeting process by inducing governments to provide information on the use of public money, which is normally not available, as well as to ensure continuity of the practice, avoiding its interruption due to political change, as documented by Sharp and Broomhill (2002) in the Australian case study.

As GRB is increasingly seen as a proper tool for good governance (United Nations Development Programme UNDP; Elson 2006; Hewitt and Mukhopadhyay 2002; Sharp 2002), the relevance of stakeholder engagement has increased. According to academic studies on governance, the distinctive features of public governance can be summarised as follows: stakeholder involvement in the definition and implementation of public policy (Bovaird 2005; Bovaird and Löffler 2002); coordination of collaborative relations internally and externally to public administration (Elander 2002); and orientation toward the outside, which introduces the notion of the public administration's accountability to its citizens (Meneguzzo 1997).

Dialogue among stakeholders constitutes the basis of this framework; individuals and organisations may thus exercise power over decisions concerning their interests and well-being. This continuous communication shapes rules and practices in decision-making and opens a wide debate on collective problems; a debate that was usually confined to public authorities. The engagement of stakeholders in order to change policy priorities and budgets (so as to enhance gender equality) makes it possible to locate GRB within the public governance scenario. The next section investigates this framework.

3. The Conceptual Framework

"Since the establishment of the paradigm of public governance (. . .), stakeholders' mapping and engagement have become a well-established practice in policy making." (Barreca 2012). As described in the previous section, a common feature of GRB and public governance principles is stakeholder involvement mainly during the design and implementation phases.

To understand how stakeholders engage in GRB, it is necessary to identify (map) them and determine their importance to the organisation. Some studies have identified three categories of stakeholders: interface stakeholders (board members); internal stakeholders (managers, employees); and external ones (funders, beneficiaries, suppliers, competitors, partners, and others) (Van Puyvelde et al. 2012; Savage et al. 1991). Although most studies concerning stakeholder theory have been developed in for-profit organisations, over time some authors have tried to classify various non-profit stakeholders (Ben-Ner and Van Hoomissen 1991; Bryson 2004; Van Puyvelde et al. 2012).

Adopting Freeman's (Freeman 1984) broad definition of stakeholders, we consider them to be all groups or individuals who may affect or are affected by achievement of the public administration's gender policy. At the same time, the definition and description of the level of engagement implicitly identify the importance of each of them. According to Pedersen (2006, p. 140), stakeholder engagement, or stakeholder dialogue (for some authors), entails "the involvement of stakeholders in the decision-making processes that concern social and environmental issues".

GRB practices require different involvement in each phase of the implementation process. According to the models of participation described by Osborne et al. (2008), in an "expert-bureaucratic" system, probably just one group of stakeholders (who lead the process) is involved in the decision-making process. In this approach, gender experts carry out only an impact assessment of the gender implications of policies and activities. By contrast, the "participative-democratic" model entails co-participation in governance mechanisms and systems from the beginning of the process, thus incorporating the widespread consultation and participation of multiple interest groups.

Despite the presence of these different approaches, the distinction is not at all clear due to the "complexities and ambiguities of the consultation exercise" (Osborne et al. 2008). In order to clarify the participation process, Noland and Phillips (2010) identified ethical strategic engagement as a way to integrate moral involvement with a business strategy. This trend goes beyond Habermasian scholars that ensure communication uncorrupted by power differences and strategic motivations. In public organisations, business strategies are far from pursuing financial goals, although these are prerequisites for citizens' welfare. The community is implicitly involved in local government, but participation cannot be taken for granted when the administration adopts voluntary practices. Similar practices also require the voluntary participation of stakeholders interested in gender issues. The sharing strategy assures free discussion about gender values and strategies in order to furnish sustainable welfare policies and services. Ethical strategic engagement has the same basis as a "participative-democratic" gender mainstreaming strategy.

According to frameworks (Bryson et al. 2012; Cumming 2001; Foo et al. 2011; Nabatchi 2012), stakeholder participation is not just a statement; it is also a specific process organised by the public administration. Clearly, the adoption of a practice (i.e., the GRB tool) requires a procedure that follows a change in stakeholder engagement from one-way communication (i.e., from public administration to stakeholders) to two-way communication (i.e., from/to public administration and from/to stakeholders).

Nabatchi (2012) suggests a process whose initial phase involves only communication to stakeholders on the project undertaken (i.e., the information step). The following steps involve a two-way dialogue, although the strategy, method, and timing of the process are in the public administration domain until the collaboration phase. The collaborative relationship fosters empowerment behaviours, thereby increasing the level of stakeholder confidence and responsibility concerning the entire process of implementation and its outcome.

The promotion of decentralised decision-making and participation by citizens (i.e., women and men) is not a costless process, but it ensures that policies "might be more realistically grounded in citizen preferences" (Irvin and Stansbury 2004). In GRB terms, this means that the entire community and other organisations may actively participate in the *mise en oeuvre* of gender policies, guaranteeing the principles of the welfare state. The existing literature underlines the complexity of the GRB incremental process, describing the audit phase and the budget phase as the opposite ends of a sort of continuum. The features of gender auditing are distant from those of a review of principles and policies; but when public administrations are willing to share ex-ante decision-making acts (i.e., the budgeting phase), this means that the auditing and budgeting phases generate an interactive cycle that increases the level of accountability.

4. Materials and Methods

Contrary to what happened in other countries, where central governments have performed the role of promoting actors, in Italy gender initiatives have been promoted at the subnational level. They therefore involve provincial administrations, municipalities, and, more rarely, regional governments (Bettio et al. 2002; Villagomez 2004).

To carry out the present study, we adopted the ground theory principles (Corbin and Strauss 1990) by first defining the phenomenon to analyse and then identify an appropriate site of research. The Italian municipality in which our study took place, Bologna, has 390,000 inhabitants, while its metropolitan area has a population of about 1 million. Bologna has a long-standing social tradition evidenced by numerous non-governmental organisations and voluntary associations working in the urban context. Therefore, it is not by chance that Bologna was the first Italian local government to produce a social report. Often, in the Italian and European context, Bologna has been a well-known entity for specific initiatives, such as in the fields of education and the elderly. As Bologna has promoted the GRB initiative since 2005, it provides distinctive evidence in the European area. In 2014, during the Forum of Public Administration supported by the Italian central government, Bologna was officially recognised as one of the well-developed gender experiences. In relation to gender issues, Bologna is undertaking both stages of the GRB process (auditing and budgeting), including these practices in regular accounting and control procedures.

Gathering data from multiple sources should allow for a deep comprehension of a phenomenon that is developed in practice but under-investigated by academia (Yin 2003). The present research began with a documentary analysis (secondary data) of official reports, policy guidelines, public statements, electronic helpdesk records, and other GRB documents available in the public domain (the local government's website). The documentary data collection and analysis took place between October 2011 and June 2013.

The documentary analysis was useful for drawing up an interview agenda (primary data) with the key actors involved in the GRB process. Semi-structured interviews with the internal technical staff who led the project were carried out face to face, by telephone and e-mail between April and June 2013 (Kvale 1996; Morgan and Symon 2004; Hunt and McHale 2007). These interviews made it possible to gather further documents and information about the methods, strategies, and timing for the involvement of stakeholders, as well as the decisions and actions resulting from their engagement and the agenda that allowed for the implementation of gender budgeting. All the interviews have been recorded and fully transcribed.

For the interpreting process, we combined open and literature coding based on the analysis of documents, interviews, and notes. In particular: (i) each interview was read and listened to several times by each author in order to become familiar with the text and eliminate the non-relevant parts of text, and all the researchers got a sense of the whole situation from reading all the transcriptions and documents; (ii) each author listed the topics that considered the substance of the information described by the actors/documents; (iii) later, the researchers discussed this preliminary coding to compare and share their intuition and interpretation, and a joined and selected list emerged; (iv) furthermore, each author carefully read the extant literature, taking notes about topics regarding GRB features and stakeholder involvement in GRB; and finally, (v) all the researchers returned to the data, identifying the final coding to use for the analysis of the case study.

5. Results

The municipality of Bologna was the first Italian local government to issue social reporting (in 1997, see Marcuccio and Steccolini 2009), while its gender initiatives fit the track of the Gender Feasibility Study published by the Emilia Romagna Region in 2001. The mandatory programme for the years 2004–2009 emphasised gender issues as public values and incorporated gender into programme guidelines, while in 2005 the municipality published a gender feasibility study focused on services for children.

> The short-term aim is to recognise that the municipality of Bologna requires a unitary process, both of steerage and organization, which adopts and implements this approach [gender mainstreaming]. This process, still entirely to be constructed, must necessarily work crosswise (. . .). But the introduction of gender difference policies wants to be more: it wants also to be an autonomous driver of policies and action in all fields and all activities (. . .), assuming and revising the traditional powers of government, administrative and managerial, in regard to difference policies, from a standpoint entirely addressed to the future and change in the life of the city. (Municipality of Bologna 2005, p. 100)

Nonetheless, only since 2008 has GRB been a stable component of the Forecasting Planning Report. Since the issue of 2008, GRB has employed the same social report matrix to reinforce the link between social sustainability reports, actions, and services with a direct or indirect impact on equality between men and women.

> The adoption of the Gender Budget is addressed to the need of visibility about the impact of the distribution of resources (e.g., financial, for services, opportunities, participation, etc.) on the life-conditions and relative disadvantage of women. (. . .) GRB is a tool that promotes the alignment between gender policy and the local government values fostering effective and efficient actions. Moreover, the aim to make Gender Budget as a managerial 'routine' is part of a more general commitment to social auditing as an essential means to plan and to connect with civil society (. . .). (Municipality of Bologna 2008, p. 6)

From the outset, GRB has been conceived as a participatory process with the involvement of internal and external stakeholders.

> The process has been characterized by close linkage with the municipality's mandatory programme and not only procedural attention to participation by leading gender-policy players: the city executive committee and council, associations and boards. (Municipality of Bologna 2008, p. 9)

Gender auditing initiatives have been developed with the involvement of the mayor and his board, stressing the political commitment of the process. The Elected Women's Commission and the internal staff have fostered the methodological formulation of the process and women's associations in the city have been consulted to assess the direct and indirect impacts of public expenditures.

> (. . .) 4. The Commission submits to the Council proposals and observations on issues with a bearing on the female condition and that may be developed into equal opportunities policies. To this end, it may consult women's associations, community organizations, and experts with proven competence and/or professional experience.
>
> 5. The Municipal Executive Committee may obtain a Commission opinion about the guidelines containing the actions addressed to the female population. (Statute of the (Municipality of Bologna 1991, art. 22) "Elected Women's Commission")

According to these purposes, the internal staff organised an open seminar (held on 9 November 2007) with the participation of women's associations engaged with the Bologna Women's Network. During the seminar, priorities were set for female issues, and the proposal was made to select a district in the city as a "laboratory" for the development of a gender budget (formal meeting notes). The observations and findings from the seminar were borne in mind; in fact, in 2010 a first attempt was made to draw up a gender budget in Bologna's Savena district.

At the beginning of 2013, the municipal council decided to formulate a GRB for 2014, linking it with the performance management cycle in which each public institution measures and assesses its performance with regard to its organisational units and its employees, stressing internal and external accountability. Accordingly, the GRB process is developed by the Planning Department, which manages all accounting flows and statistical data, supporting the Directorate-General in the performance management cycle as well as in the participatory process at the central and suburb levels.

The Planning Department's choice is of strategic value given its role in the management of decision-making processes on the budget, social reporting and public participation, as well as its links with the administration as a whole. Recent years have seen substantial cutbacks in the resources available to the municipality, thus raising issues, more forcefully than in the past, of how to select lines of action and to allocate resources. At the same time, the gender budget was drawn up in light of experience, incorporating the gender perspective into planning activities. According to this new scenario, the GRB approach is now a strategic tool driving the allocation of public resources, inducing the local government to redesign the GRB process and its various phases.

(. . .) We can't allow this thing [the wastage of resources] to go on any longer . . . This is a cultural revolution . . . But when we take a step (. . .) we mustn't lose time (. . .) this project should be part of a process, so it must start from the awareness of what it means to plan at municipal level, and from there make claims together, and this means work for them [associations] as well. (Electronic Interview 14 May 2013)

Consistently with the performance management cycle, the construction of the gender budget was preceded by the reclassification of all the Planning Department's activities in accordance with the gender perspective. This reclassification significantly increases both the gender and overall accountability of the municipality in terms of the actors involved, responsibilities, resources allocated, and outcomes.

After this reclassification, the gender budgeting process involves the relevant stakeholders in the selection ("call of ideas", Interview 21 June 2013) of the projects to be given priority in gender terms, which are then used as the basis for constructing the gender budget. The main actors involved in the process are:

- Political actors: executive committee and council, Elected Women's Commission, including the female members of district councils;
- Technical actors: Planning Department; and
- Community actors: relevant and representative associations.

The community actors are selected from the associations enrolled in the municipal register whose statutes make specific reference to gender. Hence, unlike in the past, exclusively "female" associations are not selected; rather, in order to expand the dialogue, associations sensitive to "gender" issues (from the feminist perspective to the gender perspective) are chosen.

Associations are chosen if they have consolidated relations with the municipality in terms of financial and other resources made available to them by the latter (for instance, public premises for use by the associations). Representativeness—in terms of their capacity to impact the community—is assessed by the department heads, councillors, and the presidents of the district councils. Because they work in close contact with the associations, they are better able to assess their potential impact.

(. . .) we have one thousand six hundred associations working in the community, each of which does something or other (. . .) It's obvious that we know which the hundred associations with important representativeness are (. . .) and we can also tell from the accounting figures on transfers to these associations (. . .) selection of the hundred important associations is also made by the department heads, the councilors who have relations with the sector, the presidents of the district councils. (Interview 21 June 2013)

This is therefore a qualitative and quantitative enlargement of the stakeholders involved. However, the change also concerns the relationship with the latter. In fact, the Planning Department required the associations to participate in the selection of projects to be included in the GRB. Moreover, the associations participated in implementing the projects selected, by contributing their own resources. Since the intent is to work concretely on the projects, the involvement concerns associations willing to establish a partnership with the municipality according to a horizontal subsidiarity approach. The head of the Planning Department argued that:

the associations must realize that they are not there to ask what we can do for them, but (. . .) they must play their part as well (. . .) The objective is to specify the extent already in the gender budgeting phase as policies are devised (. . .) and we expect to work together (. . .) and get involved, not just asking us for money (which we don't have any more) but bringing us commitments and ideas. (Interview 21 June 2013)

This approach—profoundly different from the previous relationship—also affects the associations, because it induces them to reconsider and assess proposals to submit to the public administration in relation to their resources and priorities. This obliges them to acquire greater awareness of the gender impact of their activities by reconsidering their projects in gender terms. While for the "female" associations this process is rather natural, for all the others it entails a more profound re-thinking. In this regard, a member of the planning team said (with reference to social collectives):

> I expect them to take account of gender in the planning phase (…) they should conceive their activities bearing in mind that they have differing impacts on men and women (…) they should involve the cultural point of view in their activities (…) they'd give great added value to their association and the city. (Interview 21 June 2013)

The selection of projects by associations is influenced by the fact that they must then make their resources available for those projects. On the one hand, this constrains the activities of associations, but on the other it enables them to undertake projects in concert with the local government in terms of both design and implementation.

6. Discussion

The case study evidences the transition described by Hofbauer Balmori (2003) and Sharp (2002) from a gender auditing to a gender budgeting approach, with the increasing incorporation of gender topics into the planning and allocation of resources by the municipality. This process, partly stimulated by the rationing of state transfers, entails a public-private revision of the relationship; but it also gives the gender budget greater incisiveness in the local government's management. The shift from the assessment of the gender impacts (direct and indirect) of public policies to their ex-ante definition in gender terms implies a greater involvement of stakeholders. The executive committee and council have given strategic value to the gender budget as a means of enabling better management of increasingly scarce resources.

Moving from gender auditing to gender budgeting entails a change of strategy by the municipality, which provides the basis for incorporating ethics (value and moral principles) into every aspect of its decision-making process (Noland and Phillips 2010). The actors who manage this adoption process are internal and external stakeholders that, in pursuing gender equality, cooperate to achieve a common public aim.

Consequently, stakeholder involvement shifts from being internal to external in that it includes a larger number of actors, and especially those with a different relationship with the municipality. It seems that the adoption of GRB has followed two strategies: in the first phase, the "expert-bureaucratic" model prevailed; in the second, the "participative-democratic" strategy drives the development of the gender budget. In this regard, the GRB developed in the municipality of Bologna demonstrates the existence of a third way that combines aspects of both these models. In most cases, Italian GRBs provide for the use of a mixed method that enhances the participation of gender experts located generally within and outside institutions (Equal Opportunities Department; Elected Women's Commission) and the contribution of the community as represented by civic groups and voluntary associations with an interest in gender issues, i.e., the GRB stakeholders.

With reference to Figure 1, gender auditing foresees a stakeholder engagement based on communication, or indeed consultation, as evidenced by the first experience of Bologna. In fact, the latter has issued information on the principle followed, but it has also addressed the needs of citizens through a two-way communication. GRB requires greater involvement and cooperation in the design and implementation of projects, as highlighted by the development of the initiative in Bologna. The process described above, by which associations are selected and involved in the choice of significant gender policies, and the manner in which they are implemented, moves in this direction. It has now reached the "collaborate" stage involving the co-production of services in which public resources and those of associations are coordinated to implement projects whose strategic value is jointly shared.

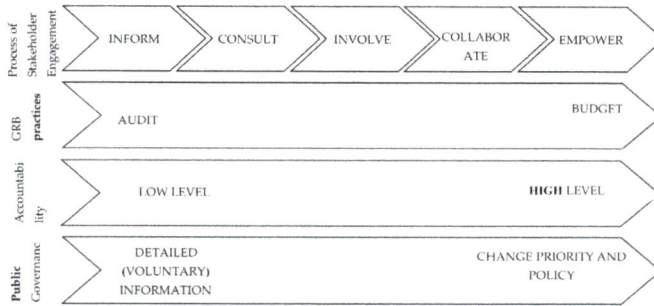

Figure 1. Summary of the above considerations on stakeholder engagement.

Moving toward collaboration, and then to potential empowerment, requires the administration to give marked strategic and operational clarity both to its interior and in its relations with stakeholders. The complex gender-based reclassification of the activities and projects undertaken by the municipality of Bologna configures a pervasive accountability procedure that lays the bases for greater transparency of processes, and their joint assessment with internal and external stakeholders. The concept of professional accountability, as defined by Gray and Jenkins (1993), can therefore be found, according to which communication toward the outside to create some sort of social pact between local governments and the external environment acquires consensus and resources.

As Foo wrote (Foo et al. 2011, p. 712), "Co-production by local administrations and stakeholders is congruent with the recent government policies to facilitate users' choice and personalisation in public service provision. In addition, involving stakeholders in co-production may increase their confidence and so lead to increased participation". The elements cited in the quotation quite clearly express one of the distinctive features of public governance, which—by involving external stakeholders through a participative process—defines new forms of strategic dialogue and collaboration in the management of resources. This requires the administration to move from voluntary reports to a change in priorities, and to policies co-governed by the public administration and stakeholders on participative bases. Consequently, accountability must be strengthened and must give account to activities from their design to their implementation.

As this paper has sought to show, GRB in Bologna has impacted governance and planning not only by the municipality, but also by the associations themselves, doing so in a potentially virtuous circle, which may generate projects of real importance for the community. Hence, the thoughts of Noland and Phillips (2010) receive valid support because the engagement of stakeholders must be integral to local governments' strategies without a distinction between morality and strategy.

7. Conclusions

Presently, public governance agendas indicate equality as one of the most important goals in creating opportunities for all citizens. The present study contributes to the existing literature as it investigates how GRB may be a tool to fulfil the public governance agenda.

Equality is accomplished when the decision-making process is aware of the different needs, characteristics, and priorities of men and women. If governments at national or local levels insist on gender-blind budgets, they will not be able to achieve the goal of an efficient and effective allocation of resources. In terms of accountability, GRB makes institutions more aware of the consequences of their decisions on civil society, thus giving citizens a new tool to evaluate the use of public resources.

Furthermore, the involvement of stakeholders from the outset supports a dialogue on how local governments decide and act in promoting activities addressed on gender issues and closer to citizens' concerns. This entails an analysis of relevant stakeholders (which would guarantee citizens' needs and the community's well-being) and a shared process of cultural change. In other words, it has sought to clarify the communication process in stakeholder engagement because participative processes require increased involvement in order to guarantee accountability for decision-making acts and outcomes. The municipality of Bologna has provided useful evidence of the positive impact of GRB on gender policy.

First, stakeholder engagement creates, in various stages of GRB adoption, both a cycle of accountability and a co-production of (gender) policies and activities. Second, the process with which associations and other stakeholders have been selected and included for the choices of these policies and activities has an impact on their effectiveness. Third, GRB within a stakeholder engagement strategy addresses the challenges of diversity and gender inequalities. In this way, GRB gives effectiveness to the public decision-making processes, contributing to a greater incisiveness of the local government's management and creating gender-sensitive governance processes.

Because there is little existing knowledge on GRB practices and public governance mechanisms, this study encourages research in Italian and international public settings. Other examples of the use of stakeholder theory in GRB initiatives are also desirable.

From the practical point of view, this paper underlines the need to involve stakeholders in the entire process of GRB adoption, promoting a participative gender mainstreaming strategy as the basis for an in-depth recasting of public policies and activities.

Author Contributions: Conceptualisation, G.G., G.V.B. and C.C.; Methodology, G.V.B.; Project administration, G.G.; Validation, C.C.; Writing—original draft, G.V.B. and C.C.; Writing—review and editing, G.G.

Funding: This research received no external funding.

Conflicts of Interest: The authors declare no conflict of interest.

References

Barreca, Manuela. 2012. Stakeholders' Involvement in Cultural Districts: A Multiple Case Studies Analysis. Paper presented at Euram Conference, Rotterdam, The Netherlands, June 6–8; Available online: http://euram2012.mindworks.ee/public/papers/paper/629 (accessed on 28 June 2013).

Beck, Tony. 1999. *Using Gender-Sensitive Indicators. A Reference Manual for Governments and Other Stakeholders.* London: Commonwealth Secretariat. ISBN 0-85092-594-0.

Ben-Ner, Avner, and Theresa Van Hoomissen. 1991. Nonprofit organizations in the mixed economy. *Annals of Public and Cooperative Economics* 62: 549–50. [CrossRef]

Bettio, Francesca, Annalisa Rosselli, and Giovanna Vingelli. 2002. *Gender Auditing dei Bilanci Pubblici.* Bergamo: Fondazione A. J. Zaninoni.

Bovaird, Tony. 2005. Public governance: Balancing stakeholder power in a network society. *International Review of Administrative Sciences* 71: 217–28. [CrossRef]

Bovaird, Tony, and Elke Löffler. 2002. Moving from excellence models of local service delivery to benchmarking of 'good local governance'. *International Review of Administrative Sciences* 68: 9–24. [CrossRef]

Brody, Alyson. 2009. *Gender and Governance: Overview Report.* London: Bridge Development-Gender. ISBN 978-185864-576X.

Bryson, John M. 2004. What to do when stakeholders matter. Stakeholder identification and analysis techniques. *Public Management Review* 6: 21–53. [CrossRef]

Bryson, John. M., Kathryn S. Quick, Carissa Schively Slotterback, and Barbara C. Crosby. 2012. Designing public participation processes. *Public Administration Review* 73: 23–34. [CrossRef]

Budlender, Debbie. 2000. The political economy of Women's Budgets in the South. *World Development* 28: 1365–78. [CrossRef]

Budlender, Debbie. 2002. A Global Assessment of Gender Responsive Budget Initiatives. In *Gender Budgets Make Cents: Understanding Gender Responsive Budgets.* Edited by Debbie Budlender, Diane Elson, Guy Hewitt and Tanni Mukhopadhyay. London: Commonwealth Secretariat. ISBN 0-85092-696-3.

Budlender, Debbie. 2007. *Gender-Responsive Call Circulars and Gender Budget Statements.* Guidance Sheet Series, No. 1. New York: United Nations Development Fund for Women (UNIFEM).

Budlender, Debbie, and Guy Hewitt. 2002. *Gender Budgets Make More Cents: Country Studies and Good Practice.* London: Commonwealth Secretariat. ISBN 0-85092-734-X.

Budlender, Debbie, and Guy Hewitt. 2003. *Engendering Budgets. A Practitioners' Guide to Understanding and Implementing Gender Responsive Budgets.* London: Commonwealth Secretariat. ISBN 0-85092-735-8.

Budlender, Debbie, Rhonda Sharp, and Kerry Allen. 1998. *How to do a Gender Sensitive Budget Analysis: Contemporary Research and Practice.* London: Commonwealth Secretariat. ISBN 0-86803-615-3.

Budlender, Debbie, Diane Elson, Guy Hewitt, and Tanni Mukhopadhyay. 2002. *Gender Budgets Make Cents: Understanding Gender Responsive Budgets.* London: Commonwealth Secretariat. ISBN 0-85092-696-3.

Corbin, Juliet, and Anselm Strauss. 1990. Grounded Theory research: Procedures, canons and evaluative criteria. *Qualitative Sociology* 13: 3–21. [CrossRef]

Council of Europe. 2005. *Gender Budgeting: Final Report of the Group of Specialists on Gender Budgeting.* Strasbourg: Council of Europe.

Council of the European Union. 2006. *Renewed EU Sustainable Development Strategy.* Brussels: Council of the European Union.

Cumming, Jane Fiona. 2001. Engaging stakeholders in corporate accountability programmes: A cross-sectoral analysis of UK and transnational experience. *Business Ethics: A European Review* 10: 45–52. [CrossRef]

Elander, Ingemar. 2002. Partnerships and urban governance. *International Social Science Journal* 172: 191–204. [CrossRef]

Elson, Diane. 1998. Policy Arena: Integrating gender issues into national budgetary policies and procedures: some policy options. *Journal of International Development* 10: 929–41. [CrossRef]

Elson, Diane. 1999. *Gender Budget Initiative.* London: Commonwealth Secretariat.

Elson, Diane. 2002. Gender Responsive Budget Initiatives: Key Dimensions and Practical Examples. In *Gender Budget Initiatives: Strategies, Concepts and Experiences.* Coordinated by Jennifer Klot, Nathalie Holvoet and Elizabeth Villagomez. Edited by Karen Judd. New York: United Nations Development Fund for Women (UNIFEM). ISBN #0-912917-60-1.

Elson, Diane. 2006. *Budgeting for Women's Rights: Monitoring Government Budgets for Compliance with CEDAW.* New York: United Nations Development Fund for Women (UNIFEM). ISBN 1-932827-47-1.

Foo, Loke-Min, Darinka Asenova, Stephen Bailey, and John Hood. 2011. Stakeholder engagement and compliance culture. An empirical study of Scottish private finance initiative projects. *Public Administration Review* 13: 707–29. [CrossRef]

Freeman, R. Edward. 1984. *Strategic Management: A Stakeholder Approach.* Boston: Pitman. ISBN 978-0-521-15174-0.

Municipality of Bologna. 2008. Gender Auditing Report 2008. Available online: http://www.iperbole.bologna.it/rendicontazione-sociale/genere/docs/BILANCIO_DI_GENERE_DOCUMENTO_2008.pdf (accessed on 4 February 2010).

Gray, Andrew, and Bill Jenkins. 1993. Codes of accountability in the new public sector. *Accounting Auditing and Accountability Journal* 6: 52–67. [CrossRef]

Hewitt, Guy, and Tanni Mukhopadhyay. 2002. Promoting Gender Equality through Public Expenditure. In *Gender Budgets Make Cents: Understanding Gender Responsive Budgets.* Edited by Debbie Budlender, Diane Elson, Guy Hewitt and Tanni Mukhopadhyay. London: Commonwealth Secretariat. ISBN 0-85092-696-3.

Himmelweit, Susan. 2002. Making visible the hidden economy: The case for gender-impact analysis of economic policy. *Feminist Economics* 8: 49–70. [CrossRef]

Hofbauer Balmori, Helena. 2003. *Gender and Budgets: Overview Report.* London: Bridge Development-Gender. ISBN 1-85864-461-5.

Hunt, Nigel, and Sue McHale. 2007. A Practical Guide to the E-Mail Interview. *Qualitative Health Research* 17: 1415–21. [CrossRef] [PubMed]

Irvin, Renée A., and John Stansbury. 2004. Citizen participation in decision making: Is it worth the effort? *Public Administration Review* 64: 55–65. [CrossRef]

Krafchik, Warren. 2002. Can Civil Society Add Value to Budget Decision-Making? In *Gender Budget Initiatives: Strategies, Concepts and Experiences.* Coordinated by Jennifer Klot, Nathalie Holvoet and Elizabeth Villagomez. Edited by Karen Judd. New York: United Nations Development Fund for Women (UNIFEM). ISBN #0-912917-60-1.

Kvale, Steiner. 1996. *Interviews: An Introduction to Qualitative Research Interviewing.* Thousand Oaks: Sage. ISBN 13-978-0803958197.

Marcuccio, Manila, and Ileana Steccolini. 2009. Patterns of voluntary extended performance reporting in Italian local authorities. *International Journal of Public Sector Management* 22: 146–67. [CrossRef]

Meneguzzo, Marco. 1997. Ripensare la modernizzazione amministrativa e il New Public Management. L'esperienza italiana: Innovazione dal basso e sviluppo della governance locale. *Azienda Pubblica* 6: 587–627.

Morgan, Stephanie J., and Gillian Symon. 2004. Electronic interviews in organizational research. In *Essential Guide to Qualitative Methods in Organizational Research*. Edited by Catherine Cassel and Gillian Symon. London: Sage Publications. ISBN 0 7619 4888 0.

Municipality of Bologna. 1991. Statute of the Municipality of Bologna. Available online: http://www.comune.bologna.it/media/files/statuto_consolidato.pdf (accessed on 28 June 2013).

Municipality of Bologna. 2005. Mandatory Programme 2004–2009. Available online: http://www.comune.bologna.it (accessed on 24 January 2012).

Nabatchi, Tina. 2012. Putting the "Public" back in public values research: Designing participation to identify and respond to values. *Public Administration Review* 72: 699–708. [CrossRef]

Noland, James, and Robert Phillips. 2010. Stakeholder engagement, discourse ethics and strategic management. *International Journal of Management Reviews* 12: 39–49. [CrossRef]

Osborne, Katy, Carol Bacchi, and Catherine Mackenzie. 2008. Gender analysis and community consultation: The role of women's policy units. *The Australian Journal of Public Administration* 67: 149–60. [CrossRef]

Pedersen, Esben Rahbek. 2006. Making Corporate Social Responsibility (CSR) Operable: How Companies Translate Shareholder Dialogue into Practice. *Business and Society Review* 111: 137–63. [CrossRef]

Rubery, Jill, Colette Fagan, Damian Grimshaw, Hugo Figueiredo, and Mark Smith. 2002. *Indicators on Gender Equality in the European Employment Strategy*. Manchester: European Work and Employment Research Centre, Manchester School of Management UMIST.

Rubin, Marilyn Marks, and John R. Bartle. 2005. Integrating Gender into Government Budgets: A New Perspective. *Public Administration Review* 65: 259–72. [CrossRef]

Savage, Grant T., Timoty W. Nix, Carlton J. Whitehead, and John D. Blair. 1991. Strategies for assessing and managing organizational stakeholders. *Academy of Management Executive* 5: 61–75. [CrossRef]

Sharp, Rhonda. 2002. Moving Forward: Multiple Strategies and Guiding Goals. In *Gender Budget Initiatives: Strategies, Concepts and Experiences*. Edited by Karen Judd. Coordinated by Jennifer Klot, Nathalie Holvoet and Elizabeth Villagomez. New York: United Nations Development Fund for Women (UNIFEM). ISBN #0-912917-60-1.

Sharp, Rhonda. 2003. *Budgeting for Equity. Gender Budget Initiatives within a Framework of Performance Oriented Budgeting*. New York: United Nations Development Fund for Women (UNIFEM). ISBN 0-646-42521-8.

Sharp, Rhonda, and Ray Broomhill. 2002. Budgeting for equality: The Australian experience. *Feminist Economics* 8: 25–47. [CrossRef]

Sharp, Rhonda, and Sanjugta Vas Dev. 2004. *Bridging the Gap between Gender Analysis and Gender-Responsive Budgets: Key Lessons from a Pilot Project in the Republic of the Marshall Islands*. Working paper Series, No. 25. Adelaide: University of South Australia, Hawke Research Institute.

United Nations Development Programme (UNDP). 1999. *Human Development Report 1999*. New York: Oxford University Press. ISBN 0-19-521562-1.

Van Puyvelde, Stijn, Ralf Caers, Clind Bois, and Marc Jegers. 2012. The governance of nonprofit organizations: Integrating agency theory with stakeholder and stewardship theories. *Nonprofit and Voluntary Sector Quarterly* 41: 1–21. [CrossRef]

Villagomez, Elizabeth. 2004. Gender Responsive Budgets: Issues, good practices and policy options. Paper presented at the Regional Symposium on Mainstreaming Gender into Economic Policies, Geneve, Switzerland, January 28–30.

Yin, Robert K. 2003. *Case Study Research. Design and Methods*. Thousand Oaks: Sage Publications. ISBN 0-7619-2553.

Zuckerman, Elaine. 2005. An Introduction to Gender Budget Initiatives. Available online: http://www.genderaction.org/images/Intro_to_Gender_Budget_InitativesFINAL.pdf (accessed on 2 November 2018).

administrative
sciences

MDPI

Article

Female Entrepreneurship in Perspective: A Methodological Issue

Paola Paoloni [1] and Gabriele Serafini [2,*]

[1] Department of Law and Economics of productive activities, Sapienza Università di Roma, 00185 Rome, Italy; paola.paoloni11@gmail.com

[2] Department of Economics and Business, Niccolò Cusano University, 00133 Rome, Italy

* Correspondence: gabriele.serafini@unicusano.it

Received: 23 August 2018; Accepted: 30 October 2018; Published: 3 November 2018

Abstract: A methodological approach to the concept of female entrepreneurship concept has not yet been treated: is female entrepreneurship an individual or collective concept? Is it considered a social or natural variable? The purpose of this research is to clear up these alternatives, which are preparatory questions for any research into female entrepreneurship that wishes to measure its features and effects. The article starts with the proposal of an identification procedure, necessary to identifying the variables of female entrepreneurship. It proceeds by classifying the concept of female entrepreneurship into four different modes and discussing their characteristics. The originality of this research consists in its fourfold classification of the concept of female entrepreneurship, intended as a preparatory step prior to the analysis of its characteristics and measures.

Keywords: female entrepreneurship; entrepreneurship; economic variable classification

1. Introduction: The Identification of Female Entrepreneurship

An analysis of the recent literature revealed methodological issues not yet treated regarding female entrepreneurship (Serafini 2018). It is, in fact, not yet clear whether female entrepreneurship is an individual or collective concept, or whether it is considered a social or natural variable. The first alternative deals with the problem that although entrepreneurship is, in the literature, considered an individual characteristic (Screpanti and Zamagni 2005)—even when its characteristics are related to, or depend on, macroeconomic variables (Parker 2018, p. 88)—the term female refers to a gender quality that is collective. The second alternative relates to the nature of entrepreneurship, since it can be considered an historically originated characteristic and a social creation (Bettio and Verashchagina 2008), or a feature that can be taken for granted because it remains qualitatively unchanged throughout time (Barker and Kuiper 2003), even if it changes quantitatively throughout time (Parker 2018, p. 451). The purpose of this article is to clear up these alternatives, which are preparatory questions for any research into the features of female entrepreneurship and their measurement. This is why the classification and definition of the concept of female entrepreneurship are related to individuation and the (eventual) measurement of its features, as it is not possible to study a variable independently of its classification and definition. Unfortunately, the classification and definition of the subject matter of a study is, in turn, not an undisputed issue in economic theory (Hausman 2008, p. 1), because "what is" an economic variable is strictly connected to the economic model and its theoretical assumptions, elaborated by the researcher who poses the question (Boniolo and Vidali 2003, pp. 31, 35). It is then important to state the subject matter identification procedure of a variable, which includes its classification and definition as a first step, being aware that "there is a boundary between me and my objects only on a conscious, secondary process level of organization; on a primary process level, I *am* my objects and my objects and I are always, necessary, inseparable" (Mitchell 2014, p. 44). Only after having determined that an adequate identification procedure is essential to the measurement of its characteristics, will it be possible to deal with alternative possible classifications of the characteristic, which will be addressed in the next paragraph.

Since classification can be intended to mean the demarcation of the external environment with respect to the variable, the definition of the variable can be intended as the boundaries of the variable. In this way, classification matches an inward perspective from the exterior and definition matches an outward perspective from the interior, where both are affected by coexistent theoretical assumptions. This first step has to be followed by a second step, dedicated to the identification of the characteristics of the variable and their classification, definition and eventual measurement. The subject matter identification procedure can therefore be constituted by the two steps displayed in Table 1.

Table 1. Subject matter identification procedure.

Step	Research Subject Matter
1	Classification and definition: boundaries from exterior and interior.
2	Characteristics: classifications, definitions, (eventual) measurement.

The two-step procedure can be a support when reasoning about the qualification of economic variables and their features, but in our specific case the only aim of the article is the classification and definition of the concept of female entrepreneurship. This is because the recent economic literature on female entrepreneurship directly focuses on characteristics, waiving the classification and definition step and revealing this lack of qualification. This is the consequence a fact that according to (Swedberg 2000, p. 7)) it is worth noting, namely that "most people who are not economists probably expect the economics literature to be full of analyses of entrepreneurship, since economics after all is the social science that deals most directly with contemporary economic reality. This, however, is not the case". Once the necessity of an identification procedure has been clarified, we should deal with the issue of its classification, in the knowledge that with regard to entrepreneurs and entrepreneurship, "there is no general agreement about the meaning of these terms" (Parker 2018, p. 6).

2. Results: Two Alternatives and a Fourfold Qualification

The term female relates to gender issues and collective characteristics but, in this context of economic variables, it is placed next to the term *entrepreneurship*, which is usually intended as an individual variable, even when collective variables influence its performance (Parker 2018, p. 300). By focusing on the name, we could thus perceive an oxymoron, but by means of a literature analysis we can state that research into female entrepreneurship has not yet investigated whether it is an individual or collective variable, and whether it has a social or natural derivation (Serafini 2018). This is why the nature and qualifications of the concept of female entrepreneurship has remained untapped until now, although the importance of the research into this concept has a dual meaning. (1) Since in the literature "entrepreneurship" is defined as a variable pertaining to individuals (see the following quotation), the concept female entrepreneurship suggests a collective qualification for this variable. The point is that in the recent literature about female entrepreneurship its collective character is not problematized. Screpanti and Zamagni (2005, pp. 181–82) say that in the modern economics model "the economy is made up of a plurality of agents who are present on the market either as consumers or as suppliers of productive services or as entrepreneurs [. . .] Clearly, there is no place in this model for the notion of social class. On the contrary, there are just two groups of individuals: the consumers and the entrepreneurs, distinguished solely by the different decisions they are called upon to take." (2) In the recent literature on female entrepreneurship, gender differences between entrepreneurs are not investigated with regard to their social or natural origins. That is, it is not investigated whether the gender differences between female and male entrepreneurship are due to historical constructions or natural differences between the two sexes—if we can refer to the traditional two sexes, which are called to mind by the term female. These two points indicate why the methodological issue mentioned above is preparatory to any recognition and classification of the characteristics of female entrepreneurship and, as we will see in the next paragraph, these two mentioned alternatives produce four different classification modes. Only one of these corresponds to the traditional definition of entrepreneurship as an individual variable that evolves over time.

Since the economic literature, at least from the last decades of the nineteenth century, qualifies entrepreneurship from an individual rather than a collective point of view, reflection is needed in order to classify it as individual or collective. Joseph A. (Schumpeter 1991, p. 855)) wrote that, according to the economic paradigm, which has dominated since that period, "all social phenomena resolve themselves into decisions and actions of individuals that need not or cannot be further analyzed in terms of superindividual factors." Nowadays, on the contrary, it is necessary to clarify whether female entrepreneurship has a social or natural character. This is because, regardless of whether it is individual or collective, the qualification may be the result of social evolution, which has created the features of female entrepreneurship, or the result of natural sex differences. According to the social evolution hypothesis, both male and female entrepreneurs can have entrepreneurship characteristics and the label of male or female entrepreneurship depends on the gender of the individual having a certain quantity of these characteristics. This means that social evolution determines variations in these characteristics and their quantities, since the classification as male or female entrepreneurship is not connected with a person's birth sex. On the other hand, according to the natural character hypothesis of male or female entrepreneurship, male entrepreneurship cannot also have characteristics classified as female entrepreneurship because of their naturally different origin. From this perspective, birth determines the possibility and characterization of males and females. Table 2 at the end of this paragraph sets out the four cases.

In order to depict the importance of prior classification, we can refer to the classical problem of linking an economic variable with the consequences of its use. Only after the decision regarding the classification of female entrepreneurship has been made, will it be possible to establish typical male and female entrepreneurial characteristics. Only after having established these, will it be possible to understand the links between characteristics and value creation, i.e., correlation (pure or spurious) or causation. For example, only after having established female entrepreneurship as a collective variable will it be possible to exclude that differences in value creation between male and female entrepreneurs are due to individual differences, instead of gender. Table 2 presents the fourfold classification of the concept of female entrepreneurship, from which it emerges that if female entrepreneurship is a collective variable, it is considered a substitute for the entrepreneurship concept because it is not of an individual nature. At the same time, if female entrepreneurship is considered a natural variable, it is unchangeable over time and in different historical periods.

Table 2. Classification of female entrepreneurship (FE).

	Individual	Collective
Social	FE is the same concept as entrepreneurship	FE substitutes the individual concept and its characteristics can be had by male entrepreneurs
Natural	FE is an omothetic concept with respect to entrepreneurship	FE substitutes the individual concept and its characteristics cannot be had by male entrepreneurs

3. Discussion. Individual Entrepreneur or Gender Variable

The economic literature maintains that an entrepreneur combines productive factors and obtains profit because of her/his particular—not general—abilities, since she/he does not have a particular productive factor, and she/he is not an individual representing any social group. (Walras 2006, p. 319)) maintains that entrepreneur is the fourth role (alongside workers, capital owners and land owners) that combines productive factors. In this way, a multitude of independent agents acts in every economic system, with every agent trying to assert her/his capacity to profitably combine productive factors. According to the economic literature, value creation and capital enhancement depend on individual qualities rather than gender qualities.

While value creation has been studied in relation to female entrepreneurship, an entrepreneur's profit is implicitly considered the result of gender qualities and differences, not individual qualities and differences. This even hypothesizes individual differences depending on the different qualities of each entrepreneur, because this cannot invalidate the original common matrix of gender differences. This hypothesis underlies research into gender issues in business and economics. In this case, the qualification of female entrepreneurship as a social or natural variable becomes necessary, as in the economic literature there is no consensus on this issue. (Barker and Kuiper 2003, p. 1)), for example, indicate that feminist economics is "reconceptualizing what economics is". This is because the feminist point of view implies a different vision of economic categories, and gender difference takes on a different and natural meaning if the gender perspective is not recognized as being filtered through particular lenses. We think that the following quotation can be read in this way: "we intend to participate in moving feminist economics out of the margin and into the center: to become economics, unmodified" (ibidem). From this point of view, the feminist vision does not stand alongside a male-dominated vision and believes that it is a universal point of view. Therefore, when the concept of female entrepreneurship changes, it changes due to the affirmation of a more general point of view and gender differences are considered natural differences.

The book edited by Bettio and Verashchagina (2008) can be placed in contrast to this. According to these authors, gender questions have a social nature, that is, they depend on the historical factors that created them. Pat Hudson writes, "gender is a social rather than a biological construction, and it has a history" (Bettio and Verashchagina 2008, p. 21). As a social construction, female entrepreneurship is a variable with characteristics that can also be had by male entrepreneurs, even if to such an extent that they do not qualify them as female entrepreneurs. As a gender variable it is still a super-individual variable, but its collective nature has a definite historical connotation.

The importance of the qualification of the concept of female entrepreneurship in terms of one of the four proposed classifications is also closely linked to the consequences it has on the classification of linked economic variables and concepts. For example, it has consequences for the concept of competition, because a competitive market is typically populated by a myriad of individuals, each with different tastes and aims, whereas a standardized qualification of individuals changes the market features, definitions and functions. From a preliminary assessment of the nature of female entrepreneurship, we can infer that if it is considered a collective quality, then the concept of competition—which includes the economic situation characterized by the presence of a set of small businesses, each of which it is not able to influence fundamental economic magnitudes—cannot be scientifically defined as the limit towards which the economic system tends. This is because every economic system, according to this point of view, is not characterized by the presence of independent entrepreneurs, as they have autonomous characteristics and compete on markets due to their different aims. The economic system, on the contrary, is characterized by the presence of entrepreneurs who are classifiable into standard types. Therefore, the market would be populated by subjects who behave according to standard qualities that cancel the individual essence that characterizes an ideal entrepreneur, who can be described as independent of other entrepreneurs and consumers. *Standard* qualities and gender differences, rather than *particular* qualities and gender differences, limit the individual differences that characterize a competitive market. The essence of an entrepreneur, in this context, would no longer be individual, even if considering that each entrepreneur has the same characteristics as the others, but held in different quantities. This is because the essence of gender is what remains once individual particularities are neglected, which are neglected precisely because entrepreneurship is defined as a gender variable. It is necessary to completely understand this alternative: if female entrepreneurship is considered an individual quality, you cannot trace and measure it within gender-based research, whereas if it is considered a gender and standardized quality, you cannot explain the qualities of economic systems through individual entrepreneurs.

4. Methods: Qualification of Female Entrepreneurship and Measurement of its Limits

This article has a methodological focus because it states, for the first time in the literature (Serafini 2018; Paoloni and Demartini 2016; Parker 2018), the inadequacy of the study of the characteristics and features of female entrepreneurship, which often proceeds without the premise of a statement about the nature of the variable female entrepreneurship. The literature has mainly focused on the differences between male and female entrepreneurship (Barker and Kuiper 2003, p. 145 ff), discrimination against female scholars (Madden 2002, p. 4 ff), or the measurement of the features of female entrepreneurship (Serafini 2016, p. 1919), but has not reflected on the possibilities of classifying the concept of female entrepreneurship.

This is why the framework of the article had a twofold purpose: (a) to clarify that it is not correct to study and measure a variable if it is not explicitly identified (Leti 1983; Bracalente et al. 2009); and (b) stimulate scholars to reflect on the nature of female entrepreneurship in order to make it distinctively measurable.

Due to the term "female", female entrepreneurship can be intended as a gender-based field of research, or research into the standardized qualities and functions of standardized human beings, rather than research into a particular function that characterizes individuals. This qualitative difference, moreover, distinguishes subsequent quantitative research, because it is preparatory to the possibility of measuring the research object; thus the research has a wider significance.

The two alternative determinations of female entrepreneurship as an individual or gender economic variable, in fact, also pose a theoretical problem at the aggregate level, not just at the company level. This is because at the "corporate level, a decrease in sales prices results in a decrease of the value created. On the contrary, in comparisons in constant prices, this decrease is not measured at macroeconomic level" (Serafini 2014, p. 3090). Moreover, "even if female entrepreneurship is considered a variable that creates value, its contribution can't be measured at an aggregate level since we won't be able to adequately separate a change in price from a change in wealth" (Serafini 2017, p. 957). As a consequence, national accounting systems cannot measure the contribution of entrepreneurship to value creation, due to price variations, accounting rules and theory. We cannot establish whether a price variation for a commodity represents, at the aggregate level, a relative price variation or an increase in wealth inserted into an economic system. In the case of female entrepreneurship, a preceding identification problem emerges, i.e., the previous qualification of what should but cannot be measured. The research into the field of female entrepreneurship, therefore, indicates a path to follow for a more general and methodological reflection on the nature of entrepreneurship in general. This is because the expression of female entrepreneurship itself indicates implied research attention to a super-individual level of analysis of economic variables that directly involves all economic research, not just gender issues.

In conclusion, the individual or collective nature and social or natural classification of female entrepreneurship is, in the literature, only insinuated and not methodologically questioned. This lack of explicit reflection causes various difficulties regarding the definition, classification and measurement of its features, at both the business and aggregate levels. We proposed an identification procedure and a fourfold classification hypothesis with the aim of supporting the future debate on this fundamental issue in business and economics.

Author Contributions: Paola Paoloni provided the literature analysis and Gabriele Serafini specified the female entrepreneurship classification methodology. Both Authors wrote the paper.

Funding: This research received no external funding.

Conflicts of Interest: The authors declare no conflicts of interest.

References

Barker, Drucilla, and Edith Kuiper. 2003. *Towards a Feminist Philosophy of Economics*. London and New York: Routledge.
Bettio, Francesca, and Alina Verashchagina. 2008. *Frontiers in the Economics of Gender*. London and New York: Routledge.

Boniolo, Giovanni, and Paolo Vidali. 2003. *Introduzione alla filosofia della scienza*. Milano: Mondadori.

Bracalente, Bruno, Massimo Cossignani, and Anna Mulas. 2009. *Statistica Aziendale*. Milano: McGraw-hill.

Hausman, Daniel M. 2008. *The Philosophy of Economics: An Anthology*. Cambridge: Cambridge University Press.

Leti, Giuseppe. 1983. *Statistica Descrittiva*. Bologna: Il Mulino.

Madden, Kirsten. Kara. 2002. Female contribution to Economics. *History of Political Economy* 34: 1. [CrossRef]

Mitchell, Stephen A. 2014. *Relationality. From Attachment to Intersubjectivity*. New York: Psychology Press.

Paoloni, Paola, and Paola Demartini. 2016. Women in management: Perspectives on a decade of research (2005–2015). *Palgrave Communications*. [CrossRef]

Parker, Simon C. 2018. *Economics of Entrepreneurship*, 2nd ed. Cambridge: Cambridge University Press.

Schumpeter, Joseph A. 1991. *History of Economic Analysis*. London: Routledge.

Screpanti, Ernesto, and Stefano Zamagni. 2005. *An Outline of the History of Economic Thought*. Oxford: Oxford University Press.

Serafini, Gabriele. 2014. Intellectual Capital Value Creation and Economic Theories. In *Knowledge and Management Models for Sustainable Growth*. Edited by Daniela Carlucci, J. C. Spender and Giovannni Schiuma. Matera: Institute for Knowledge Asset Management, pp. 3090–110.

Serafini, Gabriele. 2016. Neoclassical Theory and Female Entrepreneurship as Independent Factor of Production. A Systematic Review of the Economic Models. In *Towards a New Architecture of Knowledge: Big Data, Culture and Creativity*. Edited by J.C. Spender, Giovanni Schiuma and Jörg Rainer Noennig. Matera: Institute for Knowledge Asset Management, pp. 1918–28.

Serafini, Gabriele. 2017. Business economics vs political economics: Why female entrepreneurship value creation is underestimated at macroeconomic level. In *Knowledge Management in the 21th Century: Resilience, Creativity and Co-Creation*. Edited by J.C. Spender, Giovanni Schiuma and Jörg Rainer Noennig. Matera: Institute for Knowledge Asset Management, pp. 957–61.

Serafini, Gabriele. 2018. A fourfold classification of Female entrepreneurship concept. In *Advances in Gender and Culture Studies in Business and Economics*. Edited by Paola Paoloni and Rosa Lombardi. Heidelberg and New York: Springer, in press.

Swedberg, Richard. 2000. *Entrepreneurship: The Social Science View*. Oxford: Oxford University Press.

Walras, Marie Esprit Léon. 2006. *Elementi di economia politica pura*. Milano: Milano Finanza Editori, I grandi classici dell'economia, vol. 11.

MDPI

St. Alban-Anlage 66

4052 Basel

Switzerland

Tel. +41 61 683 77 34

Fax +41 61 302 89 18

www.mdpi.com

Administrative Sciences Editorial Office

E-mail: admsci@mdpi.com

www.mdpi.com/journal/admsci

www.ingramcontent.com/pod-product-compliance
Lightning Source LLC
Chambersburg PA
CBHW041217220326
41597CB00033BA/5995